MW00635131

# A CASE FOR THE BOOK *of* MORMON

A CASE FOR THE

# BOOK *of* MORMON

TAD R. CALLISTER

SALT LAKE CITY, UTAH

Visit us at deseretbook.com

---

**Library of Congress Cataloging-in-Publication Data**

Names: Callister, Tad R., 1945– author.
Title: A case for The Book of Mormon / Tad R. Callister.
Description: Salt Lake City, Utah : Deseret Book, [2019] | Includes bibliographical references and index.
Identifiers: LCCN 2018050802 | ISBN 9781629725659 (hardbound : alk. paper)
Subjects: LCSH: Book of Mormon—Criticism, interpretation, etc. | The Church of Jesus Christ of Latter-day Saints—Apologetic works. | Mormon Church—Apologetic works.
Classification: LCC BX8627 .C325 2019 | DDC 289.3/22—dc23
LC record available at https://lccn.loc.gov/2018050802

---

Printed in the United States of America
Lake Book Manufacturing, Inc., Melrose Park, IL

10 9 8 7 6 5 4 3 2

# CONTENTS

## PART IV: Gaining a Personal Testimony of the Book of Mormon



## PART V: Summary

# PREFACE

The primary purpose of this book is to present a case for the Book of Mormon—both intellectually and spiritually. In so doing, I have highlighted many evidences of the Book of Mormon's divine authenticity and its remarkable capacity to influence our lives for good. In addition, I have responded to many criticisms made against the Book of Mormon and addressed many of the fallacies underlying those arguments.

To accomplish these purposes, I have drawn from books and talks I have previously published, as well as unpublished talks and further research on the subject. Hopefully, this consolidates in one place an analysis of the Book of Mormon that can be rewarding both intellectually and spiritually.

It is hoped that the evidences presented will (1) further strengthen the testimony of those who already believe the Book of Mormon to be true, (2) help resolve issues for those who may have some honest questions about its divine origin, (3) provide insights for those who seek answers for their family members and friends who have been or may be exposed to false claims against the Book of Mormon, (4) stimulate the interest of those who have not yet feasted upon its profound doctrine and witness of Christ, and (5) give the critics pause to reconsider the Book of Mormon as God-given.

Although some evidences cited here refer to particular locations in the Americas, there is no intended endorsement of any specific location where the Book of Mormon people may have lived.

While I have received helpful suggestions from many in the creation of this book, a special thanks goes to my wife, Kathy, who has prayed for me, reviewed multiple manuscripts, given me many valuable insights, and encouraged me every step of the way.

Also, a special thanks goes to my assistant, Kathy Densley, who has cheerfully typed numerous copies of the manuscript and given helpful input in that process. Also, thanks to Jacquie Noriega, who has helped on occasion with the typing.

Brian Hansbrow and Ted Barnes have made multiple reviews of the manuscript as it was in progress, given invaluable suggestions on style and substance, and painstakingly reviewed and prepared numerous footnotes.

I also want to thank the many others who have meticulously reviewed the manuscript and contributed much in terms of factual accuracy, rationale, and editing, and have made many other practical and spiritual suggestions: Jeremy T. Callister, Lynn C. Callister, Reed R. Callister, Richard T. Callister, Wayne Christofferson, Devin G. Durrant, Keith A. Erekson, Matthew J. Grow, Richard G. Hinckley, Kerry Hull, Larry R. Lawrence, Laurel Lawrence, David B. Marsh, Elder James B. Martino, Carol F. McConkie, Curtis Oscarson, Virginia H. Pearce, Elder Kevin W. Pearson, Neal Rappleye, Linda S. Reeves, Elder Michael T. Ringwood, Matthew P.

Roper, Michael Skinner, and John W. Welch. Without the help of these people, this book would not have been possible.

I also express my appreciation to Book of Mormon Central and FairMormon, and their respective staffs, who have provided invaluable research into the Book of Mormon.

Finally, thanks to the team at Deseret Book who have worked to make this book a reality. Lisa Roper has ably overseen the project from its earliest stages. Emily Watts, who has excellent editing skills, has provided many suggestions that have been most helpful. Heather Ward's design, Richard Erickson's art direction, and Rachael Ward's meticulous typesetting have created a pleasing look and feel for the book.

Although I have tried to accurately state the facts and present correct doctrine, this is my own work, and if there are errors, they are mine.

PART I

# Introduction

CHAPTER 1

# Is There Room for Middle Ground?

## A Book for All Seasons

The Book of Mormon is a book for all seasons. It is for all men and all women of all nations and races. If we are lonely or discouraged, its words can soothe our "wounded soul[s]" (Jacob 2:8). If we feel the stain of sin or guilt, it can lead us to the Savior's cleansing powers. If our testimonies are wavering, it can shore them up. If we have been incorrectly influenced by the philosophies of men, it can restore the truth. And if we desire to become more like Christ, it can be our spiritual catalyst. Whatever our circumstance or need, it can provide us with a remedy of superior healing power. It is God's divine gift to every soul who wants to return to Him and become more like Him.

## The Book of Mormon Still Stands

Metaphorically, the Book of Mormon has been in the "boxing ring" of critical analysis for almost two hundred years. It has been through fifteen rounds of analyzing, critiquing, and criticizing, but never a knockdown has occurred.[1] It is an invincible opponent that knows no compromise. It carries no white flag. Rather, it is resolute and unapologetic in its claim that it is a divine work of God.

Hugh Nibley, one of the great scholars of The Church of Jesus Christ of Latter-day Saints (also referred to in this book as "the Church"), made this observation about the Book of Mormon: "The outrageous daring of its title page is the very thing that should whet the appetite of a real scholar: here is a book that is asking for a fight, so to speak, and if it is as flimsy as it looks at first glance any competent schoolman should have little trouble polishing it off in an hour or so."[2] Ironically, however, the hours have turned into days, the days to months, the months to years, and the years to decades, and yet the Book of Mormon still stands—a formidable foe that cannot be ignored or conquered.

Critics may selectively cite historical or cultural issues that seemingly provide them with some limited anti-Mormon traction, but until they can explain away the Book of Mormon, they cannot explain away The Church of Jesus Christ of Latter-day Saints. Why? Because the Book of Mormon is the crux, the kingpin, the keystone of the truth or falsity of the Church. As long as it stands, the Church stands. In other words, the Book of Mormon and the Church are inextricably tied; people cannot separate one from the other in their search for truth.

## Is the Book of Mormon a Divine Work or a Fraud?

Years ago, my great-great-grandfather picked up a copy of the Book of Mormon for the first time. He opened it to the center and read a few pages. He then declared, "That book was either written by God or the devil, and I am going to find out who wrote it." He read it through twice in the next ten days and then concluded, "The devil could not have written it—it must be from God."[3]

Another way to frame this conclusion of my grandfather is to say that the Book of Mormon is either a divine work or a fraud. And a fraud is what many critics believe Joseph Smith and the Book of Mormon to be.[4] Since a fraud is a deceit composed of one or more lies, the implied argument of the critics is that such a book is "of the devil" because the devil is the father of deceits and lies (see Acts 5:3; Revelation 12:9; 2 Nephi 2:18; Alma 12:4–5).

Part of the genius of the Book of Mormon is that it leaves little if any room for middle ground on the issue of whether it is a divine work or a fraud. This is not because there can't be middle ground on such an issue but because, in this case, the circumstances and claims surrounding it preclude such a conclusion. In essence, there are only two possibilities from which to choose. Either the angel Moroni appeared to Joseph Smith or he did not. Either Joseph Smith received golden plates containing a record of the Nephites or he did not. Either Nephi, Alma, and Moroni lived as prophets of God in ancient America or they are fictional characters. Either Christ appeared to the people of the Americas or the story is a fabrication. Because of these and many similar claims made by Joseph Smith and the Book of Mormon, there are only two reasonable conclusions that can be reached: either this book is a divine truth of infinite worth or it is a fraud of exponential proportions. It does not leave itself open to compromise on that issue.

Nonetheless, some propose that the Book of Mormon is neither a fraud nor a divine work.[5] I fail, however, to follow this line of reasoning. If there were no golden plates or angel Moroni or Nephite civilization, then every name and place and event in the Book of Mormon is an untruth, and every written word is a deception, because it is all presented as though it were the actual history of an ancient civilization and the actual words of prophets of God. Such would be a fraud, and frauds do not lend themselves to godly works. On the other hand, if there were golden plates, an angel Moroni, an ancient civilization, prophets of God, and a visit of Christ, all as described in the Book of Mormon, then, subject to any minor imperfections of men, it is the divine work of God.[6]

C. S. Lewis observed a similar dilemma faced by someone who must choose whether to accept or reject the Savior's divinity—where there is likewise no middle ground:

"I am trying here to prevent anyone saying the really foolish thing that people often say about Him: 'I'm ready to accept Jesus as a great moral teacher, but I don't accept His claim to be God.' That is the one thing we must not say. A man who was merely a man and said the sort of things Jesus said would not be a great moral teacher. . . . You must make your choice. Either this man was and is the Son of God: or else a madman or something worse. . . . But let us not come with any patronizing nonsense about His being a great human teacher. He has not left that open to us. He did not intend to."[7]

Likewise, how could one say that the Book of Mormon is a fine moral treatise on one hand and yet at the same time allege there were no golden plates, no angel who delivered them, no prophets who actually existed, and no visit of Christ to the Americas. A fraud does not produce a fine moral treatise (see Matthew 7:16–20). In the words of C. S. Lewis, God "has not left that open to us. He did not intend to."

For a moment, I invite you to take a test that will help you determine whether the Book of Mormon is from God or is a fraud influenced by the devil. Ask yourself if the devil would be the author or instigator of the following statements from the Book of Mormon:

- "They who are filthy are the devil and his angels" (2 Nephi 9:16).

- "The devil . . . [is] the founder of murder, and works of darkness" (2 Nephi 26:22).
- "That which is evil cometh from the devil" (Omni 1:25).
- "The devil will not support his children at the last day, but doth speedily drag them down to hell" (Alma 30:60).
- "Yea, cry unto him against the devil, who is an enemy to all righteousness" (Alma 34:23).
- "The devil . . . rewardeth you no good thing" (Alma 34:39).

This is hardly a collection of accolades on behalf of the devil. What is the probability that the devil—the most arrogant, egotistical, and narcissistic of all beings—"prompted" Joseph to write these harsh condemnations against himself? In addition, ask yourself if the devil would be the author of the following:

- "Feast upon the words of Christ; for behold, the words of Christ will tell you all things what ye should do" (2 Nephi 32:3).
- "And now, my sons, remember, remember that it is upon the rock of our Redeemer, who is Christ, the Son of God, that ye must build your foundation" (Helaman 5:12).
- "What manner of men ought ye to be? Verily I say unto you, even as I [Christ] am" (3 Nephi 27:27).
- "Come unto Christ, and be perfected in him" (Moroni 10:32).

Could these statements from the Book of Mormon possibly have been authored by the evil one—words that castigate the devil on one hand and, on the other hand, invite us to worship Christ and come unto Him? Some might argue that Satan tells half-truths and uses reverse psychology as part of his devilish strategy. That is true, but his methods always have a purpose, and that purpose is to ultimately draw people unto him and his ways. Thus, the key question becomes: does the Book of Mormon draw people unto the devil? And the resounding, unequivocal answer is no! To the contrary, millions are witnesses, including myself, that the Book of Mormon inspires every honest seeker of truth to live a more Christlike life.

After the Savior cast out certain devils, the Pharisees claimed that He did so by the power of the devil. The Savior responded that such a conclusion was nonsensical: "Every kingdom divided against itself," He said, "is brought to desolation; and every . . . house divided against itself shall not stand." And then His compelling climax: "And if Satan cast out Satan, he is divided against himself; how shall then his kingdom stand?" (Matthew 12:25–26).

If the scriptures from the Book of Mormon teach us to reject and cast out Satan and to worship, love, and serve the Savior, which they do, how then can they be from the devil? If so, he would be divided against himself and thus be destroying his own kingdom, the very condition the Savior said could not exist.

When all is said and done, the Book of Mormon is God's crowning witness of Jesus Christ. In fact, the testimony of this book, as confirmed by the Spirit, is the single most powerful and compelling witness we have of the divinity of Jesus Christ, the prophetic calling of Joseph Smith, and the absolute truth of the Church.

## Reason and the Spirit

There are many witnesses of the divinity of the Book of Mormon. Of course, the greatest and most crucial witness is the Spirit, who leaves us with an undeniable conviction of its truthfulness. Elder B. H. Roberts, an author and scholar of The Church of Jesus Christ of Latter-day Saints, spoke to this point. He said that the Holy Ghost "must ever be the chief source of evidence for the truth of the Book of Mormon. All other evidence is secondary to this." He then added by way of clarification that secondary evidences "in support of truth . . . may be of first rate importance, and mighty factors in the achievement of God's purposes."[8] In other words, secondary evidences can be wonderful supplements to our testimonies, but they do not replace or supersede the witness of the Spirit. President Boyd K. Packer spoke of the need for both reason and revelation in our search for truth: "Each of us must accommodate the mixture of reason and revelation in our lives. The gospel not only permits but *requires* it."[9]

Austin Farrer, an Anglican theologian, gave us this important insight: "Though argument does not create conviction, lack of it destroys belief. What seems to be proved may not be embraced; but what no one shows the ability to defend is quickly abandoned. *Rational argument does not create belief, but it maintains a climate in which belief may flourish.*"[10] In other words, reason does not necessarily bring about conviction, but a lack of it creates a climate for doubt, while the presence of it creates a climate for belief.

In that spirit, I have set forth in the beginning chapters of this book some of the critics' primary arguments against the Book of Mormon and some responses and evidences that are intended to shed further light on the full truth. Hopefully, these responses and evidences will create a welcoming climate for further investigation of the Book of Mormon and, more important, become the impetus for a spiritual testimony of its truthfulness. The concluding chapters focus on the consummate witnesses of the book's veracity—its doctrine, its divine language, the personal testimonies of its truthfulness, and the witness of the Holy Ghost.

## The Investigation

Hugh Nibley made this salient observation: "The Book of Mormon is tough; it thrives on investigation; you may kick it around like a football, as many have done; and I promise you it will wear you out long before you ever make a dent in it."[11] The following chapters will discuss some of that kicking—the intense, probing investigation the book has undergone and is still undergoing, its incredible resiliency to such attacks, and the existing as well as emerging evidences of its divine authenticity, capped by the most significant evidence of all—the witness of the Spirit. In essence, this book is intended to be a truthful and persuasive case for the Book of Mormon.

The reader is now invited to seriously consider and weigh the many evidences of the Book of Mormon's divine authenticity as presented in the following chapters and determine if these evidences are not both intellectually convincing and spiritually compelling.

---

NOTES

1. For example, no one has presented a compelling argument as to the origin of the Book of Mormon other than the story as told by Joseph Smith himself—namely, that he translated it by the gift and power of God. For more on this subject, see chapter 2.
2. Nibley, "Preface," xii.
3. Willard Richards, in LeGrand Richards, *A Marvelous Work and a Wonder,* 81, 82.
4. John E. Clark, a Latter-day Saint scholar, noted: "Detractors ridicule both [Joseph Smith and the Book of Mormon] as blasphemous frauds" ("Archaeological Trends and Book of Mormon Origins," 84). In 1886, Reverend M. T. Lamb opined, "The facts are, my good Mormon brother—that Book [the Book of Mormon] *has been proven a fraud beyond the possibility of question*" (*The Golden Bible,* 321; emphasis in original).
5. Some use phrases such as a "pious fraud" to describe the book. This is an oxymoron and makes no sense. The Book of Mormon cannot be both pious (meaning "holy") and a fraud (meaning "deceitful") at the same time.
6. Even though something is divinely inspired, that does not necessarily mean it is perfect. God uses imperfect mortals, such as Moses, Peter, Paul, and Joseph Smith, to serve as His prophets and as instruments in His hands. The title page of the Book of Mormon acknowledges that the book may have faults, but if so, "they are the mistakes of men; wherefore condemn not the things of God." These imperfections, however, will not be a distraction to the honest seeker of truth who can judge whether the ultimate

fruit produced is good or bad. The Bible has some errors. Nonetheless, most Christians recognize it as the supreme word of God. Likewise, whatever minor errors the Book of Mormon may contain are insignificant compared to the monumental work of God it is. Moroni addressed this issue as follows: "Whoso receiveth this record, and shall not condemn it because of the imperfections which are in it, the same shall know of greater things than these" (Mormon 8:12; see also 1 Nephi 19:6; Mormon 8:17; 9:30–31).

7. Lewis, *Mere Christianity,* 40–41.
8. Roberts, *New Witnesses for God,* 2:vi. See also Welch, "B. H. Roberts: Seeker after Truth," 56–62.
9. Packer, "I Say unto You, Be One"; emphasis in original.
10. Farrer, "Grete Clerk," 26; emphasis added.
11. Nibley, "A Twilight World," 153.

PART II

# Critics' Arguments and Responses to Them

CHAPTER 2

# Man-Made or God-Given?

## The Keystone of Our Religion

The Prophet Joseph Smith declared that "the Book of Mormon was the most correct of any book on earth, and the keystone of our religion, and a man would get nearer to God by abiding by its precepts, than by any other book."[1] Because the Book of Mormon is the keystone of The Church of Jesus Christ of Latter-day Saints, it has become the focal point of attack by many of the Church's critics.

On one hand, if the critics can prove that the Book of Mormon is man-made, then by implication the Church is also man-made. On the other hand, if the Book of Mormon is God-given, then Joseph Smith was a prophet, and if he was a prophet, that gives credence to the fact that The Church of Jesus Christ of Latter-day Saints is of divine origin.

Once we have a foundational testimony of the Book of Mormon, as confirmed by the Spirit, then any question or challenge we confront in life, however difficult it may seem, can be approached with faith, not doubt. Why? Because the keystone of our religion—the Book of Mormon and its witness of Jesus Christ—has also become the keystone of our testimony, holding our testimony securely in place.

Thus, there exists an unrelenting attack by many critics to disprove the Book of Mormon in hopes of disproving the Church and undermining faith and testimonies. That is essentially what Joseph Smith acknowledged: "Take away the Book of Mormon and the revelations, and where is our religion? We have none."[2]

But this effort to disprove the Book of Mormon is no easy task—in fact, it is impossible, because the Book of Mormon is true. At least eleven witnesses, in addition to Joseph Smith, saw the golden plates; external and internal evidences of the book's veracity are continually emerging; millions of believers have testified of its truthfulness; and, most important, the book is readily available for one's personal examination and testing. In the end, critics must either accept Joseph Smith's account—namely, that he translated it by the gift and power of God—or produce a viable alternative. What then are those alternative explanations presented by the critics for the origin of the Book of Mormon, and what is the truth about its origin?

## Argument 1: Joseph Smith, an Ignorant Man, Wrote the Book of Mormon

In 1831 a clergyman named Alexander Campbell proposed that Joseph Smith wrote rather than translated the Book of Mormon: "There never was a book more evidently written by one set of fingers, nor more certainly conceived in one cranium . . . than this same book. . . . I cannot doubt for a single moment that he [Joseph Smith] is the sole author and proprietor of it."[3] He also declared that Joseph was "as ignorant and as impudent a knave as ever wrote a book."[4] But this assertion that someone who was ignorant and uneducated could write such a work as the Book of Mormon seemed so preposterous to other contemporary critics that they readily dismissed it and instead presented alternative theories for the book's origin, as discussed hereafter. Even Campbell, who proposed this theory, later abandoned it in favor of another alternative.[5]

And so, the early theories about the origin of the Book of Mormon focused on the premise that Joseph Smith, an unlearned man, was simply incapable of writing such a complex book. After all, he was but twenty-three years of age, a simple plowboy from western New York who had little formal education. Consequently, the early critics concluded there must be some other explanation for the origin of the Book of Mormon than the unlikely possibility that Joseph wrote it.

## Argument 2: Someone Else Wrote It

Since Joseph Smith seemed unqualified to write the Book of Mormon, some critics proposed the theory that Joseph Smith conspired with someone who had the education, intelligence, and skills to do so. In this regard, Fawn Brodie, an avid critic of Joseph Smith and the Book of Mormon who wrote in the mid-1900s, observed: "Unwilling to credit Joseph Smith with either learning or talent, detractors of the Mormons within a few years declared that the Book of Mormon must have been written by someone else."[6] Following are some of those alleged authors.

### *Oliver Cowdery*

One candidate for its authorship was Oliver Cowdery, who was Joseph Smith's principal scribe during the Book of Mormon translation. After all, he was better educated than Joseph Smith; he was a schoolteacher and would later become a lawyer. Nevertheless, there was a major problem with this theory. Oliver never claimed to have authored any portion of the book; in fact, he testified to the contrary:

"I wrote, with my own pen, the entire Book of Mormon (save a few pages) as it fell from the lips of the Prophet Joseph Smith, as he translated it by the gift and power of God. . . . That book is *true*."[7]

We also have the historical account of Oliver attempting to translate a portion of the Book of Mormon but failing in this effort.[8] If Oliver wrote the Book of Mormon, why would there be an account of his unsuccessful attempt at translation? And if Oliver wrote the book, why the testimonies of David Whitmer and Joseph's wife Emma that they were present during a portion of the translation process and saw Oliver acting as Joseph's scribe?[9]

The original transcript of the Book of Mormon reflects the handwriting of several scribes besides that of Oliver Cowdery. To claim that Oliver was the author of the portions in his handwriting would seem to imply that there were multiple authors of the Book of Mormon besides Oliver, each writing that portion that appears in his or her handwriting. But if this is the case, why did none of these other scribes ever claim authorship or disclose the alleged fraud?

In addition, Oliver was one of the three witnesses who bore testimony "that an angel of God came down from heaven" and showed him the golden plates from which Joseph Smith translated the Book of Mormon.[10] The two other witnesses made it clear that Oliver was a fellow witness with them, not the author of the book (see chapter 7).

If Oliver wrote the Book of Mormon, then, one must ask, what was his motive? He received no fame, no money, no lasting power for writing the book and for remaining silent about its "true" authorship. In fact, eight years after the Book of Mormon was published, Oliver was excommunicated from the Church. If there were ever a time to expose Joseph Smith as a fraud, that was it—his chance to get even and to declare who the true author was. But none of that happened. To the contrary, even though it was some years before Oliver returned to the Church, he always remained true to his testimony of the golden plates and the angelic manifestation, even until his death.

For these and other reasons, the argument that Oliver Cowdery wrote the Book of Mormon receives little credence today.

### *Sidney Rigdon*

Another candidate for authorship of the Book of Mormon was Sidney Rigdon. As a Protestant minister, orator, and theologian, he seemed to critics to be a likely possibility. The supreme irony of this argument, however, is that Sidney Rigdon was converted by the very book he was supposed to have written. Parley P. Pratt, a former member of Rigdon's congregation, introduced him to the Book of Mormon in October 1830, about six months after the Book of Mormon was published. Do we have any witnesses that this is how Sidney Rigdon was converted? We do. In fact, the historical evidence is compelling.

First, Parley P. Pratt recorded Rigdon's initial reaction to the Book of Mormon: "He was much surprised, and it was with much persuasion and argument that he was prevailed on to read it, and after he had read it, he had a great struggle of mind, before he fully believed and embraced it."[11]

Second, Sidney Rigdon's daughter Nancy Rigdon Ellis was seven years old when Parley P. Pratt and Oliver Cowdery presented her father with a copy of the Book of Mormon in their home. She said she recalled the event because of the conflict that arose: "I saw them hand [my father] the book, *and I am as positive as can be that he never saw it before.* He read it and examined it for about an hour and then threw it down and said he did not believe a word in it."[12] Soon afterward, however, he did accept the divine authenticity of the Book of Mormon, joined the Church, and became one of its leaders.

Third, Rigdon's son John spoke to his father after visiting Utah in 1863 to study The Church of Jesus Christ of Latter-day Saints. He asked his father to tell him the truth about the Book of Mormon, saying, "You owe it to me and to your family." In other words, please don't perpetrate a fraud on your own family. John then recounted his father's response: "My father looked at me a moment, raised his hand above his head and slowly said, with tears glistening in his eyes: 'My son, I can swear before high heaven, that what I have told you about the origin of that book is true.'" After this tender moment, John said, "I believed him."[13] Later, John joined the Church.

Fourth, Joseph's wife Emma declared that "no acquaintance was formed between Sidney Rigdon and the Smith family till after the Church was organized,"[14] which, of course, was after the Book of Mormon had already been published.

Fifth, Phineas, Heil, and Mary D. Bronson, members of the Church, made the following corroborating statement: "We, whose signatures are affixed, did hear Elder Sidney Rigdon, in the presence of a large congregation, say he had been informed that some in the neighborhood had accused him of being the instigator of the Book of Mormon. Standing in the door-way, there being many standing in the door-yard, he, holding up the Book of Mormon, said, 'I testify in the presence of this congregation, and before God and all the Holy Angels up yonder, (pointing towards heaven), before whom I expect to give account at the judgment day, that I never saw a sentence of the Book of Mormon, I never penned a sentence of the Book of Mormon, I never knew that there was such a book in existence as the Book of Mormon, until it was presented to me by Parley P. Pratt, in the form that it now is.'"[15]

And thus, another argument fell by the wayside.

## Argument 3: The Book of Mormon Was Plagiarized from or Heavily Influenced by Other Books

Other critics have offered a different line of attack—namely, that Joseph Smith or others plagiarized or were at least heavily influenced by the historical content found in other books existing at the time. This assertion is purported to have occurred in two primary ways: (1) by borrowing concepts from existing books, and (2) by lifting exact or nearly exact language from such books.

### *The Spaulding Manuscript*

One such theory alleged that Joseph Smith conspired with Sidney Rigdon to create the historical setting of the Book of Mormon from an unpublished manuscript written about 1812 by a man named Solomon Spaulding, who had once been a Protestant minister. This document, known as "the Spaulding manuscript," is a fictional account of ancient Romans who were sailing for England but were blown off course and landed in North America.

As rumors spread about similarities between the Spaulding manuscript and the Book of Mormon, two critics of the Church, Doctor Philastus Hurlbut (a former member of the Church who had been excommunicated for immoral behavior while on a mission) and Eber D. Howe, obtained the unpublished manuscript from Spaulding's widow with the intent to print it and expose the Book of Mormon as a fraud. To their great disappointment, however, they could not find the similarities for which they had hoped. Hurlbut admitted: "I obtained a manuscript . . . which was reported to be the foundation of the 'Book of Mormon.' . . . Upon examination I found it to contain nothing of the kind, but being a manuscript upon an entirely different subject."[16] To hide the embarrassment, Howe speculated that there was a second manuscript that was the real source of the Book of Mormon, but this manuscript was allegedly lost and therefore conveniently could not be compared to see if plagiarism had occurred. Other than hearsay, there is no evidence that a second manuscript ever existed.

Eventually, the "first" and only known manuscript was found in 1884 by L. L. Rice, who many years earlier had purchased the office and supplies of the aforementioned critic, Eber Howe.[17] He discovered the alleged smoking gun among the personal papers of Mr. Howe, who had previously claimed the manuscript to be missing. Knowing of its purported connection to the Book of Mormon, Mr. Rice, James Fairchild (who was then president of Oberlin College), and others—none of whom were members of The Church of Jesus Christ of Latter-day Saints—reviewed the Spaulding manuscript and concluded: "[We] compared it with the Book of Mormon, and could detect *no resemblance between the two, in general or in detail.*"[18]

No wonder Sidney Rigdon, who was falsely alleged by some to have used the Spaulding manuscript to write the Book of Mormon, called this theory "a moonshine story . . . the most base of lies, without even the shadow of the truth."[19]

David Whitmer confirmed the foregoing historical facts in an interview with Joseph Smith III (the son of Joseph Smith Jr., the Prophet): "He [David Whitmer] states that Elder Sidney Rigdon was not known to the Elders of the Church until long after the Book of Mormon was issued; and that of his knowledge Elder Rigdon had nothing to do with the manuscript of the Book of Mormon; that he [David Whitmer] was familiar with Joseph Smith, the methods of translation, and the circumstances connected with it and the publishing of the book, and from this acquaintance knows that the Spaulding manuscript story is false and without a shadow of truth in it."[20]

With the passage of time, even various critics of the Book of Mormon have acknowledged the massive holes in this theory. For example, one such critic, Isaac Woodbridge Riley, wrote: "The commonly accepted Spaulding theory is insoluble from external evidence and disproved by internal evidence."[21]

When I was in my twenties, I saw a notice from the Church History Department stating that a copy of the Spaulding manuscript could be purchased for a dollar. I ordered a copy and likewise found no meaningful resemblance whatsoever between the two books.[22] In spite of the foregoing, a few critics continue to beat this dead-horse theory hoping it will run, even though it has not had a heartbeat for over a century.[23]

### *View of the Hebrews*

With the demise of the Spaulding manuscript theory, critics alleged that a principal source for the Book of Mormon was another book, *View of the Hebrews,* written in 1823 by Ethan Smith (no relation to the Prophet Joseph Smith) and revised in 1825.[24] This book was an attempt to prove that Native Americans were descendants of the lost ten tribes of Israel. Because some of its themes have some similarities to themes in the Book of Mormon, critics have claimed that *View of the Hebrews* provided the basic framework for the Book of Mormon.

However, one of the chief proponents of this argument, Fawn Brodie, acknowledged obvious differences between the two books: "Thus, where *View of the Hebrews* was just bad scholarship, the Book of Mormon was highly original and imaginative fiction."[25] Evidently, Brodie claims that in some mysterious, inexplicable way, Joseph Smith transformed a sow's ear (*View of the Hebrews*) into a silk purse (the Book of Mormon), hardly a rousing endorsement for an alleged act of plagiarism.

There is a simple test to determine if the Book of Mormon was copied from or relied heavily upon *View of the Hebrews*—simply compare the two books and decide for yourself. With complete academic honesty, B. H. Roberts, one of the leading scholars of The Church of Jesus Christ of Latter-day Saints, did so in the early 1920s. His desire was to inform the First Presidency of the Church of arguments that critics might make against the Book of Mormon. In this pursuit, he listed twenty-six possible parallels between the two books.[26] Critics have used these parallels to argue there must be a connection between *View of the Hebrews* and the Book of Mormon.

Hugh Nibley, however, exposed the fallacy of the argument that if two books have some parallel themes, one must have been used to create the other. He found thirty-five parallels between the Dead Sea Scrolls and the Book of Mormon. In fact, he referred to them as "perfectly staggering parallels."[27] Nonetheless, the Book of Mormon could not have been plagiarized from or influenced by the Dead Sea Scrolls, in spite of the numerous parallels, because the Dead Sea Scrolls were not discovered until more than a century *after* the Book of Mormon was published. And certainly no one is claiming that the Dead Sea Scrolls were copied from or influenced by the Book of Mormon. The similarities between the Dead Sea Scrolls and the Book of Mormon demonstrate that two records or books[28] on the same subject can have parallels, even numerous parallels, without any trace whatsoever of plagiarism or influence upon one another.

Then what accounts for the parallels? They exist because both the Dead Sea Scrolls and the Book of Mormon are records that refer to some similar historical and religious events, and thus common themes appear in their respective texts.

So it is with *View of the Hebrews* and the Book of Mormon—there are some parallels because on occasion these two books are referring to similar historical and religious events, but there is no proven connection of any reliance by one upon the other.[29] In fact, shortly before his death, B. H. Roberts declared: "Ethan Smith [the man who wrote *View of the Hebrews*] played no part in the formation of the Book of Mormon."[30]

While *View of the Hebrews* and the Book of Mormon do address some common subjects, their primary objectives and writing styles are substantially different. For example, the Book of Mormon's principal focus is to testify of Jesus Christ, declare His doctrine, and explain how we can return to Him and be saved. It is written by prophets of God. Accordingly, the historical setting is not the focus but rather the background that gives context and emphasis to the Savior and His doctrine. The principal focus, however, for *View of the Hebrews* is to historically connect the Native Americans to the lost ten tribes via archaeology, legend, and recorded histories, and to reference their prophesied gathering in the last days. In addition, *View of the Hebrews* is a series of independent quotes and examples meant to prove this theory. On the other hand, the Book of Mormon is a cohesive narrative—a story of families and prophets who sought and struggled to live God's word. The primary purpose, style, and tone of these two books differ significantly.

Perhaps the above are some of the reasons that none of Joseph Smith's contemporaries ever advanced the argument that *View of the Hebrews* was source material for the Book of Mormon. In other words, those who lived at the time when *View of the Hebrews* was in prime circulation and had its widest readership never argued there was a connection between the two books. Why? Because there was no obvious connection to be made. In fact, this argument that *View of the Hebrews* was the framework for the Book of Mormon was not first made until seventy-two years *after* the Book of Mormon was published.[31] If the connection was so obvious, why did it take the critics (many of whom were eagerly hunting for arguments to expose the Book of Mormon as man-made) seven decades to discover it?

As an additional historical note, in 1842 (twelve years after the Book of Mormon was published), the Church's newspaper, the *Times and Seasons,* under the editorship of Joseph Smith, referred to *View of the Hebrews* with seeming enthusiasm that it contained some historical information that might help confirm the authenticity of the Book of Mormon.[32] If Joseph copied from or relied upon *View of the Hebrews,* why would he publicly call attention to it?

## Argument 4: Joseph Suffered from a Mental Disorder

Some have advanced the argument that Joseph Smith suffered from a mental disorder that somehow endowed him with additional powers and skills that enabled him to write what he could not otherwise have written on his own.[33] In 1931, Harry Beardsley, a Chicago journalist, wrote, "*The Book of Mormon* is a product of . . . a mind characterized by the symptoms of the most prevalent of mental diseases of adolescence—dementia praecox,"[34] sometimes referred to as schizophrenia.

More recently, critics have postulated that Joseph suffered from childhood traumas and narcissistic personality disorder.[35] These mental disorders are supposed to have given Joseph the incentive and drive to write the Book of Mormon and also to serve as the source of the book's tone and tenor.

There are fatal defects, however, with such arguments. First, there is no credible evidence that Joseph had any form of mental disorder. Second, there is no substantiating evidence that such physical or mental conditions magically bestow upon an untrained writer such as Joseph Smith the ability to instantly become a skilled writer. Third, the book is not characteristic of the mentally ill—rather it is positive and optimistic in its tone; it expresses love for God, is filled with hope, and is consistent in these themes. Even Fawn Brodie acknowledged this fact: "Critics who insist that Joseph Smith suffered from delusions have ignored in the Book of Mormon contrary evidence difficult to override. Its very coherence belies their claims. . . . Its structure shows elaborate design, its narrative is spun coherently, and it demonstrates throughout a unity of purpose."[36]

As you would expect, the arguments that Joseph Smith suffered from a mental disorder never got much traction.

## Argument 5: Joseph Smith Was a Creative Genius Who, Shaped by His Environment, Wrote the Book of Mormon

Many critics today subscribe to the theory that Joseph Smith alone was able to compose the Book of Mormon because he was a creative genius. This is a 180-degree turnabout from the premise of earlier critics, who claimed that Joseph was too illiterate, too ignorant to write such a work on his own. In fact, in their failed efforts to find a plausible theory for the origin of the Book of Mormon, the critics have now come full circle, back to the same argument originally made by Alexander Campbell in 1831—that Joseph Smith was the sole author of the Book of Mormon, except that now Joseph Smith is considered brilliant rather than ignorant.

Fawn Brodie, perhaps the chief proponent of this argument, opined that Joseph Smith, the unschooled farm boy, was a creative genius who, fashioned by his environment and the influence of local history books and resources, personally wrote the Book of Mormon. Remarkably, Brodie wrote: "Never having written a lore of fiction, [Joseph Smith] laid out for himself a task that would have given the most experienced novelist pause. *But possibly because of his inexperience, he plunged into the story.*"[37] When one contemplates that assertion it is nothing short of mind-boggling. Was it this same inexperience that helped him create hundreds of names, weave them into a complex set of events, and then thread the narrative together in a harmonious whole resplendent with profound doctrinal insights? By her very acknowledgment of Joseph's inexperience, Brodie has magnified the improbability of Joseph writing this monumental work on his own.

Joseph Smith's wife Emma, the person who knew him better than any other, confirmed this conclusion: "Joseph Smith [as a young man] could neither write nor dictate a coherent and well-worded letter, let alone dictat[e] a book like the Book of Mormon."[38] Nonetheless, many have bought into the argument that Joseph Smith wrote the Book of Mormon because they realize that they have no viable alternative to embrace other than to admit that Joseph translated the Book of Mormon by the gift and power of God.

In order to account for the history of the Book of Mormon, many critics claim that Joseph must have read or been conversant with *View of the Hebrews,* along with a staggering number of other books, including the Apocrypha; *The Wonders of Nature* (1825), by Joseph Priest; *The Golden Pot: A Modern Fairytale* (1814), by E. T. A. Hoffman; *The Late War Between the United States and Great Britain* (1816), by Gilbert J. Hunt; *The First Book of Napoleon* (1809), by Eliakim the Scribe; *Travels Through Arabia and Other Countries in the East* (1792), by Carsten Niebuhr; and other books pertaining to ancient geography and maps. In fact, one author has listed more than 150 books about the Native Americans that could have influenced Joseph Smith or his contemporaries.[39]

The suggestion that Joseph Smith researched and read a substantial number of these books or other local resources is a far cry from his mother's observation that he was "less inclined to the perusal of books than any of the rest of our children."[40] Nonetheless, the claim is made that these books, or a discussion of the same as found in newspapers or conversations, became the basis for the historical narrative in the Book of Mormon.

Louis C. Midgley, a Church scholar, added this note: "Critics of the Book of Mormon now seem forced to follow the agenda set out by Brodie—they must locate nineteenth-century sources for all its content. And they must explain how Joseph Smith was able to locate, digest, winnow, and then fashion these materials into a coherent form."[41]

How might one counter this argument? Here is a list of questions an honest seeker of truth might raise:

- Is there any concrete historical evidence proving that Joseph read any of these books before the Book of Mormon was translated, and that such books provided resource information for the Book of Mormon? No.[42]
- Is there a single reference—just one—in Joseph's journals or letters suggesting he might have read or had conversations concerning any of these historical sources before translating the Book of Mormon? No.
- Did Emma Smith, who was married to him, ever comment that he referred to any of these books before the Book of Mormon was translated? No.
- Is there any evidence that Joseph visited the libraries where these books may have been located? No.
- Are there any independent sources who claim that Joseph discussed any of these books at any time with them before the Book of Mormon was translated? No.
- Is there any record that Joseph had any of these books or related notes present when he translated the Book of Mormon? No. Emma Smith was a firsthand witness of this. Asked in an interview if Joseph read from any books or notes while dictating, she replied, "*He had neither manuscript nor book to read from. . . . If he had had anything of the kind, he could not have concealed it from me.*"[43]

> In 1881, the *Chicago Times* reported, after an interview with David Whitmer, "Mr. Whitmer emphatically asserts as did Harris and Cowdery, *that while Smith was dictating the translation, he had no manuscript, notes or other means of knowledge save the seer stone and the characters as shown on the plates,* he [Whitmer] being present and cognizant how it was done."[44]

One might ask: How many nos does it take to expose the critics' argument as pure speculation—nothing more than a sand castle that comes crashing down when the first wave of honest questions appears on the scene?

Does anyone honestly expect us to believe that Joseph Smith, an unlearned young man of twenty-three years of age, searched out and studied all these resources on Native American life; inhaled the related conversations on the topic; ferreted out the irrelevant; organized the remainder into an intricate story involving hundreds of characters, numerous locations, detailed war strategies, and doctrinal gems; and then dictated it with perfect recollection, without any notes whatsoever—no outline, no manuscript, nothing—a fact acknowledged even among Joseph's critics?[45] And during the entire translation process, no one remembers Joseph going to libraries, bringing any such books home, or having any conversations concerning this research. Where, we might ask, is the corroborating evidence? It is nowhere to be found.

## Divine Authenticity

Emma Smith, speaking to her son, confirmed her belief regarding the divine authenticity of the Book of Mormon and the inability of Joseph to write such a book:

"*My belief is that the Book of Mormon is of divine authenticity—I have not the slightest doubt of it.* I am satisfied that no man could have dictated the writing of the manuscripts unless he was inspired; for, when acting as his scribe, your father would dictate to me hour after hour; and when returning after meals, or after interruptions, he would at once begin where he had left off, without either seeing the manuscript or having any portion of it read to him. This was a usual thing for him to do. It would have been improbable that a learned man could do this; and, *for one so ignorant and unlearned as he was, it was simply impossible.*"[46]

This may seem insignificant to some, but to me it is astounding. For thirty-four years, as a lawyer, I regularly dictated correspondence and other documents to my secretary. As I did so, I was often interrupted by a phone call or question. After such interruptions, I would invariably ask my secretary, "Where was I?" But Joseph was not dictating or writing a new work; he was translating an ancient scriptural record by the power of God and therefore did not need to ask, "Where was I?"

An honest seeker after truth must eventually ask, "If the Book of Mormon did not come forth by divine means as described by Joseph Smith, then what is the explanation for its origin?" As the theories of men become exposed and eliminated from serious consideration, Joseph Smith's explanation of the coming forth of the Book of Mormon remains the only viable option on the table—and why? Because it is as true as true can be.

In this regard, Elder Richard G. Scott offered this suggestion: "Discover for yourself that it [the Book of Mormon] is true. As you read each page ask, 'could any man have written this book, or did it come as Joseph Smith testified?'"[47]

## Who Did Write the Book of Mormon?

If neither Oliver Cowdery, Sidney Rigdon, nor Joseph Smith wrote the Book of Mormon, then who did? It was written by ancient prophets who lived in the Americas. While there were only four key engravers of the golden plates—Nephi, Jacob, Mormon, and Moroni—there were many other prophet-authors of the Book of Mormon, such as Mosiah, Alma, and Helaman. Do we have any evidence that the Book of Mormon was written by multiple authors, thus giving credence to the account of its origin as told by Joseph Smith? We do.

A form of statistical analysis called stylometrics can help discover the identity of unknown or disputed authors. Some stylometric studies have been conducted on the Book of Mormon to determine who its true author or authors might have been. Because stylometrics is an emerging science that is being refined over time, these studies have resulted in various outcomes, but certain common elements have appeared when proper methodologies have been applied.[48]

In analyzing these studies, three scholars in The Church of Jesus Christ of Latter-day Saints who have expertise in this field—Matthew Roper, Paul J. Fields, and G. Bruce Schaalje—have concluded:

"It should be understood that stylometry cannot prove that the Book of Mormon was written by multiple ancient American prophets. What it *can* reliably demonstrate, and what valid data from . . . [existing] studies collectively argue, is that (1) the Book of Mormon was written in multiple, distinct authorship styles, (2) these distinct styles are consistent with the authors designated within the text itself, and (3) none of the proposed 19th century authors [such as Sidney Rigdon or Solomon Spaulding]—including Joseph Smith himself—have writing styles that are similar to those found in the Book of Mormon."[49]

This evidence is one more witness that Joseph Smith did not author the Book of Mormon but rather translated it by the power of God.

## Intellectual Dinosaurs

As time has passed, the theories that the Book of Mormon is man-made are one by one becoming intellectual dinosaurs—extinct as viable theories. They simply cannot and do not withstand the rigors of historical inquiry, literary analysis, scientific testing, or logical scrutiny. As I evaluated these various arguments, I tried to be impartial and see the strength in each, but after doing so I was reminded of the old proverb, "The mountain rumbled and out came forth a mouse." Suffice it to say, there exists a mountain of allegations but a dearth of evidence.

Perhaps Hugh Nibley best put this in perspective when he observed: "There is no point at all to the question: Who wrote the Book of Mormon? It would have been quite as impossible for the most learned man alive in 1830 to have written the book as it was for Joseph Smith."[50]

## A Parable

In response to the various theories about the origin of the Book of Mormon, Hugh Nibley published the following parable:

"A young man once long ago claimed he had found a large diamond in his field as he was ploughing. He put the stone on display to the public free of charge, and everyone took sides. A psychologist showed, by citing some famous case studies, that the young man was suffering from a well-known form of delusion. An historian showed that other men have also claimed to have found diamonds in fields and have been deceived. A geologist proved that there were no diamonds in the area but only quartz. . . . When asked to inspect the stone itself, the geologist declined with a weary, tolerant smile, and a kindly shake of the head. . . . A sociologist showed that only three out of 177 florists' assistants in four major cities believed the stone was genuine. A clergyman wrote a book to show that it was not the young man but someone else who had found the stone.

"Finally an indignant jeweler . . . pointed out that since the stone was still available for examination, the answer to the question of whether it was a diamond or not had absolutely nothing to do with who found it, or whether the finder was honest or sane, or who believed him, or whether he would know a diamond from a brick . . . but was to be answered simply and solely by putting the stone to certain well-known tests for diamonds. Experts on diamonds were called in. Some of them declared it genuine. The others made nervous jokes about it and declared that they could not very well jeopardize their dignity and reputations by appearing to take the thing too seriously. To hide the bad impression thus made, someone came out with the theory that the stone was really a synthetic diamond, very skillfully made, but a fake just the same. The objection to this is that the production of a good synthetic diamond [in that day and age] would have been an even more remarkable feat than the finding of a real one."[51]

To suggest that Joseph Smith, a farm boy with little formal education, produced a synthetic work of God in 1829 that has baffled the brightest of critics for almost two centuries would be a more remarkable conclusion than the simple fact that he obtained golden plates from an angel of God and translated them by the gift and power of God.

Just as there is a certain test to determine the validity of a diamond, there is a certain test to determine the truthfulness of a divine work, and that test is to study it and then sincerely pray and ask God if it is true (see Moroni 10:4–5). Any other test or approach will fall short of the mark.

## Match It

After extolling the depth and expansiveness of Joseph Smith's accomplishments, not the least of which was the translation of the Book of Mormon, B. H. Roberts would sometimes say to the critics: "Match it! Match it, I say, or with hand on lips remain silent when his name is spoken."[52] In this spirit, Professor Hugh Nibley challenged some of his students to write a book comparable to the Book of Mormon. I summarize the challenge as follows:

- Write a history of ancient Tibet covering a period from 600 BC to AD 450. Why ancient Tibet? Because you know no more about Tibet than Joseph Smith (or anyone else in the 1820s) knew about ancient America.
- There is to be no research of any kind.
- Your history must be 531 pages and more than 300,000 words in length.
- Other than some grammatical corrections, and a few other minor changes, you must make no modifications in the text. The first edition, as you dictate it to your secretary, must stand forever.
- You must change your style of writing many times to represent various authors.
- Subsequent archaeological discoveries must support the truth of the objects, events, and names you refer to.
- You must invent about 280 new names of people and places that will stand up under scrutiny through the years as to their proper application and derivation.
- Thousands of great men, intellectual giants, national and international personalities, and scholars must accept your history and its teachings as true.
- Tens of thousands of salespersons (i.e., missionaries) must give eighteen months or more of their lives, paying their

own expenses and bearing witness of the truth of this book.
- You must finish writing this book in sixty-five working days or fewer.[53]

With all the claims that Joseph Smith or someone else wrote the Book of Mormon, I have never seen anyone match it. Rather than spending an entire lifetime criticizing the Book of Mormon and arguing that Joseph Smith wrote it, why don't the critics just find some brilliant person in his or her early twenties who, in sixty-five working days, can write a comparable work? Of course, in order to be comparable, it must be done without a computer or any research assistants and dictated without any notes in a single draft. In the end, this would be the critics' best evidence that the Book of Mormon could be man-made. As B. H. Roberts challenged—just "match it." But in the final analysis, this won't happen. Why? Because the Book of Mormon is matchless—it is a work of God and therefore cannot be duplicated by man.

---

NOTES

1. Joseph Smith, *Teachings of Presidents of the Church: Joseph Smith,* 64.
2. Minutes and Discourse, April 21, 1834, http://www.josephsmithpapers.org/paper-summary/minutes-and-discourse-21-april-1834/2.
3. Campbell, *Delusions,* 13.
4. Campbell, *Delusions,* 11.
5. Campbell later endorsed the argument that Sidney Rigdon wrote the Book of Mormon with the help of the Spaulding manuscript, an argument discussed and refuted in this chapter. See Midgley, "Who Really Wrote the Book of Mormon?," 132.
6. Brodie, *No Man Knows My History,* 68.
7. "Last Days of Oliver Cowdery," 48. On another occasion, Oliver Cowdery wrote, "These were days never to be forgotten—to sit under the sound of a voice dictated by the *inspiration* of heaven, awakened the utmost gratitude of this bosom! Day after day I continued, uninterrupted, to write from his mouth, as he translated, with the *Urim and Thummim* . . . the history, or record, called 'The book of Mormon'" (*Latter Day Saints' Messenger and Advocate,* October 1834, 14).

8. This is referred to in Doctrine and Covenants section 9, which was written in April 1829.
9. See Joseph Smith III, "Last Testimony of Sister Emma," 289–90; see also *Chicago Times,* October 17, 1881; cited in Cook, *David Whitmer Interviews,* 75–76.
10. See "The Testimony of Three Witnesses" in the introductory pages to the Book of Mormon.
11. Pratt, *Mormonism Unveiled,* 39.
12. Ellis, "Correspondence," 1; emphasis added.
13. In Nelson, "The Dictionary of Slander," 184.
14. Joseph Smith III, "The Spaulding Story Reexamined." Joseph's younger sister Katherine confirmed this fact: "Prior to the latter part of the year A.D. 1830, there was no person who visited with or was an acquaintance of said . . . family or any member thereof, to my knowledge, by the name of Sidney Rigdon; nor was such person known to the family or any member thereof to my knowledge, until the last part of the year A.D. 1830, or the first part of the year, 1831, and sometime after the organization of the Church of Jesus Christ by Joseph Smith Jr. and several months after the publication of the Book of Mormon" (in Vogel, *Early Mormon Documents,* 1:520; typography standardized).
15. Etzenhouser, *From Palmyra,* 388.
16. George Reynolds, "The Originator of the 'Spaulding Story,'" 263. Spaulding's widow reported that she received a letter from Hurlbut informing her that her husband's manuscript "did not read as they expected" and they decided against publishing it (see Winchester, *Plain Facts,* 17).
17. See Chase, "Spaulding Manuscript," 3:1402–3.
18. Fairchild, "Solomon Spaulding and the Book of Mormon," 173–74; emphasis added.
19. In Pratt, *Plain Facts,* 14. Oliver Cowdery offered this further damaging testimony: "Sidney Rigdon did not write it [the Book of Mormon]. Mr. Spaulding did not write it. I wrote it myself, as it fell from the lips of the prophet" ("Last Days of Oliver Cowdery," 48).
20. In Cook, *David Whitmer Interviews,* 89.
21. Riley, *The Founder of Mormonism,* 172.
22. The Spaulding manuscript is now available online for anyone to view at rsc.byu.edu/out-print/manuscript-found-complete-original-spaulding-manuscript.
23. Despite the compelling historical evidence that Sidney Rigdon did not write the Book of Mormon and that the Solomon Spaulding manuscript was not a source for that book, three researchers in 2008 conducted a stylometric study and concluded with high probability that the majority of the chapters in the Book of Mormon were written by Solomon Spaulding and Sidney Rigdon. Three Latter-day Saint scholars—Paul J. Fields, G. Bruce Schaalje, and Matthew Roper—wrote a response in which they listed and discussed eight significant problems with this study. They then demonstrated, by using the same methodology employed in the 2008 study, that there was a 99 percent probability that Sidney Rigdon wrote thirty-four of the Federalist

Papers (published five years before Rigdon was even born), a 99 percent probability that Rigdon wrote about 30 percent of the Bible, and a 99 percent probability that Oliver Cowdery wrote the very paper submitted reporting on the 2008 study. Fields, Schaalje, and Roper wrote in conclusion: "The compounding effect of at least eight major errors rendered their [the original researchers'] results utterly meaningless" ("Examining a Misapplication," 108).

24. This book is currently available for anyone to review at https://rsc.byu.edu/out-print/view-hebrews-1825-2nd-edition.
25. Brodie, *No Man Knows My History,* 48.
26. See Roberts, *Studies of the Book of Mormon,* 58. As a result of this study, some critics claim that B. H. Roberts lost his testimony of the Book of Mormon. To the contrary, subsequent statements reconfirm his testimony of Joseph Smith and the Book of Mormon. After this study he wrote an article entitled "Joseph Smith: An Appreciation," in which he said he was one "who believes in him [Joseph Smith] *without reservation.*" He continued, "To me and for me he is the Prophet of the Most High, enskied and sainted!" (81; emphasis added). How could B. H. Roberts believe in Joseph "without reservation" and simultaneously have doubts about the divine authenticity of the Book of Mormon? His final general conference address in April 1933 is an additional witness of his testimony of the Book of Mormon. He referred to it as "one of the most valuable books that has ever been preserved, even as holy scripture" (in Conference Report, April 1933, 117). See chapter 4 of this book for a discussion of the differences between *View of the Hebrews* and the Book of Mormon.
27. Nibley, "The Dead Sea Scrolls," 248; see also Nibley, "Prophets in the Wilderness," 264–69.
28. Just as the Bible is considered a book even though it is a collection of independently written gospels and epistles concerning the early Christian community, the Dead Sea Scrolls are a collection of the writings of the Qumran community and therefore referenced as a book for these purposes.
29. *View of the Hebrews* is a collection of the then-existing native American legends, history, and archaeological evidences that point to some commonality with the ancient Hebrews. Where did these legends, history, and archaeological remains originate? When the Nephite civilization was destroyed, the Lamanite civilization continued but without any substantial written records. Their traditions and history were handed down to successive generations largely by word of mouth. Some of these stories or legends were no doubt altered with time; others no doubt contained some truth. Those that contained some truth would no doubt on occasion parallel similar events in the Book of Mormon: one account through the written record of the Nephites, the other account through the oral legends and stories of the Lamanites. It is important to note that some of the theories propounded in *View of the Hebrews* have been subsequently discredited. Nevertheless, there are some segments of truth that parallel with the Book of Mormon.
30. Truman Madsen relates the following: "Just before his death in September

1933, Elder Roberts was visited at his office by a long-time friend, Jack Christensen. He placed on Elder Roberts' desk a second edition of the Ethan Smith volume. During the conversation, B. H. Roberts spoke of his Book of Mormon studies and then gave Christensen his considered judgment: 'Ethan Smith played no part in the formation of the Book of Mormon'" ("B. H. Roberts after Fifty Years," 17–18).

31. See Riley, *The Founder of Mormonism,* 124–26.
32. See Joseph Smith, "From Priest's American Antiquities," 813–14. Joseph's enthusiasm for this book suggests it was the first time he had seen it.
33. Isaac Woodbridge Riley, for example, opined that Joseph Smith was an epileptic. See Riley, *The Founder of Mormonism,* 345–66.
34. Beardsley, *Joseph Smith and His Mormon Empire,* 81.
35. See Robert D. Anderson, *Inside the Mind of Joseph Smith;* see also Morain, *The Sword of Laban.*
36. Brodie, *No Man Knows My History,* 68–69.
37. Brodie, *No Man Knows My History,* 49.
38. In Joseph Smith III, "Last Testimony of Sister Emma," 290.
39. See Vogel, *Indian Origins and the Book of Mormon,* 105–32. John E. Clark wrote: "Critical historians . . . have identified over two hundred books from which Joseph could have cribbed an idea or two. This would make the Book of Mormon something of a doctrinal dissertation written by a slick, very well-read operator with photographic recall. . . . Joseph has [now] gone from being a fool to a genius or perhaps even more than that" ("Archaeological Trends and Book of Mormon Origins," 97).
40. Lucy Mack Smith, *History of Joseph Smith by His Mother,* 82.
41. Midgley, "Who Really Wrote the Book of Mormon?" 129.
42. Some critics have argued that Joseph Smith obtained the names *Moroni* and *Cumorah* from stories of Captain William Kidd, who hunted treasure in the vicinity of the Comoro Archipelago. The city Moroni became the capital of the Comoro Islands forty-seven years after the Book of Mormon was published. Fairmormon.org observes: "Those who propose that Joseph obtained the names 'Cumorah' and 'Moroni' from stories of Captain Kidd fail to cite any sources and then demonstrate that Joseph had access to them. . . . The primary inspiration for Captain Kidd stories and legends, Charles Johnson's 1724 book *A General History of the Robberies and Murders of the Most Notorious Pirates,* fails to mention the names 'Comoro' and 'Moroni/Meroni/Maroni' in conjunction with Kidd's exploits. It is the responsibility of those who make the claim to produce some sort of documentary evidence that these names existed in stories that were available to Joseph Smith" ("Did Joseph Smith obtain the names . . . ?").
43. In Joseph Smith III, "Last Testimony of Sister Emma," 289–90.
44. In Cook, *David Whitmer Interviews,* 76.
45. Noted scholar Noel B. Reynolds observed, "All accounts agree that Joseph never paused to review even the previous page or sentence and he used no notes, books, or other reference materials" ("Shedding New Light on Ancient Origins," 29. As one critic, Dan Vogel, admitted: "Smith's method

of dictation did not allow for rewriting. It was a more-or-less stream-of-consciousness composition" (*Joseph Smith: The Making of a Prophet,* xix).

46. In Joseph Smith III, "Last Testimony of Sister Emma," 290.
47. Scott, *21 Principles,* 101.
48. In "What Can Stylometry Tell Us . . . ?" See also Roper, Fields, and Schaalje, "Stylometric Analyses of the Book of Mormon," 28–45.
49. In "What Can Stylometry Tell Us . . . ?" Matthew Roper confirmed the authorship of this article via an email to the author dated June 14, 2018.
50. Nibley, "Lehi the Winner," 123.
51. Nibley, "Lehi the Winner," 121–22.
52. In Madsen, *Defender of the Faith,* 351.
53. These ten points referred to have been slightly revised by the author, but the principal portion and substance were written by Hugh Nibley. See "Lehi the Winner," 119.

# CHAPTER 3

# Where Are the Striking Clocks?

## The Earth Will Help Confirm the Truth of the Book of Mormon

Some years ago, a friend made a presentation to our family on the Book of Mormon. He commenced by reading these lines from Shakespeare's *Julius Caesar:*

> *There is no fear in him, let him not die.*
> *For he will live, and laugh at this hereafter [clock strikes].*
> *Peace. Count the clock.*
> *The clock has stricken thrice.*[1]

At first, these lines seemed not only insignificant but also irrelevant to anything in the Book of Mormon. Then my friend made his point, that Shakespeare, one of the keenest intellects the world has ever produced, had made a mistake. There were no "striking clocks" at the time of Julius Caesar. He had placed something out of context, out of date—a mistake commonly referred to as an anachronism. Even this mastermind had momentarily stumbled.

For decades critics have placed their scholarly stethoscopes firmly against the Book of Mormon, anxiously listening for a "striking clock"—something out of date, out of context—but with the passage of time their stethoscopes have been confronted with a deafening silence. Why? Because science and linguistics and other evidentiary sources have and will continue to vindicate the Book of Mormon as a work of God. As one Latter-day Saint archaeologist observed: "The Book of Mormon looks better with age."[2]

Occasionally, there has been the cry of a "striking clock" discovered in the Book of Mormon. But then, as time and truth formed their inevitable partnership, the day of reckoning came, and what was initially presented as an anachronism in the Book of Mormon became one more confirmation of its divine origin.

Elder LeGrand Richards said in a general conference address: "I have never seen this in print, but I heard President [Charles A.] Callis make this statement: that after the Book of Mormon came forth the Prophet Joseph was terribly worried about what the world would say, and he said, 'O Lord, what will the world say?' And the answer came back, *'Fear not, I will cause the earth to testify of the truth of these things,'* and from that day until now, and only the Lord knows what is yet ahead, external evidences have been brought forth of the divinity of that book."[3]

What then are some of those alleged striking clocks in the Book of Mormon, and what have the earth and other sources produced to counter the arguments of the critics, further substantiating the book's divine authenticity?

## Alleged Striking Clock #1: A Refined and Civilized People

At the time of Joseph Smith, the ancient inhabitants of the Americas were believed to be a savage, barbaric, and uncivilized people—without trade, commerce, education, or metropolitan cities. In 1834, U.S. historian George Bancroft said of the Native Americans, "[They] were a few scattered tribes of feeble barbarians, destitute of commerce and of political connection."[4] He was referring not only to the existing Native Americans in his day and age but to their ancient ancestors as well, who presumably existed in similar societies, seemingly without change.[5] This opinion of the ancient inhabitants of the Americas was almost universally held at the time of Joseph Smith.

Matthew Roper, a scholar in The Church of Jesus Christ of Latter-day Saints, shared the following accounts of what people during the time of Joseph Smith thought of the ancient inhabitants of the Americas: "Missionary Parley P. Pratt described an 1831 encounter in which an Illinois minister dismissed the Book of Mormon for its apparent lack of archaeological evidence. 'He said there were no antiquities in America, no ruined cities, buildings, monuments, inscriptions, mounds or fortifications, to show the existence of such a people as the Book of Mormon described.' 'According to [the Book of] Mormon,' wrote a British critic in 1839, 'those native Americans could read, and write,' but 'when that country first became known to Europeans, the inhabitants knew no more about letters than a four-legged animal knows the rules of logic; and not a scrap of writing was to be found.'"[6]

In direct contrast to this view, the Book of Mormon speaks of a refined and civilized people who from time to time were "very numerous" (Mosiah 27:6), who were "building large cities" (Mosiah 27:6) and "many cities" (3 Nephi 6:7), who were constructing "many highways . . . and many roads . . . , which led from city to city" (3 Nephi 6:8), who "trade[d] one with another" (Mosiah 24:7) and had "free intercourse one with another, to buy and to sell" (Helaman 6:8), who "did raise grain in abundance" and "did raise many flocks and herds" (Helaman 6:12), who made "fine-twined linen and cloth of every kind" (Helaman 6:13), who "did receive great learning" (3 Nephi 6:12) and produced "many merchants . . . many lawyers, and many officers" (3 Nephi 6:11). The Book of Mormon painted a picture of the ancient inhabitants of the Americas showing them to be, at least in part, quite civilized. This was in startling opposition to the prevailing views of the time. Surely the critics thought they had found a striking clock.

Due to this contrast between what the world believed and what the Book of Mormon taught, David Whitmer and others were worried that people would not believe the Book of Mormon. David then shared this comforting and prophetic statement given to him and others:

"When we were first told to publish our statement [that is, The Testimony of Three Witnesses], we felt sure the people would not believe it, *for the Book [of Mormon] told of a people who were refined and dwelt in large cities; but the Lord told us that He would make it known to the people, and people should discover the ruins of the lost cities and abundant evidence of the truth of what is written in the Book.*"[7]

That prophecy is literally being fulfilled in our day. In a 2011 edition of *Popular Archaeology,* archaeologist Dan McLerran, summarizing the work of Charles C. Mann, wrote: "The pre-Columbian Americas 'were immeasurably busier, more diverse, and more populous than researchers had previously imagined.' And more 'civilized,' one might add."[8]

Mann himself, in his best-selling book, *1491* (which speaks of the inhabitants of America before Columbus), noted:

"One way to sum up the new scholarship is to say that it has begun, at last, to fill in one of the biggest blanks in history: The Western Hemisphere before 1492. [It has become] in the current view, a thriving, stunningly diverse place, a tumult of languages, trade and culture, a region where tens of millions of people loved and hated and worshipped as people do everywhere. Much of this world vanished after Columbus, swept away by disease and subjugation. So thorough was the erasure that within a few generations neither conqueror nor conquered knew that this world had existed."[9] But the Book of Mormon authors knew and recorded of such a world.

The modern view of ancient America has been corroborated by *National Geographic* and others using cutting-edge technology known as LIDAR, which is able to produce aerial laser images that can detect outlines of ancient cities buried even beneath dense jungles. Tom Clynes, a writer for *National Geographic*, wrote of one such study conducted in Guatemala:

"The results suggest that Central America supported an advanced civilization that was, at its peak some 1200 years ago, more comparable to sophisticated cultures such as ancient Greece or China than to the scattered and sparsely populated city states that ground-based research had long suggested.

"'Most people had been comfortable with population estimates of around 5 million,' said Estrada-Belli, who directs a multidisciplinary archaeological project at Holmul, Guatemala. 'With this new data it's no longer unreasonable to think that there were 10 to 15 million people there. . . . '

"Virtually all the Mayan cities were connected by causeways wide enough to suggest that they were heavily trafficked and used for trade and other forms of regional interaction. These highways were elevated to allow easy passage during rainy seasons."[10]

There is no intent here to suggest that the ancient people referred to above were the same people described in the Book of Mormon. The important conclusion is that these people who lived in ancient America in a time period that overlapped or was close to Book of Mormon times were a refined and civilized people who built large cities, constructed highways, and engaged in extensive trade. Such a realization counters the opposing view that largely existed at the time of Joseph Smith, and instead gives additional credence to the cultural and commercial environment of peoples referred to by the Book of Mormon.

### Alleged Striking Clock #2: The Existence of Metal Plates

For years, many laughed at the idea of golden plates as a medium for record keeping. It was a favorite target of detractors. Hugh Nibley referred to this in 1952 when he made this prescient forecast: "It will not be long before men forget that in Joseph Smith's day the prophet was mocked and derided for his description of the plates more than anything else."[11]

Surely Joseph Smith must have thought—like the vast majority did during his era—that ancient civilizations in the Americas recorded their histories on papyrus or parchments, not metal plates. Latter-day Saint scholar Paul R. Cheesman wrote, "At the time of Joseph Smith's remarkable discovery [of the golden plates] . . . it is evident that a knowledge of any ancient culture writing on metal, anywhere in the world, was not public knowledge."[12]

Even if there was limited knowledge before 1830 of some metal plates used for record keeping, it was obvious that the critics of Joseph's day did not know about or believe it. Otherwise, they would never have promoted the argument that the golden plates were a myth. For example, Martin Thomas Lamb, a Protestant minister, wrote, "No such records were ever engraved upon golden plates, or any other plates, in the early ages."[13]

Hugh Nibley wrote, "It is only too easy to forget that nothing in the coming forth of the Book of Mormon excited louder howls of derision than the fantastic idea of a sacred history being written on gold plates and then buried in the ground."[14]

To now argue that Joseph Smith, on a rural farm located on the then existing frontiers of America, knew of some limited findings of ancient metal plates, and used that knowledge as the basis for his story of the golden plates, while his many critics were completely unaware of such findings, seems most unlikely.

At Joseph's time, the belief that ancient civilizations did not keep records on metal plates was almost universally held. But eventually the truth was discovered. Some years after the Book of Mormon was published, discoveries of ancient metal plates began to unfold at a rapid rate, and the critics' myth was shattered. The plates of Emperor Darius I of Persia (written about 516 BC), composed of gold and silver, were found in 1933 by a German archaeologist. They were written during the same time frame as the Book of Mormon and stored in a similar stone-type box.[15] Later, a copper scroll was discovered as part of the Dead Sea Scrolls.[16] Many other metal plates recording the histories of ancient civilizations have now been discovered.[17]

John L. Sorenson, emeritus professor of anthropology at Brigham Young University, noted that "the position of orthodox archaeologists" for many years had been that metals were not used in Mesoamerica before about AD 900. Nonetheless, the years passed, and the earth continued to yield its treasured truths. Professor Sorenson then observed: "One basic lesson we learn from the experience, is that the experts were quite wrong. Metals were indeed in use in Book of Mormon times in Mesoamerica. What kind of evidence is there? The most compelling consists of actual specimens found when an early date is positively indicated. Over a dozen of these significantly precede A.D. 900. The earliest piece so far notably dates back to around the first century B.C. It is a bit of copper sheathing found on top of an altar at Cuicuilco in the Valley of Mexico."[18]

The critics' insistence that metal plates were not used to record ancient histories only magnifies the improbability that Joseph could have known of their existence. Therefore, his reference to metal plates as a medium for ancient writings is all the more astounding—nothing short of a divine disclosure.

## Alleged Striking Clock #3: Cement in Ancient America

For many years critics argued that a striking clock in the Book of Mormon was its references to the use of cement by the ancient inhabitants of America. The following scripture is an example: "The people who went forth became exceedingly expert in the working of cement; therefore they did build houses of cement, in the which they did dwell" (Helaman 3:7).

Archaeologists were certain that cement was not used in the Americas until years after the recorded history of the Book of Mormon. John L. Smith (a Christian minister) summarized this claim as follows: "There is zero archaeological evidence that any kind of cement existed in the Americas prior to modern times."[19] The Book of Mormon references to cement were simply contrary to all known scientific facts of the time. Joseph Smith, the critics alleged, had inserted something out of date, out of context—certain proof of his hoax. But then truth, as it always does, surfaced. Cement was discovered in the Americas—dating to the same time period when the Book of Mormon people lived.

Heber J. Grant, seventh President of The Church of Jesus Christ of Latter-day Saints, was once confronted by a peer who said he could not believe the Book of Mormon because it mentions cement. President Grant shared that experience in 1933 during a general conference address:

"When I was a young man, another young man who had received a doctor's degree ridiculed me for believing in the Book of Mormon. . . . He said there had never been and never would be found, a house built of cement by the ancient inhabitants of this country, because the people in that early age knew nothing of cement. He said that would be enough to make one disbelieve the book. I said: 'That does not affect my faith one particle. I read the Book of Mormon prayerfully and supplicated God for a testimony in my heart and soul of the divinity of it and I have accepted it and believe it with all my heart.' I also said to him, 'If my children do not find cement houses, I expect that my grandchildren will.' Now, since that time houses made of cement and massive structures of the same material have been uncovered [in the Americas]."

President Grant went on to say that these cement structures show "skill and ability, superior almost to anything we have today so far as the use of cement is concerned."[20]

Structural engineer David Hyman confirmed this finding: "American technology in the manufacture of cement, its mixing and placement two thousand years ago, paralleled that of the Greeks and the Romans during the same period." Hyman then observed that cement discovered in Mexico from the first century AD is a "fully developed product. . . . Technology in the manufacturing of calcareous cements in Middle America [was] equal to any in the world at the advent of the Christian Era."[21]

It is of some interest to note that David Whitmer, about forty years after his excommunication, gave further weight to the existence of cement in ancient America when he said that the golden plates were stored in "a stone box, and the stones looked to me as if they were cemented together."[22]

For a time, the critics reveled in their argument, until the earth produced the truth. Rather than accept and embrace the truth, the critics continued in their never-ending search for another striking clock.

### Alleged Striking Clock #4: Barley in Ancient America

Barley is referred to in the Book of Mormon as a crop (see Mosiah 9:9), a tribute payment to the king of the Lamanites (see Mosiah 7:22), and a means of monetary exchange (see Alma 11:7). It was clearly a basic staple of the Nephite civilization. But for years the critics were ruthless in their attacks against this Book of Mormon claim. Matthew Roper summarized some of these attacks as follows:

"In 1964 Gordon Fraser asserted, 'The only grain known in America was maize.' Elsewhere the same author described the Book of Mormon references to barley as one of numerous 'verifiable blunders' found in the Book of Mormon. In a popular anti-Mormon work published in 1979, [a] former Mormon . . . could safely affirm what previous critics already knew, that 'barley never grew in the New World before the white man brought it here!' Other Evangelical critics were even more smug, 'If there was no barley in America until the white man came, then [the Book of Mormon] must be false. If God were the one that wrote the Book of Mormon, is it not a reasonable assumption that he would have known there was no barley in the New World? The Book of Mormon . . . falls short of authenticatable [sic] truth.'"[23]

Then the shoe dropped. In 1983, barley was discovered in Hohokam Native American archaeological sites in Arizona, contrary to the unequivocal assertions of the critics that no barley existed in the Americas in pre-Columbian times. It was a domesticated form of barley known among the scientists as "little barley." The Hohokam Native Americans were believed to have existed between about 300 BC and AD 1450, thus overlapping with Book of Mormon times but predating European migrations to the Americas. Subsequently, barley was found to be native in other U.S. states as well as Mexico.[24] In the spirit of fairness, would the critics now admit that this discovery, in light of their previous stern denials, adds credibility to the authenticity of the Book of Mormon? Perhaps these critics would benefit from the counsel of an unknown source: "It ain't what you don't know that gets you into trouble. It's what you know for sure that just ain't so."

In the early 1970s, Dr. John Lund was teaching a graduate class at a Latter-day Saint institute of religion adjacent to a major university. He tells in his own words of the following experience: "One of the students working on his Ph.D. in horticulture told me privately that he could no longer believe in the Book of Mormon. He said that he had learned in his research that there was no pre-Columbian domesticated barley in the Americas." Dr. Lund counseled him: "Don't lose faith in what you know because of what you don't know!" Nevertheless, this young man lost his faith and commitment to the gospel.[25] Unfortunately, he let a partial knowledge of science trump his faith in the gospel. If only he had patiently endured a few more years, if only he had trusted his faith, his dilemma would have resolved itself. And thus, one more casualty was added to the list of those who chose to set aside their faith in favor of a limited knowledge of science.

## Alleged Striking Clock #5: Alma as a Male Name

The Book of Mormon refers to two male prophets by the name of Alma. The critics were sure they had caught Joseph Smith in an error this time. Alma was considered to be only a female name in Latin and Hebrew, not a male name. As one critic said: "Alma is supposed to be a prophet of God and of Jewish ancestry in *The Book of Mormon*. In Hebrew Alma means a betrothed virgin maiden—hardly a fitting name for a man."[26]

But then, in 1961, through the work of world-renowned archaeologist Yigael Yadin, the earth again yielded up its treasures, and a deed was found in Jerusalem dating to the early second century AD, during the same time period covered by the Book of Mormon. The deed was signed by Alma ben Yehuda, which means, in Hebrew, Alma, the son of Judah. In other words, Alma was a genuine Hebrew male name, just as revealed in the Book of Mormon.[27] What had been a seeming mistake became another witness of the Book of Mormon's divine authenticity.[28]

## Alleged Striking Clock #6: Jesus Born "at Jerusalem"

The Book of Mormon states that Jesus "shall be born of Mary, at Jerusalem which is the land of our forefathers" (Alma 7:10; see also 2 Kings 14:20; Luke 2:4). This time the critics were certain Joseph Smith had erred and they had found their striking clock. Doesn't even a child know that Jesus was born in Bethlehem, not Jerusalem? But, as always, the day of reckoning came.[29]

Once again, the earth yielded up its treasured truths. In 1887 (fifty-seven years after the Book of Mormon was published), some ancient Near Eastern documents dating back to the fourteenth century BC, known as the Amarna letters, were discovered. Near Eastern scholar D. Kelly Ogden described these texts as follows: "El Amarna letter #287 . . . mentions the 'land of Jerusalem' several times. And—like Alma—the ancient writer of El Amarna letter #290 even *refers to Bethlehem as part of the land of Jerusalem*."[30] Joseph was totally vindicated. He was merely translating language common to the usage of the time. Once again, the earth had come to the rescue.

## Alleged Striking Clock #7: "And It Came to Pass"

Mark Twain once poked fun at the Book of Mormon by commenting that if you removed the oft-repeated phrase "And it came to pass" from the book it "would have been only a pamphlet."[31] But even Mark Twain's jab has become an additional testimony of the Book of Mormon's divine authenticity.

The people of the Book of Mormon originated from Jerusalem; hence they were immersed in Hebraic culture. So, if the Book of Mormon is true, you would expect it to be filled with Hebraic expressions, representative of the culture from where the people came. How does this relate to the phrase "And it came to pass"? This phrase appears 1,404 times in the Book of Mormon, thus triggering Mark Twain's comment. With such repetition, one might appropriately ask, "Does this phrase also appear with repetition in the Hebraic culture of the Old Testament?" It does. In fact, the Hebrew word from which the phrase is translated appears 1,204 times in the Old Testament.[32] In the book of Genesis the phrase "And it came to pass" appears eight times in chapter 39 alone. What many thought to be a boring, overtaxed phrase, unrepresentative of the scriptures—a striking clock—is in fact totally consistent with the scriptures and a reflection of the Hebraic culture from which the Book of Mormon people claim their origins.

How did Joseph Smith know this? Was he so brilliant that he made this connection? Was he lucky? Or rather was he the instrument in God's hands who translated a divine book, just as he claimed?

## The Critics' Response

How do critics respond to these discoveries? Not surprisingly, their response is similar to that of skeptics described in the Book of Mormon who rejected the prophets who had foretold of signs to accompany the Savior's birth. Rather than rejoice and accept these prophecies as they were being fulfilled, the critics responded: *"Some things they may have guessed right, among so many; but behold, we know that all these great and marvelous works cannot come to pass, of which has been spoken"* (Helaman 16:16; emphasis added). Contrary to the critics' assertion, every single prophecy was fulfilled, including that of a day, a night, and a day without darkness.

You can almost hear the critics now: "Oh, Joseph may have guessed right on golden plates, cement, barley, Alma's name, and a few other things; he was a very lucky guesser, you know. But surely all these names, places, objects, and events spoken of in the Book of Mormon cannot be true."[33] But once again they will be proven wrong, because in the Lord's timetable the earth will yield up its treasures, and no doubt many additional names, places, objects, and events in the Book of Mormon will be confirmed.

## What About Names, Places, Objects, and Events Not Yet Confirmed?

Critics have now become relatively mute as to the previous arguments, due to the overwhelming evidence emerging in favor of the Book of Mormon. Instead, they now claim that there are many items referred to in the Book of Mormon that have not yet been discovered in archaeological excavations, such as horses, cattle, steel, and the names of Nephite cities, and therefore they assert that the Book of Mormon cannot be true.

For example, one critic made the following bold assertion: "Anachronisms: horses, cattle, oxen, sheep, swine, goats, elephants, wheels, chariots, wheat, silk, steel, and iron *did not exist in pre-Columbian America during Book of Mormon times.* Why are these things mentioned in the Book of Mormon as being made available in the Americas between 2200 B.C.–421 A.D.?"[34] This seems like a somewhat rash statement when one recalls that "experts" in prior years were absolutely certain there were no such things in the Book of Mormon times as metal plates, cement, barley, or men named Alma, until the same science on which they built their criticism proved them in error. This reminds me of the observation of George Santayana: "Those who cannot remember the past are condemned to repeat it."[35]

While some of the items mentioned by critics are currently in dispute as to whether or not they have been discovered,[36] I have no doubt that in the future many more of these items, such as horses, cattle, wheels, or steel, will be discovered and confirmed with certainty. Time and science are great allies of the Book of Mormon, and no doubt the earth will continue to reveal its treasures and produce further witnesses of the book's divine authenticity.

To some extent, these critics unwittingly do Joseph Smith and the Book of Mormon a great service. Every time they accuse Joseph of an anachronism (such as metal plates, cement, or barley), they strengthen Joseph's prophetic claim. Why? Because in their dogged certainty that they know the "real" truth as supported by science (only later to be proven wrong), they have heightened the probability that Joseph could not have known the real truth except through divine means.

The fact is that very few of the known archaeological sites in ancient America have been excavated. George Stuart, a leading scholar on the Maya who worked for National Geographic for almost forty years, did an interview in 2001 on *National Geographic Live.* In the course of his interview, he made the following revealing comment: "We hardly know anything, really, about the Maya. *You know, there's almost 6000 archaeological sites and we've dug at 40 of them.*"[37] That is less than one percent.

Kerry Hull, a professor of ancient scripture at Brigham Young University, made this observation: "When my colleague Mark Wright here at BYU talked to George Stuart about this [the number of sites excavated], he told Mark it was about 1%. So, a safe estimate would be around 1–2% of Maya sites have been partially excavated, and none has been fully excavated, or even anything close to that. When you figure all the other ancient Mesoamerican cultures into this equation (Olmec, Zapotec, etc.) from Book of Mormon time periods, *the number goes down to a fraction of one percent.*"[38]

Other non–Latter-day Saint archaeologists have confirmed these estimates of minimal archaeological work done on ancient American sites. Edwin Barnhart wrote: "Less than one percent of Mesoamerica has been professionally surveyed."[39] And William Saturano added: "What percentage of Maya sites have been excavated? Of all the Maya sites that we know to exist, we have excavated less than 1% of them. . . . The sites themselves that we've done excavation at, we've excavated less than 10% of those sites, so of all the remains that we possibly could excavate, we are at 10% of 1% or one-tenth of a percent."[40]

Suppose I were to tell you that a man surveyed 2 percent or less of the geography in the United States and then made the unequivocal assertion that there are no everglades in the U.S., no mountains above 10,000 feet, no large lakes, no gold mines, no oil fields, and no volcanos, because in his survey he did not see any of these things. You would likely respond to such an assertion: "How foolhardy to categorically state that no such things exist when 98 percent of the U.S. had never even been seen by him!" Likewise, how foolhardy to unequivocally claim there were no horses, cattle, steel, or the like in Book of Mormon lands and times when at least 98 percent of archaeological sites in ancient America remain unearthed. Biblical historian and archaeologist Edwin Yamauchi summed it up pretty well when he said, "The absence of archaeological evidence is not evidence of absence."[41]

Recognizing the limited archaeological work done to date, one would expect that there would be many new discoveries in the future, and that, following the pattern of the past, there will be many more evidences of the truthfulness of the Book of Mormon. The earth, as well as cultural, linguistic, historic, and other evidence, will continue to testify of the truth of the Book of Mormon.[42]

Perhaps the time will come when the evidences of the Book of Mormon will be so irrefutable that, like the fulfillment of the three days of darkness prophesied of by Samuel, "there should be no cause for unbelief among the children of men" (Helaman 14:28).

## Are the Archaeological Findings to Date a Representative Sample?

Some critics might respond that the approximately 2 percent (actually much less) of archaeological excavations that have been conducted on ancient American sites provide a "representative sample" of all the existing sites. Therefore, they might conclude that since horses, steel, and the like have not been discovered in this representative sample, we can safely assume that such items will not be found in any site. This argument, however, is severely flawed for at least the following reasons:

First, there are no doubt numerous archaeological sites that are buried beneath jungles or lakes or mountains, about which current archaeologists have no knowledge. Therefore, the total number and size of archaeological sites is a moving target. This knowledge, coupled with recent discoveries made possible by advanced technology, has caused archaeologists to now opine that we have unearthed only a fraction of 1 percent of possible sites. Suffice it to say, it is impossible to draw a true "representative sample" from a population whose actual size we do not know.

Second, a representative sample, to be truly representative of the whole, must be carefully selected so that it does not over- or under-represent one or more segments of the population. However, I can find no reference to a central archaeological organization that has a master plan of what sites in the Americas should be excavated, and in what order, so as to constitute a representative sample. In truth, much of the excavation work is driven by special interest groups, governments, or educational institutions based on available funding, manpower, and local interests. For example, is there any evidence that the excavation of Hohokam Indian sites in Arizona is a coordinated effort with excavations occurring in Bolivia as part of a master plan to find representative samples? If not, we end up with many random samples rather than a coordinated representative sample.

Third, how does one decide on representative samples from Book of Mormon culture if we don't know for certain whether Book of Mormon people lived in Mesoamerica or the midwestern United States or somewhere else? How does one draw a master plan to make a representative sample from an undetermined base?

Finally, if archaeologists already possess a representative sample, why are they surprised by new and major discoveries such as the finding of domesticated barley (in Hohokam Indian sites and elsewhere) and the degree of culture and civilization in ancient America (as evidenced by the recent LIDAR findings in Guatemala)? Archaeologist Chris Fisher recently wrote: "Everywhere you point the lidar instrument, you find new stuff and that is because we know so little about the archaeological universe in the Americas right now. Right now, every textbook has to be rewritten, and two years from now (they're) going to have to be rewritten again."[43] Such an admission strikes at the heart of the argument for a representative sample.

Perhaps archaeologist Kerry Hull summed it up best when he said: "The very notion of a representative sample is problematic in the best of circumstances, and it becomes even more tenuous with greater chronological time periods, just as we have in Mesoamerica. We're nowhere near having a 'representative sample,' whatever that even means."[44]

## An Additional Evidence That Supports the Veracity of the Book of Mormon: Chiasmus

In the summer of 1967, John W. Welch was serving as a missionary for the Church in Regensburg, Germany. He convinced his companion on preparation day to attend a lecture at a local theological seminary offering a literary analysis of the New Testament. In that class, he learned of an ancient form of writing called chiasmus—particularly utilized and highly developed in Hebrew literature. In simple terms, chiasmus is an inverted type of parallelism. Brother Welch has provided the following examples: "He that (a) findeth his life shall (b) lose it" with the next line inverted to read "And he that (b) loseth his life for my sake shall (a) find it." Or the maxim, "He who fails to prepare" and then the inversion "prepares to fail." These are simple, two-element reversals. Chiasmus is a type of parallelism that can be extended in the following type of pattern:

A
  B
    C
      D
      D
    C
  B
A

In Hebrew literature, the elements could go on for verses, even chapters.

Brother Welch tells of being awakened early one morning about two weeks later by a voice that said: "If it [chiasmus] is evidence of Hebrew style in the Bible, it must be evidence of Hebrew style in the Book of Mormon."[45] With some trepidation, he picked up his Book of Mormon and commenced his treasure hunt. He started in Mosiah, where he and his companion had been reading the night before. After about fifteen minutes or so, the first golden nugget leaped from the page—in Mosiah, chapter 5. The central portion of it reads as follows:

**A.** And now it shall come to pass, that whosoever shall not take upon him the *name of Christ*
  **B.** Must be *called* by some other name;
    **C.** Therefore, he findeth himself on the *left hand of God*.
      **D.** And I would that ye should *remember* also, that this is the name that I said I should give unto you
        **E.** That never should be *blotted out*,
          **F.** Except it be through *transgression*;
          **F.** Therefore, take heed that ye do not *transgress*,
        **E.** That the name be not *blotted* out of your hearts.
      **D.** I say unto you, I would that ye should *remember* to retain the name written always in your hearts,
    **C.** That ye are not found on the *left hand of God*,
  **B.** But that ye hear and know the voice by which ye shall be *called*,
**A.** And also, the *name* by which he shall call you (Mosiah 5:10–12).

There it was—an elegant, purposeful chiasmus in the Book of Mormon. Brother Welch and his companion returned to the professor and asked, "How strong an evidence is chiasmus of Hebraic origins?" He replied, "Very strong." They then showed him two passages in Mosiah. He read them through and said, "That's very good." However, upon realizing this was from the Book of Mormon, he said, "Oh, you are Mormons, get out."[46]

Since then Professor Welch and others have found chiasms sprinkled liberally throughout the entire Book of Mormon, with heavy doses in 1 Nephi, Mosiah, and Alma. In fact, the whole structure of Alma, chapter 36, is composed in this literary style.[47]

Once again, the Book of Mormon had been vindicated. Does anyone really believe that Joseph Smith, who couldn't write a coherent letter, not only knew of this ancient form of writing but also creatively imitated it? Even if he somehow had done so, why did not he or one of his supporters bring it to the attention of the world as an evidence of the truth of the Book of Mormon when it was first published? Why leave it to "chance" discovery over 130 years later?

## The Lord Gives Signs and Evidences to Strengthen Testimonies

Only a sampling of Book of Mormon evidences has been presented thus far. Many others exist, such as additional archaeological finds, Hebraic word patterns, internal consistencies, and the like.[48] But one might ask, "Are these signs and evidences necessary in light of our ability to have the confirmation of the Spirit?" The Lord, in His mercy, realizes that we are not perfect spiritually—that sometimes we need a stimulus to get us going in the right direction or a "tangible" confirmation to support our spiritual inclinations, and that role can be filled by physical and intellectual evidences, also known as signs.

Samuel the Lamanite prophesied that as evidence of Christ's birth, there would be (1) a day, a night, and a day without darkness, (2) a new star, and (3) many other signs and wonders in heaven. And then Samuel gave the reason for such signs: "That ye might know of the signs of his coming, to the intent that ye might believe on his name" (Helaman 14:12; see also Helaman 14:20–28; 16:4–5). There is a great lesson in this disclosure. On occasion, the Lord gives us physical or intellectual signs to help us believe on Him—not as a replacement of the Spirit but as a supplement to it.[49] For this same reason the resurrected Savior invited the Nephites to thrust their hands into His side and feel the prints of the nails in His hands and feet. Why? So that these signs would help them "know of a surety . . . that it was he, of whom it was written by the prophets, that should come" (3 Nephi 11:15).

In like manner, physical evidences played a significant role in the conversion of many Lamanites. They witnessed a "cloud of darkness," "a pillar of fire," and angels who "came down out of heaven and ministered unto them" (Helaman 5:40, 43, 48). They shared these experiences with other Lamanites, who "were convinced of them, because of the greatness of the evidences which they had received" (Helaman 5:50).

The evidences described in this chapter are, in essence, signs that we might more fully believe in the Book of Mormon.[50] Signs from heaven serve two key purposes: one, to strengthen the faith of the believer, and two, to serve as a witness against the unbeliever who has hardened his or her heart (see Helaman 14:28–29).

## A Double Standard for the Bible and Book of Mormon

### *Archaeology*

Despite the many evidences and signs witnessing the truth of the Book of Mormon, many people who accept evidence in support of the Bible seem to hold the Book of Mormon to a different, even higher standard. For example, there is no current historical or archaeological evidence of Moses or the exodus of hundreds of thousands of Israelites from Egypt or their forty years of wandering in the wilderness, even though we know the approximate locations of some of their campsites. According to *Harper's Bible Dictionary*: "Our only source of knowledge about an individual named Moses is in the Bible. Archaeology has not unearthed objects bearing his name, nor do ancient Near Eastern documents contain references to him."[51]

In addition, two respected archaeologists, Israel Finkelstein and Neil Asher Silberman, concluded: "We have no clue, not even a single word, about early Israelites in Egypt; neither in monumental inscriptions on walls of temples, nor in tomb inscriptions, nor in papyri. The possibility of a large group of people wandering in the Sinai Peninsula is also contradicted by archaeology. . . . Repeated archaeological surveys in all regions of the peninsula . . . have yielded only negative evidence, not even a single sherd, no structure, not a single house, no trace of an ancient encampment. . . . The conclusion—that the Exodus did not happen at the time and in the manner described in the Bible—seems irrefutable when we examine the evidence at specific sites where the children of Israel were said to have camped for extended periods during their wandering in the desert (Numbers 33) and where some archaeological indication—if present—would almost certainly be found."[52]

How does the Christian community respond to this current lack of archaeological support of Moses and the Exodus? Do most Christians lose their testimony of the Bible and its divine origin? No—and rightfully so. They respond by proposing (1) that biblical archaeology is still in its infant stages and as more excavation is completed, the truth will be revealed; and (2) that many scholars are biased against the Bible and, therefore, their conclusions are tainted and unreliable. Does this reasoning sound like it might also apply to the Book of Mormon? *Virtual Christian* magazine justified the lack of evidence for the Exodus and other biblical stories as follows:

"Many critics who doubt the historicity of the Exodus share a problem: overreliance on what archaeology can prove. . . .

"Archaeologist Edwin Yamauchi points out the limits of the science [archaeology] when he explains: (1) Little of what was made or written in antiquity survives to this day; (2) few of the ancient sites have been surveyed and a number have not even been found; (3) *probably fewer than 2 percent of the known sites have been meaningfully excavated;* (4) *few of these have been more than scratched;* and (5) *only a fraction of the fraction that have been excavated have been published and data made available to the scholarly world.*"[53]

If this is true for the Bible, what about Book of Mormon lands, where archaeological research did not start until many decades after biblical archaeology, and where no known sites could be used as starting points?

The purpose of this example is not to question the divinity of the Bible, for which I have a sacred regard as an inspired book, but to point out that there is not a level playing field when it comes to critical analysis of biblical archaeology as compared to Book of Mormon archaeology.

### *Mistakes of Men*

But this is not all. There is another significant example of the double standard employed by some Christians. The title page of the Book of Mormon states, "If there are faults they are the mistakes of men; wherefore, condemn not the things of God, that ye may be found spotless at the judgment-seat of Christ" (see also Mormon 8:12, 17).

Some contend that because there were numerous corrections made to the Book of Mormon since its original printing (the vast majority of which were minor printing and grammatical errors), this book cannot be true, because God is perfect and therefore makes no errors.

The fact is that the Bible—which we, like most of the Christian world, believe to be the word of God—has similarly undergone numerous corrections. The King James Version of the Bible was first published in 1611, but few people use this original edition. Most people are surprised to learn that the 1769 edition of the King James Version produced by Benjamin Blayney, which is in common use today, contains approximately 16,000 corrections from the original 1611 edition. The Revised Version of the Bible, another popular edition of the King James Bible, contains another 36,000 changes.[54] One might wonder how the critics who revere their King James or Revised Version of the Bible, with its multitudinous corrections, can at the same time disparage the Book of Mormon with its similar type corrections. Clearly there is a double standard in effect.

The errors and imperfections in both the Bible and the Book of Mormon, however, are of men, not God. Certainly God, who is perfect in every way, works with imperfect men to accomplish His work. Moses, Peter, Paul, and many others were called to the ministry in spite of their weaknesses. Accordingly, God performed His work of bringing about the Bible through good but imperfect prophets and translators. Such is also the case with the Book of Mormon. To illustrate this point, I share an observation made by my wife, Kathy:

"In the Louvre Museum in Paris, France, there is a majestic marble statue commonly referred to as *Winged Victory*. A Greek sculpture from the 2nd century BC, it is one of the most famous statues in the world. Towering at the top of a sweeping staircase near the entrance to the museum, it is breathtaking at first sight. Even though severely damaged—missing her head, arms, and feet—with her gracefully outstretched wings and robes, seemingly fluttering in the wind, she is stunningly beautiful. President M. Russell Ballard, speaking at President Boyd K. Packer's funeral, said that President Packer loved the *Winged Victory* and had a small replica in his office. President Packer had once said 'he liked this work of art because even though it is less than perfect in appearance, it is still a masterpiece.'"[55]

Suffice it to say, if people focus only on the minor imperfections in the Bible and Book of Mormon, they will miss the mark—they will never see the masterpiece; they will never recognize it as the handiwork of God. No doubt that is why the prophet Moroni said of the Book of Mormon, "Whoso receiveth this record, and shall not condemn it because of the imperfections which are in it, the same shall know of greater things than these" (Mormon 8:12; see also Moroni 8:17).

## The Spirit Is the Only Sure and Certain Witness

If I were to ask my Christian friends how they unquestionably know the Bible is the word of God, I believe that most would refrain from citing archaeological discoveries or linguistic connections with ancient Hebrew or Greek as their prime evidence (although these things may provide evidence), but rather they would make reference to the Spirit. It always comes back to the Spirit. The Spirit that helps me know the Bible is true is the exact same Spirit that helps me know the Book of Mormon is true. Nephi taught, "If ye shall believe in Christ ye will believe in these words [the Book of Mormon], for they are the words of Christ" (2 Nephi 33:10). The same Spirit emanates from both books.

When all is said and done, the Spirit is the ultimate evidence. It is the decisive, determining factor—not archaeology, not linguistics, and certainly not the theories of man. The Spirit has no bias, no prejudice; rather, it has but one driving concern—to bear witness of the truth, regardless of the difficulty one may have in accepting it. In essence, the Spirit is that one indisputable piece of evidence in the courtroom of truth that cannot be discredited, diluted, or denied. It speaks for itself without the need of any external confirmation or corroboration.

---

NOTES

1. Shakespeare, *Julius Caesar,* act 2, scene 1, lines 198–201.
2. Clark, "Archaeological Trends," 94.
3. Richards, in Conference Report, April 1955, 123.
4. Bancroft, *History of the United States,* 1:3.
5. See Mann, *1491: New Revelations of the Americas,* 16.
6. Roper, "Joseph Smith, Central American Ruins, and the Book of Mormon."
7. In Cook, *David Whitmer Interviews,* 96.
8. McLerran, "Lost Civilizations of North America."
9. Mann, *1491: New Revelations of the Americas,* 31.
10. Clynes, "Laser Scans Reveal Maya 'Megalopolis.'"
11. Nibley, "Lehi the Winner," 107.
12. Cheesman, *Ancient Writing on Metal Plates,* 11. While some metal plates had been discovered before 1830, this knowledge was not widely known; as William J. Hamblin observed, "It . . . would be unlikely for a young frontier farm-boy to have had access to this knowledge" ("An Apologist for the Critics," 463).
13. Lamb, *The Golden Bible,* 11.
14. Nibley, *Since Cumorah,* 57.
15. Sorenson, *An Ancient American Setting,* 278–88.
16. See Lundberg, "The Copper Scroll."
17. For further information on metal plates, see Hamblin, "Sacred Writing on Metal Plates," 37–54. Hugh Nibley observed, "The discovery of writings on plates of precious metal, once the hardest thing to swallow in Joseph Smith's story, has become almost commonplace in the Near East" ("New Approaches to Book of Mormon Study," 76).
18. Sorenson, *An Ancient American Setting,* 278. Professor Sorenson also referred to several ancient American languages that had a word for metal and then concluded: "Work in comparative linguistics shows that metals must have been known and presumably used, at least as early as 1500 B.C. That date extends back to the time of the Jaredites" (*An Ancient American Setting,* 279).
19. John L. Smith, "What about Those Gold Plates?" 8.
20. Grant, in Conference Report, April 1929, 129.
21. Hyman, *Precolumbian Cements,* ii. See also "When Did Cement Become Common . . . ?"
22. In Cook, *David Whitmer Interviews,* 23.

23. Roper, "Right on Target."
24. See Livingston, "Another Look at Barley in the Book of Mormon."
25. Lund, *MesoAmerica and the Book of Mormon,* 215.
26. Martin, *The Maze of Mormonism,* 327.
27. See Roper, "Right on Target."
28. At least one critic has discounted this as evidence, pointing out that a simple internet search produces many references to Alma as a male name. Of course, Joseph Smith would have had no access to an internet search. Further, if Alma was commonly known as a male name, why did multiple critics raise the argument that it was only a female name?
29. It is important to note that Alma 7:10 does not say that Jesus was to be born *in* Jerusalem, but rather *at* Jerusalem, which was then further described "as the land of our forefathers." The word "at" can also mean "near," and Bethlehem was certainly near Jerusalem—approximately eight miles to the south.
30. Ogden, "Why Does the Book of Mormon Say That Jesus Would Be Born in Jerusalem?," 52. Neal Rappleye, a Book of Mormon scholar, wrote: "In [El Amarna letter #290], Abdu-Heba [the king of Jerusalem] mentioned 'a town of the land of Jerusalem, Bit-Lahmi by name.' W. F. Albright, the translator, felt that Bit Lahmi was 'an almost certain reference, to the Town of Bethlehem'" ("Why Did Alma Say Christ Would Be Born in Jerusalem?").
31. Twain, *Roughing It,* 127–28.
32. The Hebrew word that is translated "and it came to pass" appears 1,204 times in the Hebrew Bible, but in 477 of those cases, the King James translators used other expressions, such as "and it happened" or "and . . . was" (see Parry, "Why Is the Phrase 'and It Came to Pass' So Prevalent in the Book of Mormon?," 29).
33. "For critics, finding such items [as ancient American barley] are often seen as 'lucky guesses' on the part of Joseph Smith" (Ash, "Archaeological Evidence and the Book of Mormon").
34. Runnells, "Letter to a CES Director."
35. Santayana, *Life of Reason,* 284.
36. For example, a horse bone found in Mexico has been carbon dated to about 500 BC (see "New Evidence for Horses in America").
37. Stuart, "Interview: George and David Stuart."
38. Email from Kerry Hull to author, Mar. 30, 2017; emphasis added.
39. Barnhart and Liulevicius, *Maya to Aztec,* 325.
40. William Saturano, "The Thrill of the Find."
41. Yamauchi, "The Current State of Old Testament Historiography," 34.
42. To repeat what was said in the preface, any evidence cited thus far is not an attempt to pinpoint where the events of the Book of Mormon took place. Rather, it is to expose the fallacy of the critics' arguments and to explain that minimal archaeological work has been done on Book of Mormon sites, wherever those sites may be.
43. As quoted in Davis, "Laser scanning reveals." In an email from Kerry Hull to the author dated September 26, 2018, Dr. Hull explained that the

proposition for a representative sample is further countered by the facts that (1) massive looting has occurred and is still occurring on current sites, (2) inordinate focus has been placed on excavating at city centers rather than rural areas, and (3) no single site has been fully excavated.

44. Email from Kerry Hull to author, Sept. 26, 2018.
45. Welch, "The Discovery of Chiasmus in the Book of Mormon," 79.
46. Welch, "The Discovery of Chiasmus in the Book of Mormon," 81. In March 2018, Brother Welch reviewed this description of his discovery of chiasmus in the Book of Mormon and made some corrections to help ensure its accuracy.
47. Welch argues convincingly for chiasmus as an evidence of the divinity of the Book of Mormon: "Even assuming that Joseph Smith had known of chiasmus, the following observation, which I made in 1981, still stands: 'There would still have remained the formidable task of composing the well-balanced, meaningful chiastic structures . . . which are found in precisely those portions of the Book of Mormon in which one would logically and historically expect to find them.' To me the complexity of Alma 36 seems evidence enough of this point. Imagine the young prophet, without notes, dictating extensive texts in this style that was unnatural to his world, while at the same time keeping numerous other strands, threads, and concepts flowing without confusion in his dictation" ("How Much Was Known about Chiasmus in 1829?," 80).
48. There are many wonderful sources to explore these evidences, including fairmormon.org and bookofmormoncentral.org.
49. The Lord has cautioned us that we should not seek signs, declaring that they come "by the will of God" (see D&C 63:7–10).
50. Paul also spoke of the role of signs or evidences in building faith when he said: "Faith is the substance of things hoped for, the evidence of things not seen" (Hebrews 11:1).
51. *Harper's Bible Dictionary,* "Moses," 659.
52. Finkelstein and Silberman, *The Bible Unearthed,* 60–63.
53. Seiglie, "The Exodus Controversy," 11; emphasis added; see also Yamauchi, *The Stones and the Scriptures.*
54. See Gordon Campbell, *Bible: The Story of the King James Version,* 235.
55. In Walch, "President Monson, Others."

## CHAPTER 4

# Partial Truths Presented as the Whole Truth

President Russell M. Nelson shared the following story highlighting the need to tell the whole truth. He said: "I was serving as a consultant to the United States government at its National Center for Disease Control in Atlanta, Georgia. Once while awaiting a taxi to take me to the airport after our meetings were over, I stretched out on the lawn to soak in a few welcome rays of sunshine before returning to the winter weather of Utah's January. Later I received a photograph in the mail taken by a photographer with a telephoto lens, capturing my moment of relaxation on the lawn. Under it was a caption, 'Governmental consultant at the National Center.' The picture was true, the caption was true, but the truth was used to promote a false impression. Yes, truth can even be used to convey a lie."[1]

Suffice it to say, a partial truth, when intentionally presented as the whole truth, is an untruth. Unfortunately, there are some who are so concerned about winning an argument or promoting an ideology that they present only a partial truth, perhaps afraid that if they presented the whole truth, it would dilute or even negate their argument. When they do so, that partial truth becomes an untruth.

This criticism is not intended to apply to those who present truths line upon line (that is, as milk before meat) with the honest intent to eventually disclose the whole truth. Nor does it apply to those who are writing within limited space but provide citations for people so they might obtain additional critical information on the subject. It is designed for those who intentionally withhold certain key facts that are essential to making an informed decision on the subject.

This principle applies not only to critics of The Church of Jesus Christ of Latter-day Saints but to all of us. If we have presented only a partial truth, then we should do our best to correct it. In the end, an honest answer, even though not fully supportive of one's position, will usually appeal to an honest person.

Following are a few examples of cases in which only a portion of the facts were disclosed as though they were the whole truth, resulting in an untruth.

## Archaeology

### *Partial Truth*

Critics claim that the Book of Mormon cannot be true because there is no archaeological evidence that certain things mentioned in the Book of Mormon—such as horses, cattle, elephants, silk, and steel—existed in pre-Columbian America.[2]

### *The Omissions*

As mentioned in chapter 3, what the critics have failed to disclose is that fewer than two percent of the archaeological sites of ancient America have been unearthed. Failure to disclose this critical fact is a gross omission that severely distorts one's understanding of the whole picture. At the same time, the critics have failed to disclose that among the approximate two percent that has been excavated, significant discoveries have been made that help confirm the veracity of the Book of Mormon, such as cement, metals, and barley, all of which were ridiculed at one time as being nonexistent in ancient America. Why these glaring omissions by the critics? Simply stated, the partial truths of the critics, when presented in isolation as the whole truth, are untruths.

## Parallels with *View of the Hebrews*

### *Partial Truth*

Critics cite parallels between *View of the Hebrews* and the Book of Mormon, thus suggesting that Joseph plagiarized concepts or themes from that book.

### *The Omissions*

Critics are quick to list the parallels between these two books, but they fail to list any of the obvious and significant "unparallels"—details or themes that are essential to the central message of *View of the Hebrews* but do not appear in the Book of Mormon. This is a significant point because if Joseph Smith used *View of the Hebrews* as the framework for the Book of Mormon, as some critics claim, it seems unlikely that he would fail to include several of its most essential points—even contradicting some of them. Professor John Welch has summarized some of the many key "unparallels," a few of which are listed below:

"Chapter 2 [of *View of the Hebrews*] lists many prophecies about the restoration of Israel, including Deuteronomy 30; Isaiah 11, 18, 60, 65; Jeremiah 16, 23, 30–31, 35–37; Zephaniah 3; Amos 9; Hosea and Joel. These scriptures are essential to the logic and fabric of *View of the Hebrews,* yet with the sole exception of Isaiah 11, none of them appear in the Book of Mormon.

" . . . *View of the Hebrews* asserts repeatedly that the Ten Tribes came to America via the Bering Strait, which they crossed on 'dry land.' According to *View of the Hebrews,* this opinion is unquestionable, supported by all the authorities. In direct contrast to this, the Book of Mormon speaks of its migrations by means of boat across the ocean. . . .

"*View of the Hebrews* reports that the Indians are Israelites because they use the word 'Hallelujah.' Here is one of the favorite proofs of *View of the Hebrews,* a dead giveaway that the Indians are Israelites. Yet the word is never used in the Book of Mormon.

" . . . A table showing thirty-four Indian words or sentence fragments with Hebrew equivalents appears in *View of the Hebrews.* No reader of the book could have missed this chart. If Joseph Smith had wanted to make up names to use in the Book of Mormon that would substantiate his claim that he had found some authentic western hemisphere Hebrew words, he would have jumped at such a ready-made list! Yet not one of these thirty-four Hebrew/Indian words (e.g., *Keah, Lani, Uwoh, Phale, Kurbet,* etc.) has even the remotest resemblance to any of the 175 words that appear for the first time in the Book of Mormon."[3]

## *The Late War*: Common Events

Critics have compared the Book of Mormon with a book by Gilbert Hunt titled *The Late War between the United States and Great Britain* (a history of the War of 1812). They conclude that Joseph Smith was influenced by events it describes and the language it uses, claiming that there exist "shared events" between them.[4] Two prime examples of claimed "shared events" are (1) a story of 2,000 courageous soldiers and (2) an account of a cataclysmic event involving earthquakes, thunder, and darkness.

*Partial Truth: 2,000 Soldiers*

Both the Book of Mormon and *The Late War* tell of an army of 2,000 soldiers who fight courageously for their country. Critics claim that the account of the 2,000 stripling warriors found in the Book of Mormon is taken from *The Late War* account. Below is a comparison of the two accounts as set out by the critics. The bolded words are the critics' attempt to show that this is a "shared event."

| ***The Late War*** | **The Book of Mormon** |
|---|---|
| *Chapter 35:5–6*<br>Immediately Jackson took **two thousand** hardy **men** who were called volunteers, because they fought freely for **their country** and led them against the savages. Now the men **of war** that followed after him were mostly from the state of Tennessee, and **men of dauntless courage**. | *Alma 53:18–20*<br>Now behold, there were **two thousand** of those young **men**, who entered into this covenant and took their weapons of war to defend **their country**. And now behold, as they never had hitherto been a disadvantage to the Nephites, they became now at this period of time also a great support; for they took their weapons **of war**, and they would that Helaman should be their leader. And they were all young **men**, and they were exceedingly **valiant for courage**, . . . |

*The Omissions*

The following chart lists the similar words and phrases highlighted by the critics, along with a response to each:

| **"two thousand . . . men"** |
|---|
| It is true that both accounts initially speak of 2,000 men (the Book of Mormon later speaks of 2,060), but the critics fail to highlight that in one case the 2,000 are hardy men and in the other case the 2,000 are very young men, who had never fought in battle. |

| "their country" |
|---|
| One might honestly ask: how would this show plagiarism, since who else would men normally fight for but their families and/or country? |
| **"of war"** |
| Who would expect two different people to write about battles and not use the word "war"? |
| **"courage"** |
| How many times have authors used the word "courage" to describe men in battle? In fact, *The Late War* uses the words "courage" or "bravery" or similar terms about 100 times to describe men in battle. Why then is this word, which is so common to battles, a notable parallel with the Book of Mormon? |

But more important than the above, the critics have failed to mention that the crux of the story of the 2,000 stripling warriors is that it is a significant faith-promoting experience that resulted in a series of remarkable miracles. This key feature is totally absent from *The Late War* account. This striking omission alone should make it apparent that these two accounts are not a "shared event." Following are some of the principal differences in these two accounts:

- The 2,000 "very young" men (Alma 56:46) choose a prophet of God as their leader (Helaman). No such prophet-leader is found in *The Late War* account.
- The 2,000 young men had faith that God would "not suffer that [they] should fall" (Alma 56:46). No mention of faith in God is mentioned in the allegedly similar account of *The Late War.*
- The 2,000 young men "had been taught by their mothers, that if they did not doubt, God would deliver them"

(Alma 56:47). No such mention of mothers and their teaching is made in *The Late War* account.

- The miracle and climax of the story of the 2,000 young men in the Book of Mormon is that not one of them was slain in the heat of battle, while 1,000 of their cohorts were slain (see Alma 57:25–26). Somehow, the critics conveniently forgot to mention that no such miracle occurred in *The Late War* account, in direct contrast to the primary point of the Book of Mormon story.

To suggest that the inclusion of 2,000 hardy men in *The Late War* is a "shared event" with the 2,000 very young men of the Book of Mormon is a significant stretch of one's imagination, and misses the heart and core of the Book of Mormon account.

## *The Late War*: Cataclysmic Event

### *Partial Truth*

Critics claim that another event in *The Late War* is similar to a cataclysmic event in the Book of Mormon, suggesting the possibility of plagiarism. Below is the comparison as cited and bolded by the critics.[5]

| ***The Late War*** | **The Book of Mormon** |
|---|---|
| *Chapter 19:37–44*<br>. . . **thunders** . . . as the mighty **earthquake** which **overturneth cities** and the **whole face of the earth** overshadowed with **black smoke; so that, for a time**, one man saw not another . . . sharp rocks **had fallen upon them**: | *3 Nephi 8:6–23*<br>. . . **thunder**, . . . **did shake the whole earth** . . . **cities were sunk, and** . . . **the face of the whole earth** . . . could feel the **vapor of darkness** . . . **so that** . . . **for the space of three days** that there was no light seen; . . . great destruction . . . **had come upon them**. |

### *The Omissions*

Here is what the critics do not disclose about these two events:

- The event in *The Late War* was evidently an accidental explosion of an ammunition depot during the course of a battle, while the event in the Book of Mormon was a divinely directed series of calamities, given as signs of Christ's death. There is no similarity in the cause or consequence of these events. One is an accident; the other was divinely prophesied of years in advance.
- The selected language from *The Late War* is scattered across ten paragraphs, while the common words selected from the Book of Mormon account are scattered over approximately twenty-five verses. These comparisons are initially presented as though they came from a single paragraph in each book. This alone is deceptive. The likelihood that the similarities are a result of chance is greatly expanded in a large block of text.
- The critics point to certain words or phrases such as *thunder*, *earthquake*, and *black smoke* as being similar in both books, but fail to disclose the significant difference in usage and context of such words. For example, the word *thunder* in *The Late War* is used metaphorically to describe an explosion that sounds like "the noise of a thousand thunders."[6] In the Book of Mormon, however, the word *thunder* is used literally: "terrible thunder" in the heavens "that it did shake the whole earth as if it was about to divide asunder" (3 Nephi 8:6). Likewise, the words *earthquake* and *black smoke* that are associated with an ammunition explosion have a completely different magnitude of meaning than the Book of Mormon experience of a massive regional earthquake that caused entire cities

> to be destroyed and "the face of the whole earth . . . [to be] deformed" (3 Nephi 8:17), or a vapor of darkness that resulted in a total absence of light for three days (see 3 Nephi 8:19–23). The difference in scope and power of these events is monumental.

Unfortunately, this is another partial truth presented as though all the pertinent facts were honestly presented.

## *The Late War*: Similarity of Names

### *Partial Truth*

Critics suggest that *The Late War* provided Joseph Smith with ideas for some of the unique names in the Book of Mormon. For example, some compare *Moravian Town* (a place) in *The Late War* with *Morianton* (a person) mentioned in the Book of Mormon. They also suggest a similarity between *Tecumseh* in *The Late War* and *Teancum* in the Book of Mormon.[7]

### *The Omissions*

The first glaring omission is that the critics fail to mention that there is not one common name between the two books (excluding references to biblical names or noted historical figures). The best the critics can come up with is two possible names that they claim have some similarity. One can judge for oneself whether *Morianton* is a derivative of *Moravian Town,* or whether *Teancum* could be likely construed as a plagiarism of *Tecumseh.*

If the critics, however, really want a fair test to determine if Joseph copied names from *The Late War,* let them set forth all the names in *The Late War* and see if any of them also appear in the Book of Mormon. For this purpose, the names of all persons mentioned in *The Late War,* excluding biblical names or noted historical figures, are set forth in endnote 8.[8] How many of these names are related to Book of Mormon names? I found *none, absolutely none.* If Joseph plagiarized names from *The Late War,* he did a mighty poor job of it. Once again, presenting a partial truth as the whole truth in order to win an argument is nothing less than an untruth.

## Comparisons between Certain Books and the Book of Mormon

I doubt that Joseph read any of the books alleged by the critics to be sources for the Book of Mormon before the translation process commenced. There is no historical evidence confirming that he did so. But even if he did, the magnitude of differences between these books and the Book of Mormon—especially when comparing lack of commonality of names, places, doctrine, and objectives—is significant, if not staggering. In the event that Joseph read any of these books, no doubt he learned some words or phrases that enhanced his vocabulary that would be available for future use in translation—that would seem natural to me. But to suggest, for example, that the story of the 2,000 hardy men who fought in the War of 1812 is the basis for the story of the 2,000 very young men known as the sons of Helaman, or that the explosion of an ammunition depot is the genesis for the story of the divine calamities at the time of Christ's death, seems like a futile attempt, driven by predetermined ideology, to transform some worldly experience into a spiritual one as described in the Book of Mormon.

## Nature of the Godhead

### *Partial Truth*

Critics claim that when Joseph Smith wrote the Book of Mormon he expressed a Trinitarian view of the Godhead—namely, that God the Father, Jesus Christ, and the Holy Ghost are one being or substance. They further claim that Joseph's views were later modified to refer to a Godhead of three separate personages.[9] To support this criticism, four main scriptures from the Book of Mormon are cited: Mosiah 15:1–4, Mosiah 16:15, Alma 11:38–39, and Ether 3:14–15. In each of these scriptures the titles of "Father" and "Son" are used as appropriate titles for Jesus Christ.

### *The Omissions*

I can see how people might be confused about the Godhead if the scriptures cited by the critics were the only scriptures on this subject in the Book of Mormon—but they are not.

Suppose someone showed you a very small portion of a picture of a lion (such as the tail) and then claimed, without showing you the rest of the picture, that the remainder was identical to the portion you have already seen. You would immediately know this to be false and deceptive. Likewise, it is deceptive when critics cite only a few scriptures describing one aspect of the Godhead but fail to reference the dozens of other scriptures that help reveal the full picture.

Because the Father and Son are perfectly united in will and purpose and equal in knowledge and power, They rightfully refer to Themselves as one, just as the scriptures refer to a husband and wife as one (see Mark 10:6–10), or to the laborers in the mission field who share a common goal as "one" (see 1 Corinthians 3:8–9), or to believers as of "one heart and of one soul" (Acts 4:32) or "one spirit" (1 Corinthians 6:17) or "one mind" (2 Corinthians 13:11). These references from the Bible are not a declaration of oneness in person, but of oneness in unity and purpose and will. In a similar sense, the Father and Son are perfectly one with each other in unity and purpose and will, but, contrary to the Trinitarian view, the Book of Mormon clearly and repeatedly teaches that God the Father and His Son Jesus Christ are two separate beings.

If critics really want to present the whole truth, they should also cite some of the many other scriptures in the Book of Mormon that clearly confirm that the Father and Son are two distinct beings. Below is a brief synopsis of 3 Nephi 11, which describes the Savior's appearance to the Nephites, and in which this doctrine is unmistakably taught. (Emphasis has been added.)

| Scripture | Explanation |
|---|---|
| 3 Nephi 11:7: "*Behold my Beloved Son, in whom I am well pleased*, in whom I have glorified my name." | What sense would it make for the Father to say, "Behold my Beloved Son" or that He was "well pleased" with His Son if in fact He is referring to Himself? This scripture assumes the necessity of two beings to make sense—the Father and a separate Son. |
| 3 Nephi 11:11: "I [the Savior] have drunk out of that bitter cup *which the Father hath given me* . . . in the which I *have suffered the will of the Father*." | What would it mean for the Savior to drink out of a cup *given* to Him if He is the same person who *gives* the cup? How could the Savior be both giver and receiver at the same time? And how could He submit His will to the Father if in fact He is the same person as the Father? Submission requires at least two distinct persons. |
| 3 Nephi 11:14: "Arise and come forth unto me, that ye may thrust your hands into my side, and also that ye may feel the prints of the nails in my hands and in my feet, that ye may know that I am the God of Israel, and the God of the whole earth, and have been slain for the sins of the world." | If the resurrected Christ has a body of flesh and bones, how can He be the same being or substance as the Holy Ghost, who is a spirit? This contradicts the Trinitarian doctrine, which claims that all members of the Godhead are of the same substance. |

| Scripture | Explanation |
|---|---|
| 3 Nephi 11:32: *"And this is my doctrine, and it is the doctrine which the Father hath given unto me."* | How could the Father give the doctrine to the Son unless they were separate persons and beings? |

Many other scriptures in the Book of Mormon teach the same doctrine about the Godhead as taught in 3 Nephi 11. The Savior acknowledged on multiple occasions that He was commanded by the Father (3 Nephi 15:15–16, 19; 16:3; 18:27). Why would the Father command the Son if They were the same person? Do we command ourselves to do things? In 3 Nephi 17:14–15, the Savior knelt and prayed to the Father. Why engage in such an act if He is merely speaking to Himself? In other words, why pray to the Father if He is the same being as the Father? In 3 Nephi 18:27 the Savior said, "I must go unto my Father" (see also 3 Nephi 27:28). Why would He need to go anywhere to be with the Father if He and the Father were the same being? In 3 Nephi 9:15, we read that the Son "was with the Father from the beginning." What would it mean for the Son to be "with" the Father if He were, in fact, the same person as the Father? And why would the Savior instruct the Nephites to "be perfect even as I, or your Father who is in heaven is perfect" (3 Nephi 12:48) if He and the Father were one and the same?

In addition, the Savior is referred to as one who advocates our cause (see Moroni 7:28) and as our "Mediator" (2 Nephi 2:27) with the Father, but with whom does He advocate or mediate if He sits on both sides of the table as the same person? In other words, it would be impossible to fulfill those roles if He and the Father were the same being.

All of these scriptures cited from the Book of Mormon witness the separate and distinct identities of the Father and Son. Lest there be any question, a multitude of scriptures in the Book of Mormon explain that the members of the Godhead are three distinct persons, who are one in every way *except identity of being*. If someone is trying to be fair rather than promote an ideology, why would he or she fail to make reference to at least some of these scriptures, all of which are in direct opposition to the claim that the Book of Mormon teaches a Trinitarian view of the Godhead?

## Statements Outside the Book of Mormon Text

On occasion, statements have been innocently but incorrectly made that extrapolated beyond the Book of Mormon text. It is important to keep in mind, however, that when this occurred, the need for correction did not apply to the inspired Book of Mormon text but rather to the statements made that were not clearly supported by actual Book of Mormon language. Below are two examples:

### *Coinage*

Some critics note that earlier editions of the Book of Mormon referred to the word *coinage* and allege that such a reference is an anachronism because coins were evidently not used in ancient America or in Israel when Lehi left Jerusalem. The text of the Book of Mormon, however, does not refer to coins; rather it refers to a system of weights and measures, as described in Alma 11. The word *coinage* is used only in the chapter heading, which is not part of the inspired Book of Mormon text. Chapter headings were added several years after the initial translation to give an overview of each chapter for the convenience of the reader.[10]

Elder Bruce R. McConkie, who supervised the creation of the chapter headings for the 1981 Latter-day Saint edition of the scriptures, wrote:

"[As for] Joseph Smith Translation items, the chapter headings, Topical Guide, Bible Dictionary, footnotes, the Gazetteer and the maps . . . none of these are perfect; they do not of themselves determine doctrine; there have been and undoubtedly now are mistakes in them."[11]

Daniel C. Peterson, a scholar on the Book of Mormon, also addressed this issue: "The text of the Book of Mormon never mentions the word 'coin' or any variant of it. The reference to 'Nephite coinage' in the chapter heading to Alma 11 is not part of the original text and is mistaken."[12] Consequently, in 2013 the chapter heading to Alma 11 was revised, and "Nephite coinage" was changed to read, "The Nephite monetary system is set forth," in order to make it consistent with the original text.[13]

As an aside, John W. Welch has noted that a Near Eastern monetary system based on weights and measures, similar to the system described in the Book of Mormon, was discovered more than 100 years after the Book of Mormon was published. In ancient Mesopotamia, the laws of Eshnunna (a city-state) provided that "one kor of barley is (priced) at one shekel of silver." The Book of Mormon states that "a senum of silver was equal to a senine of gold, and either for a measure of barley, and also for a measure of every kind of grain" (Alma 11:7). Professor Welch then noted that the "primary conversion in ancient Babylonia was between barley and silver,"[14] similar to that in the Book of Mormon—another evidence of the Book of Mormon's ancient roots and authenticity.

### *DNA*

For decades, many Church members believed that Native Americans were direct descendants of the Lamanites described in the Book of Mormon, even though the Book of Mormon makes no such claim. Consistent with this belief, the Introduction to the Book of Mormon (not part of the original record translated by Joseph Smith) stated that the Lamanites were the "principal ancestors of the American Indians."

DNA studies, however, have suggested that most Native

Americans have primarily Asian DNA.[15] Putting aside the issue of the reliability and completeness of such DNA studies (which is a serious issue),[16] and assuming that the Book of Mormon peoples were the only ones in the Americas during the recorded history of the Book of Mormon, then one might come to the conclusion that the lack of greater DNA evidence from the Near East or West Asia (where Book of Mormon migrations commenced) among Native Americans is a strike against the Book of Mormon account.

But this assumption that Book of Mormon peoples were the only ones living in the Americas at that time is incorrect. The Book of Mormon does not make such a claim. In fact, in 1929, before any related DNA studies were being conducted, President Anthony W. Ivins, a member of the First Presidency of the Church, wrote:

"We must be careful in the conclusion that we reach. *The Book of Mormon . . . does not tell us that there was no one here before [the civilizations it describes]. It does not tell us that people did not come after.* And so, if discoveries are made which suggest differences in race origins, it can very easily be accounted for, and reasonably, *for we do believe that other people came to this continent.*"[17]

As early as the 1950s, Hugh Nibley made a similar observation: "The fact that the Jaredites were led to the land of promise at the time of the dispersion [from the Tower of Babel] gives us no right to conclude that no one else was ever so led, either earlier or later than they. It is nowhere said or implied that even the Jaredites were the first to come here. . . . It is significant that the Prophet [Joseph Smith] was not reluctant to recognize the possibility of other migrations than those mentioned in the Book of Mormon."[18]

Whether or not the Lamanites were the principal ancestors of the Native Americans, we do not know for sure. Accordingly, the statement in the Introduction to the Book of Mormon that the Lamanites were the "principal ancestors of the American Indians" has been corrected to read that they were "among the ancestors of the American Indians."[19]

In cases like these, when individuals have extrapolated beyond the text of the Book of Mormon, then statements that could not be fully substantiated by the Book of Mormon text or subsequent revelations have been corrected or revised. However, such corrections or revisions do not alter the text of the Book of Mormon or undermine its truthfulness.

## Conclusion

While I disagree with the Church's critics on most points, I recognize that among them are good, intelligent people. My assertions in this book are not intended as attacks against them as individuals. Rather, they are intended as criticisms of arguments when they become ad hominem attacks instead of rational ones, when their methodologies present partial truths as the whole truth, or when their conclusions simply do not harmonize with the facts or logic—in essence, when promoting an ideology takes precedence over disclosing "the whole truth and nothing but the truth."

---

NOTES

1. Russell M. Nelson, "Truth—*and More,*" 71.
2. See Runnells, "Letter to a CES Director."
3. Welch, "View of the Hebrews: 'An Unparallel,'" 84–85.
4. See Johnson and Johnson, "A Comparison of the Book of Mormon and The Late War."
5. See Johnson and Johnson, "A Comparison of the Book of Mormon and The Late War."
6. Hunt, *The Late War,* 103.
7. See Johnson and Johnson, "A Comparison of the Book of Mormon and The Late War."
8. Names of People Mentioned in *The Late War*:
   Thomas Jones, George, Carrol, Henry, Russell, Gibbs, Keane, Hume, Rogers, Crane, Boyle, William Hull, Brock, Miller, Snelling, Brush, Isaac Hull, Dacres, Porter, Pakenham, Bellinger, Woolsey, Elliot, Cuyler, Stephen

Van Rensselaer, Chrystie, Ogilvie, Wool, Scott, Wadsworth, Fennick, Fink, Gibson, Alexander, Whinyeates, Jones, Carden, Decatur, Harrison, Dearborn, Russel, Hopkins, Tupper, Campbell, Williams, Winchester, Proctor, Round-Head, Lambert, Mix, Bainbridge, Sampson, Armstrong, Guy, Lawrence, Peake, Chauncey, Zebulon Pike, Forsyth, Sheaffe, Fraser, Ordonneaux, Bissel, Roman, Cesar, German, Scot, Gaul, Hibernian, Briton, Cockburn, O'Neil, Cassin, Kirby, Gallatin, Bayard, Henry Dearborn, Lewis, Boyd, M'Comb, Winder, Chandler, Perry, Yeo, Prevost, Marquis of Tweedale, Broke, William, Augustus Ludlow, White, Crowninshield, Boerstler, Chapin, Warren, Bishop, Wilkinson, Palmer, McDonough, Hampton, Murray, Mooers, George Croghan, Goliah, Diron, Allen, Maples, Burrows, Blythe, Oliver Perry, Barclay, Yarnell, Nelson, McArthur, Tecumseh, Johnson, Prince Regent, Shelby, Beasley, Joshua Penny, Coffee, Tallushatches, Floyd, Claiborne, Wetherford, Manahoee, Pearson, Brown, Covington, Swift, Coles, Purdy, Ripley, Swartwout, Atkinson, McClure, Leonard, Hillyar, Warrington, Wales, Blakeley, Cochrane, Macomb, Izard, Appling, Wellington, Riall, Drummond, Jessup, Morgan, Gaines, Hardy, Ross, Barney, Willet, Stewart, Gordon, Biddle, Parker, Reid, Sumter, Downie, Macdonough, Grosvenor, Hamilton, Riley, Cronk, Brooks, Richards, Smith, Strong, Sproul, Samuel Smith, Stricker, Stansbury, O'Boyle, Harris, Stiles, Findley, Armistead, Lloyd, Morris, Adams, Woodbine, Daniel Patterson, Robert Fulton, Livingston

9. Contrary to such an assertion, Joseph declared in June 1844: "I have always declared God to be a distinct personage, Jesus Christ a separate and distinct personage from God the Father and that the Holy Ghost was a distinct personage, and a Spirit, and these three constitute three distinct personages, and three Gods" (http://www.josephsmithpapers.org/paper-summary/history-1838-1856-volume-f-1-1-may-1844-8-august-1844/107).
10. At the beginning of modern editions of the Book of Mormon is a section titled "A Brief Explanation about the Book of Mormon." It makes clear that chapter headings are not part of the original text: "Introductions in italics, such as in chapter headings, are not original to the text but are study helps included for convenience in reading."
11. McConkie, *Doctrines of the Restoration,* 289–90.
12. Peterson, "Chattanooga Cheapshot," 55. For further information on this topic, see "Money and the Book of Mormon" at fairmormon.org.
13. For more information on revisions to the 2013 edition of the Book of Mormon, see lds.org/scriptures/adjustments.
14. Welch, "The Laws of Eshnunna and Nephite Economics," 147–48.
15. See "Book of Mormon and DNA Studies," Gospel Topics, topics.lds.org.
16. See "Book of Mormon and DNA Studies," Gospel Topics, topics.lds.org.
17. Ivins, in Conference Report, Apr. 1929, 15.
18. Nibley, "A Permanent Heritage," 249–50.
19. An essay on lds.org on the topic of "The Book of Mormon and DNA Studies" gives this helpful summary: "Nothing is known about the extent of intermarriage and genetic mixing between Book of Mormon peoples or their

descendants and other inhabitants of the Americas, though some mixing appears evident, even during the period covered by the book's text. What seems clear is that the DNA of Book of Mormon peoples likely represented only a fraction of all DNA in ancient America." And then this concluding thought: "Nothing is known about the DNA of Book of Mormon peoples. Even if such information were known, processes such as population bottleneck, genetic drift, and post-Columbian immigration from West Eurasia make it unlikely that their DNA could be detected today" (Gospel Topics, topics.lds.org). For these reasons, no DNA study can reasonably, let alone conclusively, state that there was no group of people from the Near East or Western Asia who inhabited ancient America. For further information on this subject, see "Why Hasn't Lehi's DNA Been Found?"

PART III

# Additional Evidences of the Book of Mormon

CHAPTER 5

# Where Did Joseph Get the Doctrine?

## Transition: From Defense to Offense

The previous chapters were designed as responses to some of the principal arguments made by critics against the Book of Mormon—in essence, responses to an agenda largely driven by those critics. To some extent, this requires one to play defense, even though many of the answers to their arguments produce a viable and positive confirmation of the veracity of the Book of Mormon.

The critics, however, cannot always have the ball. If they want to have credibility, they must also defend the tough questions the Book of Mormon poses for them, which happen to be same questions that lead to credible evidences for the divine authenticity of the Book of Mormon. Accordingly, the remaining chapters in this book take the offense. They are designed to highlight many evidences of the Book of Mormon that the critics seem reluctant to address or for which they have minimal responses. Of even greater significance, however, these next few chapters highlight evidences that are particularly conducive to inviting the Spirit. As one honestly and seriously considers these evidences, it will open the door for the Spirit to bear witness of their truthfulness.

## Plain and Precious Truths Removed from the Bible

Even if Joseph obtained historical facts from local libraries and resources, a claim for which there is no substantiating evidence, the real issue still remains: How did Joseph Smith create a book that permeates with the Spirit, and where did he get the deep and expansive doctrine taught in the Book of Mormon, much of which is contrary to or clarifies the religious beliefs of his time?

For example, the vast majority of Christians in Joseph's day believed that the Fall of Adam was a tragic setback that introduced "original sin" into the world, whereas the Book of Mormon declares the Fall to be a positive step forward (see 2 Nephi 2). Likewise, contrary to most contemporary beliefs, the Book of Mormon refers to a premortal existence (see Alma 13:1–11) and to a postmortal spirit world (see Alma 40:11–14).

Where did Joseph Smith get these and other profound doctrinal truths that were unknown or contrary to the prevailing doctrinal teachings of his time? Where did he get the stunning sermon on faith in Alma 32 or King Benjamin's remarkable sermon on the Savior's Atonement, one of the greatest in all of scripture (see Mosiah 2–5), or the allegory of the olive tree (see Jacob 5) with all its complexity, doctrinal richness, and historical accuracy? When I read this allegory, I have to map it out to follow its intricacies. Are we now supposed to believe that Joseph Smith just dictated these sermons off the top of his head with no notes whatsoever?

The doctrinal truths taught in the Book of Mormon are an overwhelming evidence of its divine authenticity. Nephi prophesied that in the last days many people, using the Bible alone, would "stumble" in their attempt to understand Christ's gospel message. Why? Because of the "many plain and precious things which have been taken out of the book [the Bible]" (1 Nephi 13:29; see also 1 Nephi 14:23) due to the years of apostasy following Christ's ministry and multiple translations of the Bible.

What are those plain and precious things that have been lost? They are doctrinal truths, covenants, and ordinances. Isaiah prophesied of this when he said, "The earth also is defiled under the inhabitants thereof; because they have transgressed the laws, changed the ordinance, broken the everlasting covenant" (Isaiah 24:5). This is a sad commentary, particularly when we realize that the Holy Bible in its original state "contained the fulness of the gospel" (1 Nephi 13:24).

This loss of plain and precious truths has caused most of the Christian world to stumble on many key doctrinal issues such as the Fall of Adam, baptism, the ongoing nature of revelation, the name of Christ's Church, the relationship between grace and works, and many others. Such loss of truth has contributed to the formation of hundreds of different Christian churches that exist today, each of which interprets the Bible differently. If they interpreted it the same, they would be the same church. And why this confusion? Because many plain and precious truths were removed from the Bible, causing many to stumble, exactly as the Book of Mormon prophesied. This is one reason the Book of Mormon is so essential in our pursuit of spiritual truth—to clarify the doctrinal confusion that exists in the Christian world.

While the Bible acts as one witness of Jesus Christ and His doctrine, the Book of Mormon acts as another (see 2 Corinthians 13:1). As a consequence, they complement and support each other in teaching the full truth (see Mormon 7:8–9). The following analogy demonstrates their interdependence:

How many straight lines can you draw through a single point? The answer is an infinite number. Following is a simple illustration of this (only using a few lines for demonstration purposes):

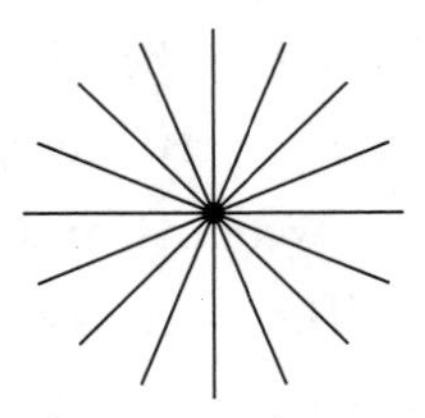

Suppose that the single point above represents the Bible, that each straight line represents a different interpretation of the Bible, and that each interpretation represents a different church.

Now ask yourself: How many straight lines can you draw between two points as shown below?

Point 1 Point 2

The answer is one. You can draw only one straight line between two points. Now assume that one point represents the Bible and the other point represents the Book of Mormon. There can be only one straight line, one doctrinal interpretation, one church between them.

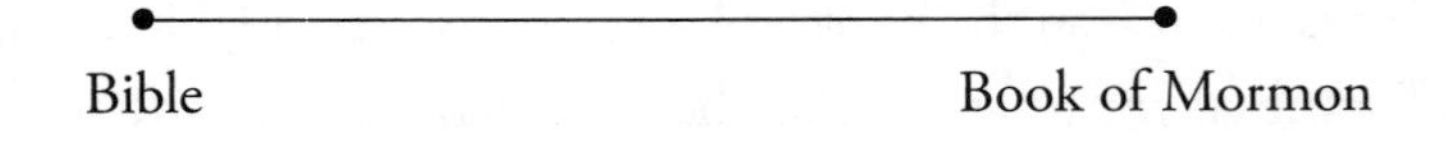


This is one reason the Book of Mormon is so crucial: because it is a second witness of Jesus Christ—a second reference point that results in one clear interpretation of Jesus Christ and His teachings.

## Evidence of Lost Truths

The Book of Mormon is not alone in its claim that many plain and precious truths have been lost from the Bible. The omissions began at an early date and were noted by early Christian writers. Origen (c. AD 185–255) was one of the most prolific of such writers. He lived at the time the early Bible manuscripts were being copied, translated, and circulated. As a firsthand witness, he made this observation about their troubling lack of accuracy and completeness: "The differences among the manuscripts have become great, either through negligence of some copyists or through the perverse audacity of theirs; they either neglect to check over what they have transcribed, or, in the process of checking, they make additions or deletions as they please."[1]

This is exactly the position advocated by Joseph Smith: "I believe the Bible as it read when it came from the pen of the original writers. Ignorant translators, careless transcribers, or designing and corrupt priests have committed many errors."[2]

It is worth noting as background information that the Bible was not produced as a single, coordinated effort—rather it is a compilation of sacred texts in many iterations and over centuries. Joseph Smith noted that some of the omissions occurred after the Bible was compiled, while others occurred before the compilation process was ever completed. While working on his inspired revision of the King James Bible, Joseph observed, "It was apparent that many important points touching the salvation of man had been taken from the Bible or lost before it was compiled."[3]

Justin Martyr, a defender of the faith who lived in the second century, once defended the divine Messiahship of Jesus Christ in a debate with a Jew named Trypho. In the course of the discussion, Justin Martyr observed that certain prophecies of Christ had been removed from the Jewish scriptures, and that Trypho was no doubt aware of such a fact, because some of these prophecies still remained in copies of the scriptures found in some of the synagogues. Speaking of one such prophecy, Justin Martyr wrote: "And again from the sayings of the same Jeremiah these have been cut out: 'The Lord God remembered His dead people of Israel who lay in the graves; and He descended to preach to them His own salvation.'"[4]

Professor Bart Ehrman, considered one of the leading experts on the ancient manuscripts of the New Testament, wrote: "We have to admit that in addition to copying scripture, they [the scribes] were changing scripture. Sometimes they didn't mean to—they were simply tired, or inattentive, or on occasion, inept. At other times, though, they did mean to make changes as when they wanted the text to emphasize precisely what they themselves believed."[5]

Omissions in the Bible are further verified by the fact that the Bible itself refers to at least thirteen missing books of scripture that are not found within its covers. The Latter-day Saint Bible Dictionary observes that these missing books of scripture "remind us that the Bible, in its present form, is rather incomplete."[6]

Did the Lord leave us with an incomplete Bible and no hope for a restoration of lost truths, or in His loving mercy did He provide a solution?

## Plain and Precious Truths Restored in the Book of Mormon

Fortunately, the Book of Mormon comes to the rescue. It promises that in the last days certain books, of which the Book of Mormon is one, "shall make known the plain and precious things which have been taken away from them [the Bible and other early scriptural records]" (1 Nephi 13:40; see also 1 Nephi 13:34). The Book of Mormon fulfills that promise again and again. Following are some examples of plain and precious truths that have been obscured or lost from the Bible but clarified or restored by the Book of Mormon.

## Was the Fall of Adam a Tragic Step Backwards?

Most of the modern Christian world, both at the time of Joseph Smith and currently, believes that if Adam and Eve had not partaken of the forbidden fruit, they would have had children in the Garden of Eden and would have resided there for eternity, raising the human family in a state of paradise.[7] In other words, they believe the Fall was a tragic step backwards in man's eternal journey. While this is a central belief in mainstream Christianity, it is contrary to the correct doctrine taught in the Book of Mormon. In 2 Nephi 2, Lehi teaches:

"And now, behold, if Adam had not transgressed he would not have fallen, but he would have remained in the garden of Eden. And all things which were created must have remained in the same state in which they were after they were created; and they must have remained forever, and had no end.

"And they would have had no children; wherefore they would have remained in a state of innocence, having no joy, for they knew no misery; doing no good, for they knew no sin.

"But behold, all things have been done in the wisdom of him who knoweth all things.

"Adam fell that men might be; and men are, that they might have joy" (2 Nephi 2:22–25).

Mainstream Christianity's misunderstanding of this doctrine was demonstrated to me in dramatic fashion in a conversation I had with someone who questioned the truth of the Book of Mormon. I asked him if there were any teachings or doctrines in the Book of Mormon that were not consistent with the Bible. He thought for a moment and replied, "Yes, there is, 2 Nephi 2 teaches that the Fall of Adam was a good thing." He then explained that this was a false teaching. He claimed that if Adam had not fallen we would all be living today in the Garden of Eden, in God's presence, in a state of eternal bliss—essentially heaven. "Adam's actions," he said, "resulted in a step backwards in man's spiritual progress."

At that point, I asked him if he believed that this "heaven" for unfallen man—the Garden of Eden—was better than the heaven for men who have fallen but have been redeemed by Jesus Christ—the heaven referred to in the New Testament? "Yes," came his response. No doubt, most of the Christian world would agree with him because they believe the Fall of Adam was a serious mistake.

I further asked if he believed that Satan would be in heaven. "Of course not," he replied. We then agreed that Satan had been cast out of heaven, for, as John said, "And [Satan and his angels] prevailed not; *neither was their place found any more in heaven. . . . And Satan . . . was cast out into the earth*" (Revelation 12:8–9; emphasis added).

I continued, "Where did Satan go when he was cast out of heaven?" There was a long silence. Finally I said, "Didn't he go to the Garden of Eden to tempt Adam and Eve?"

"Yes," he slowly replied.

"How then," I inquired, "could the Garden of Eden possibly be heaven if Satan had previously been cast out of heaven, never to return?"

To his credit, he honestly replied, "You have a point."

We then discussed that if Adam had not fallen, man would have been eternally consigned to the Garden of Eden, a "lesser" heaven than where God resides, but because Adam fell, and only because he fell, the "higher" heaven spoken of in the New Testament (where God resides) became accessible to Adam and his posterity. The Savior confirmed this truth: "In my Father's house are many mansions: if it were not so, I would have told you. I go to prepare a place for you" (John 14:2), meaning a place in heaven where God resides.

Then I asked the final question: "If fallen man can return to heaven and be with God, was Adam's choice a step backwards or a monumental step forward in man's spiritual progress?" Once again, he honestly answered: "You have a point." But this was not *my* point; rather it was the point taught by the Book of Mormon in 2 Nephi 2.[8]

C. S. Lewis, even with limited biblical scripture on the subject, came to the same conclusion as the Book of Mormon: "Redeemed humanity is to be something more glorious than unfallen humanity would have been, more glorious than any unfallen race now is."[9] In other words, the Fall was a necessary step to bring about more glorious possibilities than could have ever existed in the Garden of Eden.[10] That is the message of the Book of Mormon—in direct opposition to the vast majority of Christian beliefs of Joseph's time.

The young man with whom I had this conversation, like most of the Christian world, struggles with the Fall of Adam and its part in the divine plan because he does not understand two key points of doctrine that are missing in the Bible but taught in the Book of Mormon. One doctrine missing is that Adam and Eve "would have had no children" in the Garden of Eden (2 Nephi 2:23). The other missing doctrine corrects the misunderstanding that Adam and Eve lived in a state of unparalleled bliss while in the Garden; instead the Book of Mormon clarifies that they actually lived "in a state of innocence [meaning they had a limited knowledge of good and evil], having no joy, for they knew no misery" (2 Nephi 2:23). Accordingly, if Adam and Eve had never left the Garden, they would have been without posterity and would have remained in a state of spiritual stagnation or neutrality. Only the Fall put them into spiritual drive and thus made possible their godly progress—and ours as well.

John Fiske, a Harvard professor and philosopher, recognized the misconception of the Christian world: "Clearly, for strong and resolute men and women an Eden would be but a fool's paradise. How could anything fit to be called character have ever been produced there? . . . Unless our eyes had been opened at some time, so that we might come to know the good and the evil, we should never have become fashioned in God's image. We should have been the denizens of a world of puppets, where neither morality nor religion could have found place or meaning."[11]

The idea that the Garden of Eden is heaven may be an innocent mistake, but it is nonetheless a serious doctrinal error. President Ezra Taft Benson helped put in perspective the need for a correct understanding of the Fall: "No one adequately and properly knows why he needs Christ until he understands and accepts the doctrine of the Fall and its effect upon all mankind. And no other book in the world explains this vital doctrine nearly as well as the Book of Mormon."[12]

The Book of Mormon restores those plain and precious truths necessary for us to understand the Fall of Adam. Are we supposed to believe that Joseph Smith, without the Lord's help, defined the doctrine of the Fall with remarkable clarity when the rest of the Christian world was in utter confusion on this fundamental Christian principle?

## The Plan of Salvation Was Created in the Premortal Existence

The plan of salvation is a fundamental doctrine of the gospel of Jesus Christ. It is God's plan that describes how we might return to Him and become like Him. It is essential to our salvation.

Yet nowhere does this term or related terms appear in the entire Bible. Why such an omission? Hugh Nibley responded as follows: "This theme [the plan of salvation] as fully set forth in the Book of Mormon, enjoys almost overwhelming predominance in . . . apocryphal writings, and yet has no place in conventional Christian and Jewish theology, having been vigorously condemned by the doctors of both religions in the fourth and fifth centuries, since they would not tolerate any concepts involving preexistence of the spirit of man. Hence is found the studious avoidance of such words as 'plan' and 'probation' in our translations of the Bible." Professor Nibley then added the following observation: "On the other hand, it [the word 'plan'] appears no fewer than twenty-four times in the Book of Mormon."[13]

Just as the Savior has multiple names to describe His roles and attributes, so too the plan of salvation as described in the Book of Mormon (see Jarom 1:2; Alma 42:5) has multiple names that give us insights as to its nature and scope, such as the "merciful plan of the great Creator" (2 Nephi 9:6), confirming its divine origin; the "plan of redemption" (Alma 12:25), confirming the role of the Savior's Atonement in redeeming us from the Fall; the "plan of mercy," confirming the Savior's ability to "appease the demands of justice" (Alma 42:15); and the "plan of happiness" (Alma 42:8, 16), confirming the ultimate object of such plan, namely that "men are, that they might have joy" (2 Nephi 2:25).

The Book of Mormon also makes clear that the plan of salvation or "the plan of redemption . . . was laid from the foundation of the world" (Alma 12:25), thus suggesting its creation in a premortal existence—a doctrine that, as mentioned before, has been long lost to mainstream Christianity.

## Is Baptism Essential for Salvation?

In spite of biblical scriptures to the contrary (see John 3:3–5; Acts 2:37–40; Acts 10:47–48), much of the Christian world teaches that we are saved by grace alone, and therefore baptism is not essential for salvation. Rather, it is a symbol or confirmation of an already saved condition. As a consequence, many Christians stumble over this issue. But the Book of Mormon clearly teaches that all men "must repent, and be baptized . . . *or they cannot be saved in the kingdom of God*" (2 Nephi 9:23; emphasis added; see also 3 Nephi 11:33–34).

Not only does the Book of Mormon give definitive statements on the necessity of baptism, but it gives the underlying rationale for such need:

"And now, if the Lamb of God, he being holy, should have need to be baptized by water, to fulfil all righteousness, O then, how much more need have we, being unholy, to be baptized, yea, even by water!" (2 Nephi 31:5).

The logic is so simple yet so powerful: if the Savior who is perfect was baptized, how much greater need have we who are imperfect to be baptized? If He is our exemplar, should we not follow in His footsteps? Should there be any debate about the necessity of baptism after reading these scriptures?

What the Book of Mormon teaches about the absolute essentiality of baptism conforms with what early Christian writers taught on the subject.[14] For example, Tertullian (c. AD 200–230) wrote, "The prescript is laid down that 'without baptism, salvation is attainable by none.'"[15] And Cyprian (c. AD 200–258) added, "Unless therefore they receive saving baptism they cannot be saved."[16]

David W. Bercot, a noted scholar specializing in early Christian writings, initially believed, like many other Christians, that baptism was a symbol of one's spiritual conversion but not a necessity for salvation. He completely reversed his position, however, after reading the early Christian writers and rereading the scriptures on the subject. He then made this revealing observation:

"A person wasn't viewed [by the early Christian writers] as saved or born again until the entire process, including water baptism and receiving the Holy Spirit, were fulfilled. . . . That, in a nutshell, is what the primitive church believed, and when I say the church believed it, I mean it was universally held. In the entire set of *The Ante-Nicene Fathers*—in all ten volumes—I think just about every one of those writers somewhere discusses baptism, and every single one of them presents this same view—no exceptions."[17]

One must wonder why there is so much confusion on this subject of baptism when both the Bible and early Christian writers address it in a consistent manner. Fortunately, the Book of Mormon makes crystal clear that which is still unclear for much of the Christian world.

## What Is the Prescribed Mode of Baptism?

The majority of the Christian world embraces sprinkling or pouring as legitimate modes of baptism,[18] even though the Bible explains that the Savior was immersed at His baptism. For example, Matthew records that Christ came "up straightway out of the water" (Matthew 3:16; see also John 3:3–5; Romans 6:3–5; Acts 8:36–39). How could He come "up straightway out of the water" if He had not first gone down under the water? Lest there be any confusion on the subject, the Savior, during His visit to the Nephites, taught His disciples the correct and only divinely approved mode of baptism: "And then shall ye immerse them in the water" (3 Nephi 11:26; see also Mosiah 18:14; 3 Nephi 19:11–13). What is ambiguous for many is plain and straightforward in the Book of Mormon.

Again, early Christian writers and also key Reformers taught the same truth found in the Book of Mormon. For example, Tertullian wrote, "As of baptism itself, there is a physical act, that we are immersed in water; a spiritual effect, that we are freed from sins."[19] John Wesley, the founder of Methodism, noted in his journal, "Mary Welch was baptized, according to the custom of the first church, and the rules of the Church of England, by immersion."[20] John Calvin concurred, "The very word *baptize* . . . signified to immerse; and it is certain that immersion was the practice of the ancient Church."[21]

The Book of Mormon clarifies what is confusing in much of the Christian world, namely that baptism is essential for salvation and that immersion is the only legitimate form of baptism—all of which is consistent with the Bible as well as with many early Christian writers and Reformers.[22] Was Joseph Smith lucky again? Had he diligently read the thousands of pages of early Christian writings and discovered the key statements cited above? Or rather is the Book of Mormon a divine work of God?

## Original Sin and Infant Baptism

About the end of the second century the false doctrine of original sin emerged—teaching that all men were tainted at birth with the sin of Adam. Once this false doctrine gained acceptance, it led to the false practice of baptizing infants, not for their own sins, because they were deemed innocent, but for the "inherited" sin of Adam.[23]

Fortunately, the Book of Mormon confronts this issue square on. The Lord explained that little children are not capable of committing sin because "the curse of Adam [so-called original sin] is taken from them in me [Christ]" (Moroni 8:8). The prophet Mormon further explained, "He that saith that little children need baptism denieth the mercies of Christ, and setteth at naught the atonement" (Moroni 8:20; see also Moroni 8:5–9, 12). In other words, infant baptism is a heresy because little children are born clean due to Christ's Atonement. In addition, the Bible makes it clear that we must receive the word of God (see Acts 2:41), believe in Christ (see Acts 2:37; 8:37), and repent (see Matthew 3:8; Acts 2:38) before we are baptized. None of these conditions can be fulfilled by an infant.

Certain Reformers acknowledged that infant baptism was not initiated by Christ or His Apostles. Martin Luther wrote: "It cannot be proved by sacred scripture, that infant baptism was instituted by Christ or began by the first Christians after the apostles."[24] Menno Simons (1496–1561), an Anabaptist, wrote, "We do not find in all Scripture a single word by which Christ has ordained the baptism of infants, or that His apostles taught and practiced it, we say and confess rightly that infant baptism is but a human invention, an opinion of men, a perversion of the ordinance of Christ."[25]

How does the Book of Mormon keep getting the doctrine right, when so many at the time of Joseph Smith were totally confused?

## Baptism without Authority

Many perform baptisms without direct authority from God, claiming that sincerity alone or a theological degree is sufficient to perform this divine ordinance. The Book of Mormon dispels this false notion. It makes it clear that one must have priesthood authority to baptize, because God is a God of order.

Just as the Savior gave power to His Twelve Apostles in the Old World (see Matthew 10:1), so too He gave power to His Twelve Apostles in the New World, including the "power to baptize" (3 Nephi 11:22; see also 3 Nephi 11:25; 12:1). This priesthood authority is given to those called of God by the laying on of hands (see Alma 6:1). In Hebrews, we read that "no man taketh this honour [priesthood] unto himself, but he that is called of God, as was Aaron" (Hebrews 5:4).

The importance of having authority to baptize is illustrated in the story of King Limhi and his people, who heard the gospel and desired to be baptized, "but there was none in the land that had authority from God" (Mosiah 21:33). Note that the governing criterion was not sincerity but authority. The Book of Mormon then tells us the course of action these believers pursued: "They were desirous to be baptized as a witness and a testimony that they were willing to serve God with all their hearts; nevertheless they did prolong the time; and an account of their baptism shall be given hereafter" (Mosiah 21:35). Later they were baptized by Alma, a prophet of God who held the authority to baptize (see Mosiah 25:17–18; see also Mosiah 18:13).

The Book of Mormon's position is in harmony with the early Christian Church (see Acts 19:1–6, 13–17; Hebrews 5:4). Clarus of Mascula, a third-century bishop, spoke of heretics who baptized in Jesus's name without authority: "And therefore heretics, who neither have power without nor have the Church of Christ, are able to baptize no one with His baptism."[26]

Once again, the Book of Mormon clarified a doctrine that is misunderstood in much of the Christian world.

## Baptismal Covenants

Many Christians who are baptized have little, if any, knowledge about covenants made at the time of baptism. The Book of Mormon, however, not only tells us that at baptism "ye have entered into a covenant to serve him [Christ] until you are dead as to the mortal body" (Mosiah 18:13; see also Mosiah 5:7), but it also describes the nature of that covenant: "To mourn with those that mourn; yea, and comfort those that stand in need of comfort, and to stand as witnesses of God at all times and in all things, and in all places that ye may be in, even until death, that ye may be redeemed of God, and be numbered with those of the first resurrection, that ye may have eternal life" (Mosiah 18:9).

The well-respected *Encyclopedia of Early Christianity* speaks of certain "sacraments" such as baptism as "a transaction by which subject and deity bind themselves to each other in a sacred commitment." It then adds that early Christian writers such as "Tertullian, Cyprian, and Arnobius [believed that] baptism is a commitment [covenant] that binds the baptized to Christ in loyalty to the point of death, the baptismal creed being the terms of the oath."[27]

One must wonder, where did Joseph Smith get the specific baptismal covenants referred to above that were basically unknown to the Christian church at his time? Was he so brilliant, so creative as a theological genius that he formulated these covenants on his own? Or, rather, did the Book of Mormon once again restore a plain and precious truth lost from the Bible?

## How Does One Receive the Holy Ghost?

Many Christians believe that the gift of the Holy Ghost comes automatically after a person is baptized or makes a confession of faith, without the necessity of a physical ordinance. Again, the Book of Mormon corrects this misunderstanding as to how the gift of the Holy Ghost is received. The Lord said, "Ye shall have power that to him upon whom ye shall lay your hands, ye shall give the Holy Ghost" (Moroni 2:2).

The doctrine of the laying on of hands, as taught in the Book of Mormon, is consistent with the Bible. For example, Peter and John laid their hands on the newly baptized, "and they received the Holy Ghost" (Acts 8:17). Likewise, Paul "laid his hands" on those he baptized, and "the Holy Ghost came on them" (Acts 19:6).

Early Christian writers taught similarly. Tertullian wrote, "In the next place [following baptism] the hand is laid on us, invoking and inviting the Holy Spirit through benediction."[28] Cyprian was an additional witness of this holy ordinance: "Wherefore, in the name of the same Christ, are not hands laid upon the baptized persons among them, for the reception of the Holy Spirit?"[29] Will Durant, a noted world historian, recognized that this was a common practice in the early Church: "It was apparently the practice of the early Christians to add to baptism an 'imposition of hands' whereby the apostle or priest introduced the Holy Spirit into the believer."[30] One must ask again, how did Joseph Smith get this doctrinal truth correct when much of the Christian world in his day was in confusion on the issue?

## Did Miracles End with the Bible?

With the death of the Apostles, many Christians adopted the belief that miracles ceased.[31] These fruits of faith, they claimed, were no more than inspiring memories of the past, certainly not present-day realities. The Book of Mormon anticipated such a frame of mind among those who would claim that in the latter days, "he is not a God of miracles; he hath done his work" (2 Nephi 28:6). But the Book of Mormon counters such a heresy with this telling question: "Has the day of miracles ceased?" It then answers boldly and succinctly: "Behold I say unto you, Nay; for it is by faith that miracles are wrought" (Moroni 7:35, 37). Miracles did not end because the Bible ended; rather, miracles ended for a time because faith ceased, and when men and women again exercised faith, miracles again became a reality.

Erasmus, a respected priest of the sixteenth century, reprimanded his fellow monks because they believed that "to perform miracles is old fashioned, outworn, completely out of step with the times."[32] This is consistent with Nephi's prophecy that the time would come when churches would "put down the power and miracles of God"

(2 Nephi 26:20) and Moroni's prophecy about a future "day when it shall be said that miracles are done away" (Mormon 8:26).

In contrast to this attitude that miracles were a thing of the past, the Book of Mormon restored the truth that miracles continue in our day based on the faith of the people, just as they occurred in Christ's original Church.

## Ongoing Revelation

What about those who believe revelation ceased at the conclusion of the Bible? Moroni speaks to them with perfect logic:

"And again I speak unto you who deny the revelations of God, and say that they are done away, that there are no revelations, nor prophecies, nor gifts, nor healing, nor speaking with tongues, and the interpretation of tongues;

"Behold I say unto you, he that denieth these things knoweth not the gospel of Christ; yea, he has not read the scriptures; if so, he does not understand them.

"For do we not read that God is the same yesterday, today, and forever, and in him there is no variableness neither shadow of changing?" (Mormon 9:7–9).

If God spoke to prophets in Old and New Testament times, why would He not speak to prophets today, particularly since He is the same yesterday, today, and forever? If God has the same love today for His children that He did anciently, and the same power to speak, why would He not speak in current times, when we seem to need His counsel more than ever? This doctrinal truth as taught in the Book of Mormon makes perfect sense.

## Is the Bible the End of All Scripture?

Virtually all Christian churches teach that the Bible is the only word of God. In other words, they teach the doctrine of *sola scriptura,* meaning there is no other divine, infallible authority besides the Bible. How does their logic hold up against the reasoning of the Lord as recorded in the Book of Mormon: "Thou fool, that shall say: A Bible, we have got a Bible, and we need no more Bible. . . . Know ye not that there are more nations than one . . . and I bring forth my word unto the children of men, yea, even upon all the nations of the earth? Wherefore murmur ye, because that ye shall receive more of my word?" (2 Nephi 29:6–8; see also 2 Nephi 28:29–30).

Since God is no respecter of persons, does it not seem reasonable that He would raise up prophets whenever and wherever His people might have a listening ear? And with those prophets comes God's inspired word—the scriptures. The Book of Mormon contains the words of the living prophets in ancient America. Why should anyone murmur because they have more of the word of God? Should we not rejoice in every godly word we can receive?

## The Name of Christ's Church

There are hundreds of names used by churches today. Is there a correct name that the Savior wants us to use for His Church? The Lord spoke directly to this point in the Book of Mormon:

"How be it my church save it be called in my name? For if a church be called in Moses' name then it be Moses' church; or if it be called in the name of a man then it be the church of a man; but if it be called in my name then it is my church, if it so be that they are built upon my gospel" (3 Nephi 27:8).

That seems so reasonable—if we pray in the name of Jesus Christ, if we are baptized in the name of Christ, and if we are saved in the name of Christ, then why wouldn't His Church be named after Him? And so it is: The Church of Jesus Christ of Latter-day Saints.

## Other Doctrines Restored

The list of doctrines clarified or restored by the Book of Mormon goes on and on. The Book of Mormon provides the baptismal and sacrament prayers that were lost with time (see 3 Nephi 11:24–25; Moroni 4–5); it restores the doctrine of the premortal existence (see Alma 13:1–7), which was banned as heresy in the sixth century by the Fifth Ecumenical Council;[33] it explains that our spirits at death do not immediately go to heaven or hell but rather to an intermediate spirit world to await the Resurrection and our final judgment (see Alma 40:11–13); it explains that the gospel of Jesus Christ was not introduced for the first time in the meridian of history but was clearly taught in Old Testament times (see Jacob 4:4); it enlarges our understanding of the infinite nature of Christ's Atonement (see chapter 9 of this book); and it contains an ancient prophecy about Joseph Smith as a latter-day seer, which prophecy is omitted from the Bible (see 2 Nephi 3).

The Bible has many wonderful doctrinal insights, but again and again the Book of Mormon provides the necessary clarifications and additions that allow for an even greater understanding of Christ's doctrine. It eliminates the confusion so widespread in the Christian world.

With bewilderment, I have asked myself many times how anyone could possibly believe that Joseph Smith produced these remarkable and profound doctrinal insights on his own. This was a staggering accomplishment—nothing less than divinely directed.

## Summary Chart of Doctrine

Following is a summary of the doctrinal confusion that exists in some (but not necessarily all) of the Christian world and some clarifications and restorations of doctrine found in the Book of Mormon. It is not an exhaustive list. Hopefully this summary is sufficiently complete to convey a feel for the breadth and depth of such clarifications and restorations.

| Confusion in Some of the Christian World | Truth Clarified or Restored by the Book of Mormon |
|---|---|
| **The Fall of Adam** | |
| The Fall was a tragic step backwards in man's spiritual progress | Without the Fall and Atonement, Adam and Eve could not have had children or progressed spiritually<br>*2 Nephi 2:22–26* |
| **Man's destiny** | |
| Man cannot become like God | Man can become like God<br>*3 Nephi 12:48; 3 Nephi 27:27; Moroni 7:48; Moroni 10:32–33* |
| **The Atonement of Jesus Christ** | |
| Christ's Atonement does not perfect us | Jesus Christ, through His Atonement, has the power to perfect us as well as cleanse us.<br>*Mosiah 3:19; Ether 12:26–27; Moroni 10:32–33* |
| **Grace** | |
| Grace is sufficient to save us without works | Grace and works are both necessary to save us<br>*2 Nephi 25:23; Mosiah 4:30; Alma 12:14; Alma 24:10–14; Moroni 10:32–33* |
| **Baptism** | |
| Baptism is not essential for salvation | Baptism is essential for salvation<br>*2 Nephi 9:23; 2 Nephi 31:5–7; 3 Nephi 11:32–34* |
| Baptism may be done by immersion, sprinkling or pouring | Baptism must be done by immersion<br>*Mosiah 18:14; 3 Nephi 11:26* |

| Confusion in Some of the Christian World | Truth Clarified or Restored by the Book of Mormon |
|---|---|
| **Baptism (continued)** | |
| Baptism may be done by someone who is sincere, without priesthood authority | Baptism must be performed by one who has priesthood authority<br>*Mosiah 18:13; Mosiah 21:33–35; 3 Nephi 11:25* |
| Covenant making is not part of the baptismal ordinance | Covenants are made in connection with baptism<br>*Mosiah 18:8–10, 13* |
| Baptism of infants is necessary to eliminate the effects of original sin | Baptism of infants is a solemn mockery before God<br>*Mosiah 3:16; Moroni 8:5–26* |
| **The gift of the Holy Ghost** | |
| Comes automatically after a declaration of faith or baptism, without the necessity of a separate ordinance | Comes by a separate ordinance—the laying on of hands<br>*Moroni 2:2–3* |
| **Revelation** | |
| Ended with the Bible | Continues in modern times<br>*3 Nephi 29:6; Mormon 9:7–9* |
| **Miracles** | |
| Ended with the Bible | Continue in modern times<br>*2 Nephi 26:20; Mormon 9:15–20; Moroni 7:35–37* |
| **Apostasy and Restoration** | |
| Christ's original Church either continued or underwent some reformation | Christ's original Church was lost from the earth and needed to be restored, not just reformed<br>*1 Nephi 13:3–9; 24–29, 32–41; 1 Nephi 14:7–12* |

| Confusion in Some of the Christian World | Truth Clarified or Restored by the Book of Mormon |
|---|---|
| **Prophets** | |
| No prophets in our day | We have and need prophets today; Joseph Smith was a prophet, seer, and revelator<br>*1 Nephi 22:2; 2 Nephi 3* |
| **The spirit world** | |
| At death, we go either to heaven or to hell | At death, our spirits go to the spirit world<br>*2 Nephi 9:13; Alma 40:9–14* |
| **The Melchizedek Priesthood** | |
| Was held only by the Savior—the great High Priest | May be held by worthy men called of God<br>*2 Nephi 6:2; Alma 4:4; Alma 13:1–12* |
| **The premortal existence** | |
| There was no premortal existence for man | There was a premortal existence for man<br>*Alma 13:1–9* |
| **The Resurrection** | |
| The wicked never see God after this life | The Resurrection restores all men to the presence of God to be judged<br>*2 Nephi 9:12–13, 22; Alma 42:23; Helaman 14:17–18* |
| **The sacrament prayers** | |
| Not revealed in the Bible | Restored<br>*Moroni 4–5* |
| **America** | |
| No clear mention of its destiny | America is a choice land for the Restoration to occur<br>*1 Nephi 13:12–20, 34–37* |

| Confusion in Some of the Christian World | Truth Clarified or Restored by the Book of Mormon |
|---|---|
| **Ministry of angels** | |
| Ended with the Bible | Continues in modern times<br>*Moroni 7:29–37* |
| **The plan of salvation** | |
| The term *plan* is not mentioned in the Bible | The plan of salvation, plan of happiness, etc. are mentioned on multiple occasions<br>*Alma 42:5, 8, 16* |
| **The role of the Bible** | |
| The Bible is the only word of God | God has revealed His word to many nations and continues to do so<br>*1 Nephi 13:39–40; 2 Nephi 29:3–14* |
| **Witnesses to the Book of Mormon** | |
| No mention of these witnesses | Prophecies that there will be witnesses to the Book of Mormon<br>*2 Nephi 27:12–13; Ether 5:2–4* |
| **Christ will visit other sheep** | |
| The "other sheep" are the Gentiles | The "other sheep" are the Nephites and lost tribes of Israel<br>*3 Nephi 15:21–24; 3 Nephi 16:1–3* |
| **The name of Christ's Church** | |
| It doesn't need to include Christ's name | Christ's Church must be named after Him (i.e. Christ or God) and be built on His gospel<br>*3 Nephi 27:3–8* |
| **The introduction of Christ's gospel to mortals** | |
| Christ's gospel was first introduced during the Savior's mortal ministry | Christ's gospel was introduced before Christ's mortal ministry<br>*2 Nephi 31–32; Jacob 4:4; Mosiah 18:5–17* |

| Confusion in Some of the Christian World | Truth Clarified or Restored by the Book of Mormon |
|---|---|
| **Prophecies about the discovery and colonization of America and the Restoration of the gospel there** | |
| Not mentioned in the Bible | These prophecies were restored<br>*1 Nephi 13:12–19, 34, 39–40* |
| **The Light of Christ** | |
| Not fully defined | Explains what the Light of Christ does and who receives it<br>*Alma 28:14; Moroni 7:13–20* |
| **The nature of the Godhead** | |
| The Father, the Son, and the Holy Ghost are the same being | The Father, the Son, and the Holy Ghost are three separate beings but one in mind and will and purpose<br>*3 Nephi 11:7, 11, 32; Nephi 17:4, 13–15; 3 Nephi 18:27, 35* |
| **New Jerusalem in the last days** | |
| Only one Jerusalem—located in the East | Also, a New Jerusalem in America<br>*3 Nephi 20:22; Ether 13:3–11* |

Again, one must ask, how could Joseph have brought forth this remarkable collection of doctrinal restorations and clarifications on his own? The truthful answer: he couldn't.

On one occasion, my wife and I taught the plan of salvation to one of our teenage sons. It was obvious he was captivated by this doctrine. When we finished our discussion, he asked, "Why doesn't everyone believe this?" The Holy Ghost had borne witness to him of the plan's innate goodness, fairness, and completeness. I find myself asking the same question about many of the truths clarified or restored by the Book of Mormon: "Why doesn't everyone believe these? They are so plain and precious and powerful."

## The Doctrine Is Pragmatic

The doctrinal truths as clarified and restored in the Book of Mormon are not some abstract philosophies meant only to be debated, analyzed, and critiqued by the esoteric theologian. Rather they are down-to-earth, intensely pragmatic solutions and principles that can successfully govern our everyday lives. They give vision, they offer hope, they provide comfort, and they are the ultimate source for finding true joy. In essence, they give purpose to our lives.

## The Pieces of the Puzzle

The gospel of Jesus Christ is like a hundred-piece jigsaw puzzle. When Joseph Smith came on the scene, perhaps fifteen to twenty pieces were in place. As a result, it was impossible to see the total gospel picture—there were too many unintelligible pieces and blank spots. That is why there was, and is, so much confusion and dissension in the Christian world over doctrine. That is why there are hundreds of different Christian churches today. Each is trying to fill in the missing and confusing pieces with its own interpretation. Peter warned against such: "No prophecy of the scripture is of any private interpretation. For the prophecy came not in old time by the will of man: but holy men of God spake as they were moved by the Holy Ghost" (2 Peter 1:20–21). In other words, because scriptures came by prophets, prophets have the final word on how to interpret them.

This is one key reason Joseph Smith was called as a prophet of God—to supply many of the missing pieces of the gospel puzzle and to give the divine interpretation when necessary. He did this by translating the Book of Mormon and through other revelations he received. That is why the Lord said to Joseph, "This generation shall have my word through you" (D&C 5:10).

Some years ago, I had dinner with a retired judge who unfortunately had chosen not to be active in the Church. In the course of our conversation we found ourselves focusing on the Book of Mormon. At one point, he made this perplexing statement: "I've read the Book of Mormon and there's nothing new in it that's not already in the Bible." I was surprised, to say the least. It was obvious that he either had not read the Book of Mormon or did not understand it. If it were not for the Book of Mormon, we would fall victim to the many doctrinal misconceptions discussed previously, simply because the Bible, as inspired as it is, has lost "many parts which are plain and most precious" (1 Nephi 13:26). Fortunately, the Book of Mormon has come to the rescue. It clarifies certain doctrinal points that are ambiguous in the Bible, confirms others, and, even more importantly, fills in many of the gaps and voids that are glaringly apparent.

Even if Joseph Smith had had the uncanny ingenuity and brilliance to write the historical story of the Book of Mormon, as some claim, one must ask a yet deeper and more probing question—how did he, as a young, uneducated man, restore and clarify the confusing and missing doctrines of Christianity that had eluded and even baffled the brightest of theologians for hundreds of years? Where did he get the answers? How did he write doctrine that was contrary to or missing from the Christian religions of his time, yet was continually in harmony with the Bible as well as the works of many early Christian writers and Reformers? Was he that brilliant—that lucky? Or rather was Joseph Smith an instrument in God's hands in translating the Book of Mormon, which restored many plain and precious truths lost from the Bible, exactly as the Book of Mormon promised would happen?

## How Do Critics Respond?

Some critics claim that the doctrinal principles clarified or restored in the Book of Mormon are somewhere to be found in published nineteenth-century theological sources. These same critics further claim that Joseph Smith devised "his" theology by plagiarizing from those contemporary sources. In making such allegations, however, critics often fail to cite specific sources to prove their point.[34]

For example, who in the 1820s was teaching that Adam and Eve would not have had children in the Garden of Eden, thus necessitating the Fall, all as explained in the Book of Mormon? What source provides the exact covenants made at baptism and the exact wording of the sacramental prayers? What source speaks of the coming forth of additional scripture to accompany the Bible, such as the Book of Mormon? What source speaks of Christ's visit to the Americas in fulfillment of the Savior's prophecy in John 10:16? I am aware of no citations given by the critics as to the existence of these doctrinal truths at the time the Book of Mormon was published. Nonetheless, it would seem reasonable that in this era of widespread theological debate, some of these doctrines, as well as others referred to in this chapter, would have been discussed or written about to some extent.

Even if such sources could be found, however, there is no evidence that prior to the translation of the Book of Mormon Joseph Smith ever had possession of any of these books, that anyone recalls a conversation with Joseph concerning the same, or that Joseph ever alluded to any of these sources in his written journals or correspondence. In essence, we have nothing more than a hollow claim—a proposition without proof.

But supposing all of these sources existed and were accessible to Joseph Smith in his rural surroundings, it is astonishing to contemplate the sheer quantity of historical and theological literature that Joseph would need to have researched, consumed, and marshaled in a systematic way in order to make the critics' claim possible, let alone plausible. In essence, the critics have now transformed Joseph, the unlearned young man, into a theological scholar of exponential proportions.

And even if all the foregoing could be proven, one must still answer the difficult question: "How did Joseph put all these doctrinal fragments together into a cohesive, doctrinal whole—a rational, harmonious theology?" There is a simple answer, uncomplicated by the speculative and unproven theories of the critics: namely, that Joseph translated the Book of Mormon by the gift and power of God.

## Conclusion

I have written several books that focus on Church doctrine. Each took years to complete. I believe I have some understanding of the time and effort it takes to study and ponder the doctrine, to ask and research questions, and then to articulate and crystallize one's conclusions in the most concise, logical, and spiritual manner possible. It requires writing and rewriting—again and again. It necessitates deletions, additions, corrections, and refinements on multiple, even scores of occasions. In addition, I sought and greatly benefited from the advice of many gospel scholars who gave me invaluable input and, when necessary, corrected mistakes.

To suggest that Joseph Smith dictated more than five hundred pages of history and doctrine with no notes or rewrites (only minor changes to his original draft, and most of them grammatical), without the aid of any gospel scholars, and without the power of God, in approximately sixty-five working days, is totally incompatible and inconsistent with my experience and the experience of every doctrinal writer I know. It reminds me of the observation made by Hank Smith, a popular Latter-day Saint speaker and teacher: "A person with an experience is never at the mercy of a person with an opinion."[35] In other words, experience trumps opinion. And my experience teaches me it was not just highly improbable but impossible for Joseph Smith to write the Book of Mormon with its vast doctrinal insights under any circumstances.

NOTES

1. Origen, in Ehrman, *Misquoting Jesus,* 210.
2. *Teachings of Presidents of the Church: Joseph Smith,* 207.
3. See http://www.josephsmithpapers.org/paper-summary/history-1838-1856-volume-a-1-23-december-1805-30-august-1834/189.
4. Trypho, in *The Ante-Nicene Fathers,* 1:235.
5. Ehrman, *Misquoting Jesus,* 52.
6. LDS Bible Dictionary, "Lost Books." These books include: the book of the Wars of the Lord (Numbers 21:14), the book of Jasher (Joshua 10:13; 2 Samuel 1:18), the book of the acts of Solomon (1 Kings 11: 41), the book of Samuel the seer (1 Chronicles 29:29), the book of Gad the seer (1 Chronicles 29:29), the book of Nathan the prophet (1 Chronicles 29:29; 2 Chronicles 9:29), the prophecy of Ahijah (2 Chronicles 9:29), visions of Iddo the seer (2 Chronicles 9:29; 12:15; 13:22), the book of Shemaiah (2 Chronicles 12:15), the book of Jehu (2 Chronicles 20:34), sayings of the seers (2 Chronicles 33:19), an earlier epistle of Paul to the Corinthians (1 Corinthians 5:9), possibly an earlier epistle to the Ephesians (Ephesians 3:3), an epistle to the Church at Laodicea (Colossians 4:16), and some prophecies of Enoch known to Jude (Jude 1:14).
7. See "The Fall of Man in God's Perfect Plan," Bible.org; "Eve's 5 Mistakes," bibletalk.tv.
8. Upon reflection, I am probably more concise and articulate in this written account than in the original conversation, but the essence of what was said is accurate.
9. Lewis, *Miracles,* 122–23.
10. That is also what Paul taught: "Eye hath not seen, nor ear heard, neither have entered into the heart of man, the things which God hath prepared for them that love him" (1 Corinthians 2:9). Adam and Eve had seen the Garden of Eden, but Paul now promised that the heaven for redeemed man would be more glorious than anything any man has ever seen—better, even, than the Garden of Eden.
11. Fiske, *Studies in Religion,* 252, 266.
12. Benson, "The Book of Mormon and the Doctrine and Covenants," 85.
13. Nibley, "Checking on Long-Forgotten Lore," 188.
14. See *The Apostolic Fathers,* 472.
15. Tertullian, in *The Ante-Nicene Fathers,* 3:674–75.
16. Cyprian, in *The Ante-Nicene Fathers,* 5:566.
17. Bercot, *What the Early Christians Believed about Baptism,* as modified by David W. Bercot in a fax message to the author, Feb. 22, 2005.
18. In spite of the scriptural injunctions and examples of baptism by immersion, many churches have taken it upon themselves to authorize additional methods of baptism, as outlined in the following table (see Howells, *His Many Mansions,* back cover):

| Name of Church | Manner of Baptism Authorized |
|---|---|
| Lutheran | Sprinkling, pouring, or immersion |
| Methodist | Sprinkling, pouring, or immersion |
| Presbyterian | Sprinkling, pouring, or immersion |
| Catholic | Sprinkling, pouring, or immersion |
| Episcopal | Pouring or immersion |

19. Tertullian, in *The Ante-Nicene Fathers,* 3:94. The author of the Epistle of Barnabas (c. AD 70–132) wrote, "We go down into the water laden with sins and filth and rise up from it bearing fruit in the heart resting our fear and hope on Jesus in the spirit" (in *The Apostolic Fathers,* 148).
20. Wesley, in King, *Baptism: Sprinkling and Pouring versus Immersion,* 67.
21. Calvin, in Winebrenner, *The Ordinances,* 296; emphasis in original.
22. This is not to say that every early Christian writer and Reformer taught this, but there are sufficient patterns to suggest this was clearly the prevailing view, contrary to the views expressed in Christianity at the time of Joseph Smith. The same caveat applies to other references used herein to early Christian writers and Reformers.
23. Origen (AD 184–253) taught: "The prophets . . . tell us that a sacrifice for sin was offered even for new-born infants, as not being free from sin. They say [quoting Psalm 51:5], 'I was shapen in iniquity; and in sin did my mother conceive me'" (in *The Ante-Nicene Fathers,* 4:631). Later, Augustine (AD 354–430) taught that original sin occurred when Adam yielded to Eve's temptation, and thereafter all his descendants shared in his guilt (see Manchester, *A World Lit Only by Fire,* 9).
24. Luther, in Winebrenner, *The Ordinances,* 267.
25. Simons, *Menno Simons,* 262.
26. In *The Ante-Nicene Fathers,* 5:572.
27. *Encyclopedia of Early Christianity,* 811.
28. *The Writings of Tertullian,* 3:22.
29. Tertullian, in *The Ante-Nicene Fathers,* 5:387.
30. Durant, *Caesar and Christ,* 600.
31. The Catholics do believe, however, that miracles are necessary to achieve sainthood.
32. Erasmus, in *A Reformation Reader,* 72.
33. "Early Christian Belief in a Pre-Mortal Existence."
34. See Boylan, "Responding to a Critique."
35. Excerpt from various talks given by Hank Smith and confirmed to the author in an email dated Sept. 1, 2017.

CHAPTER 6

# A Divine Eloquence

## Messages with a Heartbeat

One of the evidences of the truthfulness of the Book of Mormon is not only the substance of the doctrine taught but the simplicity and majesty with which it is expressed. Divine language has a divine eloquence, simple but powerful, that appeals not only to the intellect but also to the heart.

Winston Churchill was an orator and author of extraordinary talent. During World War II his eloquence and passion gave strength and vision to the battle-weary people of Great Britain. Time and time again it was his words, steeled by his confidence, that lifted them from despair to hope. No wonder Edward Murrow wrote of him, "He mobilized the English language and sent it into battle."[1]

So it is with the Book of Mormon—it mobilizes the language of the Spirit and sends it into battle against Satan, against sin, against pride, against the false philosophies of men, against ignorance, against every enemy and obstacle that prevents us from returning to God and becoming more like Him.

Its divine language leaves an indelible impression upon the mind while also causing a stirring of the soul. It has a purity and conciseness of thought that prompts us to repeatedly stop and ponder the language—perhaps even memorize selected verses, highlight them in our scriptures, or place them on a mirror, refrigerator, or other visible location at home. These verses become our companions and friends in time of need or reflection. Such passages, forged from the language of the Spirit, are messages with a heartbeat—messages that live and breathe and inspire. They possess an inherent power to lift us upward. The Book of Mormon is filled with such golden nuggets—each a divine masterpiece in its own right. To suggest that Joseph Smith, who lacked formal education and struggled to write a coherent letter in his early years, was the author of such unforgettable phrases at age twenty-three is simply untenable.

Below are some inspired masterpieces from the Book of Mormon that appeal to me. If you have read the Book of Mormon, then no doubt many of these and others have stirred your soul and given you hope and comfort and direction in your time of need. As you read them, contemplate, Could Joseph Smith have written these, let alone many more of similar divine vintage? Why is it that millions of men and women quote these and other Book of Mormon phrases repeatedly? Why is it that they have such a powerful influence in our lives for good? How is it that many of them answer questions of the soul if they are merely the secular wisdom of a man?

*Can I possibly do everything the Lord commands me to do?*

> "And it came to pass that I, Nephi, said unto my father: I will go and do the things which the Lord hath commanded, for I know that the Lord giveth no commandments unto the children of men, save he shall prepare a way for them that they may

accomplish the thing which he commandeth them" (1 Nephi 3:7).

*What is the purpose of life?*

"Men are, that they might have joy" (2 Nephi 2:25).

*What shall I do when the way before me is unknown?*

"And I was led by the Spirit, not knowing beforehand the things which I should do" (1 Nephi 4:6).

*How can the scriptures make a difference in my life?*

"Feast upon the words of Christ; for behold, the words of Christ will tell you all things what ye should do" (2 Nephi 32:3).

*Why do I need the Holy Ghost when I teach?*

"When a man speaketh by the power of the Holy Ghost the power of the Holy Ghost carrieth it unto the hearts of the children of men" (2 Nephi 33:1).

*What can I do to better serve God?*

"And behold, I tell you these things that ye may learn wisdom; that ye may learn that when ye are in the service of your fellow beings ye are only in the service of your God" (Mosiah 2:17).

*How can I overcome the natural man in me?*

"For the natural man is an enemy to God, and has been from the fall of Adam, and will be, forever and ever, unless he yields to the enticings of the Holy Spirit, and putteth off the natural man and becometh a saint through the atonement of Christ the Lord, and becometh as a child, submissive, meek, humble, patient, full of love, willing to submit to all things which the Lord seeth fit to inflict upon him, even as a child doth submit to his father" (Mosiah 3:19).

*How do I know if I am a true believer?*

"And now, if you believe all these things see that ye do them" (Mosiah 4:10).

*How do I know when I have had a change of heart?*

"And they all cried with one voice, saying: Yea, we believe all the words which thou hast spoken unto us; and also, we know of their surety and truth, because of the Spirit of the Lord Omnipotent, which has wrought a mighty change in us, or in our hearts, that we have no more disposition to do evil, but to do good continually" (Mosiah 5:2).

*How can I come to know the Savior?*

"For how knoweth a man the master whom he has not served, and who is a stranger unto him, and is far from the thoughts and intents of his heart?" (Mosiah 5:13).

*How can I know if I have truly repented?*

"And behold, he preached the word unto your fathers, and a mighty change was also wrought in their hearts, and they humbled themselves and put their trust in the true and living God. And behold, they were faithful until the end; therefore they were saved.

"And now behold, I ask of you, my brethren of the church, have ye spiritually been born of God? Have ye received his image in your countenances? Have ye experienced this mighty change in your hearts?" (Alma 5:13–14).

*Can I be forgiven of my deepest, even most egregious sins?*

"And Alma said: If thou believest in the redemption of Christ thou canst be healed" (Alma 15:8).

*How can I help change the lives of others?*

"And now, as the preaching of the word had a great tendency to lead the people to do that which was just—yea, it had had more powerful effect upon the minds of the people than the sword, or anything else, which had happened unto them—therefore Alma thought it was expedient that they should try the virtue of the word of God" (Alma 31:5).

*How can I be supported in my trials?*

"I do know that whosoever shall put their trust in God shall be supported in their trials, and their troubles, and their afflictions, and shall be lifted up at the last day" (Alma 36:3).

*What difference can small things make in my life?*

"Now ye may suppose that this is foolishness in me; but behold I say unto you, that by small and simple things are great things brought to pass; and small means in many instances doth confound the wise" (Alma 37:6).

*When is the best time to learn to keep God's commandments?*

"O, remember, my son, and learn wisdom in thy youth; yea, learn in thy youth to keep the commandments of God" (Alma 37:35).

*Do my prayers make a difference?*

"Counsel with the Lord in all thy doings, and he will direct thee for good; yea, when thou liest down at night lie down unto the Lord, that he may watch over you in your sleep; and when thou risest in the morning let thy heart be full of thanks unto God; and if ye do these things, ye shall be lifted up at the last day" (Alma 37:37).

*Can I do some wicked things and still be happy?*

"Ye have sought all the days of your lives for that which ye could not obtain; and ye have sought for happiness in doing iniquity, which thing is contrary to the nature of that righteousness which is in our great and Eternal Head" (Helaman 13:38).

"Behold, I say unto you, wickedness never was happiness" (Alma 41:10).

*Are there some legitimate excuses for sinning?*

"Do not endeavor to excuse yourself in the least point because of your sins, by denying the justice of God" (Alma 42:30).

*What influence can righteous mothers have on their children?*

"Now they never had fought, yet they did not fear death; and they did think more upon the liberty of their fathers than they did upon their lives; yea, they had been taught by their mothers, that if they did not doubt, God would deliver them.

"And they rehearsed unto me the words of their mothers, saying: We do not doubt our mothers knew it" (Alma 56:47–48).

*How should I react to afflictions?*

"But behold, because of the exceedingly great length of the war between the Nephites and the Lamanites many had become hardened, . . . and many were softened because of their afflictions, insomuch that they did humble themselves before God, even in the depth of humility" (Alma 62:41).

*How can I strengthen my faith and humility?*

"They did fast and pray oft, and did wax stronger and stronger in their humility, and firmer and firmer in the faith of Christ, unto the filling their souls with joy and consolation, yea, even to the purifying and the sanctification of their hearts, which sanctification cometh because of their yielding their hearts unto God" (Helaman 3:35).

*What should be the foundation of my testimony?*

"And now, my sons, remember, remember that it is upon the rock of our Redeemer, who is Christ, the Son of God, that ye must build your foundation; that when the devil shall send forth his mighty winds, yea, his shafts in the whirlwind, yea, when all his hail and his mighty storm shall beat upon you, it shall have no power over you to drag you down to the gulf of misery and endless wo, because of the rock upon which ye are built, which is a sure foundation, a foundation whereon if men build they cannot fall" (Helaman 5:12).

*How long should we seek to find the lost?*

"Ye shall not cast him out of your synagogues, or your places of worship, for unto such shall ye *continue* to minister; for ye know not but what they will return and repent, and come unto me with full purpose of heart, and I shall heal them; and ye shall be the means of bringing salvation unto them" (3 Nephi 18:32; emphasis added).

*Whom should I strive to be like?*

"What manner of men ought ye to be? Verily I say unto you, even as I [the Savior] am" (3 Nephi 27:27).

*What is my responsibility to the poor?*

"Why do ye adorn yourselves with that which hath no life, and yet suffer the hungry, and the needy, and the naked, and the sick and the afflicted to pass by you, and notice them not?" (Mormon 8:39).

*Which comes first—a spiritual witness or faith?*

"Wherefore, dispute not because ye see not, for ye receive no witness until after the trial of your faith" (Ether 12:6).

*Can I ever overcome my weaknesses, and if so, how?*

"If men come unto me I will show unto them their weakness. I give unto men weakness that they may be humble; and my grace is sufficient for all men that humble themselves before me; for if they humble themselves before me, and have faith in me, then will I make weak things become strong unto them" (Ether 12:27).

*How can I know when I am feeling the witness of the Spirit?*

"Behold, that which is of God inviteth and enticeth to do good continually; wherefore, every thing which inviteth and enticeth to do good, and to love God, and to serve him, is inspired of God" (Moroni 7:13).

*How can I increase my love for the Savior and my fellow man?*

"My beloved brethren, pray unto the Father with all the energy of heart, that ye may be filled with this love, which he hath bestowed upon all who are true followers of his Son, Jesus Christ; that ye may become the sons of God; that when he shall appear we shall be like him, for we shall see him as he is; that we may have this hope; that we may be purified even as he is pure" (Moroni 7:48).

*In the midst of my despair, how can I have hope?*

"My son, be faithful in Christ; and may not the things which I have written grieve thee, to weigh thee down unto death; but may Christ lift thee up, and may his sufferings and death, and the showing his body unto our fathers, and his mercy and long-suffering, and the hope of his glory and of eternal life, rest in your mind forever" (Moroni 9:25).

*What does God expect me to become?*

"Yea, come unto Christ, and be perfected in him, and deny yourselves of all ungodliness; and if ye shall deny yourselves of all ungodliness, and love God with all your might, mind and strength, then is his grace sufficient for you, that by his grace ye may be perfect in Christ; and if by the grace of God ye are perfect in Christ, ye can in nowise deny the power of God" (Moroni 10:32).

## The Burning Question

I think most of us would be happy if in a lifetime we produced two or three memorable phrases that truly resonated with and touched our family and friends. The burning question then becomes: How did Joseph Smith, in his early twenties, produce this litany of memorable phrases and sage counsel as well as scores of others that have blessed millions? One might also ask: Are these phrases the words of a fraud and charlatan, one who is trying to dupe and deceive his fellow man? Or are they the words of the Spirit—words that soothe the soul, enlighten the mind, enlarge the heart, inspire to good works, and bring hope and direction to one's life? The answers to these questions will go a long way in helping you know whether the Book of Mormon is man-made or God-given. As for others, I cannot speak, but for me, these and similar phrases are the language of the Spirit.

---

NOTE

1. In *Proceedings of the International Churchill Societies,* 33.

## CHAPTER 7

# The Three Witnesses

Both the Old and New Testaments address the necessity of multiple witnesses to establish divine truth. In Deuteronomy 19:15 we read, "At the mouth of two witnesses, or at the mouth of three witnesses, shall the matter be established." The Apostle Paul referred to the same requirement: "In the mouth of two or three witnesses shall every word be established" (2 Corinthians 13:1). In conformity with this divine law, God has provided multiple witnesses of the reality and divinity of the Book of Mormon.

Nephi prophesied of the Three Witnesses to the Book of Mormon: "The eyes of none shall behold it [the book] save it be that three witnesses shall behold it, by the power of God." He then added, "There is none other which shall view it, save it be a few according to the will of God" (2 Nephi 27:12–13; see also 2 Nephi 11:3; Ether 5:2–4). Certainly, this latter reference to "a few" includes at least the additional Eight Witnesses, making a minimum of eleven in total, besides Joseph Smith, who saw the plates.[1]

The testimonies of these eleven witnesses, in addition to Joseph Smith's testimony, are a powerful evidence of the truth of the Book of Mormon. In addition, they constitute a divine fulfillment of the law of witnesses.

The Three Witnesses—namely, Oliver Cowdery, David Whitmer, and Martin Harris—testified to the following:

- That an angel of God showed them the golden plates and the engravings thereon from which the Book of Mormon was translated.
- That they heard the voice of God testify that the plates were translated by the gift and power of God. This same voice commanded them to bear record of what they had seen and heard.

The eight other witnesses did not see the angel or hear the voice of God but testified that Joseph Smith showed them the golden plates and related engravings, and that they handled and felt the plates with their own hands.

For years I had been aware of the testimonies of these eleven men placed at the beginning of the Book of Mormon and a few oft-repeated statements of these witnesses confirming their testimonies in their later years. Until recently, however, I was unaware of the many reaffirmations of their testimonies and the numerous statements made by others (in and out of the Church) affirming the integrity of these witnesses.

Again and again, at all stages of the witnesses' lives, their testimonies are consistent in the sense they reaffirm that they saw the angel or plates—or both—and constant in the sense they never denied their original testimonies.

Nevertheless, critics of the Book of Mormon are relentless in their attack against the eleven witnesses. One website alleges: "All the Mormon witnesses are as worthless as they are unreliable who recanted their testimony."[2] Hopefully, the following will help the reader have a more enlightened view on the matter.

Suppose for a moment that all I told you about the Apostle Peter was that he cut off the ear of the high priest's servant (see John 18:10), that three times he denied knowing the Savior (see Luke 22:54–62), that the Savior referred to him on one occasion as "thou of little faith" (Matthew 14:31), and that on another occasion the Savior rebuked him, saying, "Get thee behind me, Satan" (Matthew 16:23). What would you think of Peter based on those facts alone—that he was a scoundrel, a reprobate, a good-for-nothing? All of those scriptural statements are true, but when presented in isolation, they create a false representation of the entire man.

Who, then, is the "real" Peter? He is the man who left his fishing nets to follow Jesus; the man Christ chose to lead His Church; the man who saw heavenly angels; the man who healed the infirm and raised the dead; and the man who gave his life for his testimony of Jesus Christ. Only when we have all the facts before us do we gain the full picture of this man's nobility and majesty.

President Gordon B. Hinckley has spoken of those who impugn a man's character based on a portion of the truth:

"We have those critics who appear to wish to cull out of a vast panorama of information those items which demean and belittle some of the men and women of the past who worked so hard in laying the foundation of this great cause. . . .

"We recognize that our forebears were human. They doubtless made mistakes. . . . But the mistakes were minor, when compared with the marvelous work which they accomplished. To highlight the mistakes and gloss over the greater good is to draw a caricature. Caricatures are amusing, but they are often ugly and dishonest. A man may have a blemish on his cheek and still have a face of beauty and strength, but if the blemish is emphasized unduly in relation to his other features, the portrait is lacking in integrity.

"There was only one perfect man who ever walked the earth. The Lord has used imperfect people in the process of building his perfect society. If some of them occasionally stumbled, or if their characters may have been slightly flawed in one way or another, the wonder is the greater that they accomplished so much. . . .

"I do not fear truth. I welcome it. But I wish all of my facts in their proper context."[3]

Unfortunately, character denigration has monopolized the approach of many critics when it comes to the eleven witnesses. They have become obsessed with finding a wart and magnifying it, all the while missing or distorting the beauty of the witnesses' lives and testimonies. They point out that some of the witnesses were treasure hunters and perhaps gullible, that some were excommunicated from The Church of Jesus Christ of Latter-day Saints, and that some joined multiple churches. They allege that there are some inconsistencies in their testimonies, that they did not really see golden plates but only had a spiritual vision or faith-based experience, that a few contemporaries had bad things to say about them, that even Joseph Smith rebuked some of them, and that because some were related to each other there must exist an inherent conflict of interest and conspiracy mentality. All of this, the critics claim, discredits the witnesses' testimonies.[4]

It is interesting to note, as will be discussed in chapter 8, that the existing positive statements about these men and their character and testimonies outnumber the negative statements at a rate of approximately 19 to 1, yet somehow the critics seldom, if ever, quote any of these positive statements. They certainly have the right to quote the negative, but in the spirit of fairness and historical accuracy, should they not also quote at least some of the positive? This is another case in which a partial truth presented as the whole truth is an untruth.

Even if all the allegations made by the critics concerning the witnesses were true, they disclose a very small and distorted picture of who these men really were, the adversities they endured, and the price they paid to remain true to their testimonies. Below is an honest effort to disclose the "whole truth" about these men, both blemish and beauty.

In writing the following, I give thanks and credit to Richard Lloyd Anderson, who wrote *Investigating the Book of Mormon Witnesses,* and Lyndon W. Cook, who edited the book *David Whitmer Interviews.* Both of these books contain detailed and careful research on this subject, from which I draw heavily.

The Three Witnesses had their sacred experience in late June of 1829. Some years later, Lucy Mack Smith, the mother of Joseph, recorded their reaction to this experience:

"They returned to the house. It was between three and four o'clock. Mrs. Whitmer and Mr. Smith [Joseph Smith Sr.] and myself were sitting in a bedroom. I sat on the bedside. When Joseph came in he threw himself down beside me: 'Father! Mother!' said he, 'you do not know how happy I am. The Lord has caused the plates to be shown to three more besides me, who have also seen an angel and will have to testify to the truth of what I have said. For they know for themselves that I do not go about to deceive the people. And I do feel as though I was relieved of a dreadful burden, which was almost too much for me to endure. But they will now have to bear a part, and it does rejoice my soul that I am not any longer to be entirely alone in the world.' Martin Harris then came in. He seemed almost overcome with excess of joy. He then testified to what he had seen and heard, as did also others, Oliver and David.

Their testimony was the same in substance as that contained in the Book of Mormon. . . .

"Martin Harris particularly seemed altogether unable to give vent to his feelings in words. He said, 'I have now seen an angel from heaven, who has of a surety testified of the truth of all that I have heard concerning the record, and my eyes have beheld him. I have also looked upon the plates and handled them with my hands and can testify of the same to the whole world.[5] But I have received for myself a witness that words cannot express, that no tongue can describe, and I bless God in the sincerity of my soul that he has condescended to make me—even me—a witness of the greatness of his work and designs in behalf [of] the children of men.' Oliver and David also joined with him in solemn praises to God for his goodness and mercy."[6]

Lucy Mack Smith was among the most honorable of women. Does her account sound like a fabricated story, or does it ring true with the joy of those who had experienced a divine manifestation?

## Oliver Cowdery

There are some who have suggested that Oliver Cowdery was gullible because on occasion he used a divining rod or sought treasure, and therefore they claim he was abnormally prone to accept a story about angels and golden plates.[7] To make this argument in the context of twenty-first-century culture, however, is a classic case of "presentism"—the practice of imposing current cultural practices and values on prior generations. There should be no dispute that many on the frontiers in the early nineteenth century used divining rods to seek water, treasure, metal objects, and the like. Although such an action may seem strange to many now, it was certainly not a cultural anomaly in Oliver's day.

In addition, one might ask, "What evidence exists that someone who is allegedly gullible lacks the integrity to tell the truth?" But, again, the critics have not told the whole story. How gullible was Oliver, who, in a climate of limited educational opportunities on the frontier, was bright and savvy enough to become a schoolteacher and lawyer? Perhaps there is no one better than his contemporaries to answer that question. One referred to him as "shrewd and bright,"[8] while others said he was of "sound and vigorous intellect" and "unquestioned legal abilities" (as cited hereafter). Does that sound like someone who is gullible?

Critics also point out that Joseph Smith made some disparaging statements about Oliver Cowdery and some of the other witnesses. For example, in December 1838, Joseph said of Oliver (who had recently been excommunicated) and certain others, including David Whitmer and Martin Harris, "They were too mean to mention and we had liked to have forgotten them."[9] No doubt such statements were made when emotions ran high because these men, who had had so many divine witnesses, nonetheless turned against the Prophet at a time when he desperately needed and deserved their support.[10] In spite of these personal differences, none of these witnesses ever denied his testimony of the Book of Mormon—an incredible evidence of its truthfulness.

Below are the observations of some of those who knew Oliver well, along with Oliver's own statements about his divine experience. The reader can be the judge of the weight and credibility of these testimonies.

Horace A. Tenney, the editor of a Wisconsin newspaper, remembered Oliver Cowdery as "a man of sterling integrity, sound and vigorous intellect, and every way worthy, honest and capable."[11] John Breslin, a member of the Ohio House of Representatives, wrote of Cowdery's character as follows: "Mr. C. was a resident among us for a period of seven years, during which time he earned himself an enviable distinction at the bar of this place and of this judicial circuit, as a sound and able lawyer, and as a citizen none could have been more esteemed. His honesty, integrity, and industry were worthy [of] the imitation of all, whilst his unquestioned legal abilities reflected credit as well upon himself as upon the profession of which he was a member."[12]

In 1833, mobs in Missouri were destroying property, driving Saints from their homes, and even taking lives. It was a dangerous time to be a Latter-day Saint. The mob had offered a cash reward for anyone who could deliver William McClellan or Oliver Cowdery to them. In an effort to seek greater safety, McClellan travelled from Independence, Missouri, to the Whitmer family settlement a few miles to the west. McClellan then told what happened:

"There in the lonely woods I met with David Whitmer and Oliver Cowdery. I said to them, 'Brethren, I never have seen an open vision in my life, but you men say you have, and therefore you positively know. Now you know that our lives are in danger every hour, if the mob can only catch us. Tell me in the fear of God, is that book of Mormon true?' Cowdery looked at me with solemnity depicted in his face, and said, 'Brother William, God sent his holy angel to declare the truth of the translation of it to us, and therefore we know. And though the mob kill us, yet we must die declaring its truth.' David said, 'Oliver has told you the solemn truth.' . . . Said I, 'boys I believe you. I can see no object for you to tell me falsehood now, when our lives are endangered.'"[13]

Perhaps there is no greater tribute to Oliver's consistent adherence to his testimony than that of his wife, Elizabeth Whitmer Cowdery, who in reflection upon her husband's life wrote, "From the hour when the glorious vision of the Holy Messenger revealed to mortal eyes the hidden prophecies which God had promised his faithful followers should come forth in due time, until the moment when he passed away from earth, *he always without one doubt or shadow of turning affirmed the divinity and truth of the Book of Mormon.*"[14]

Even during the time Oliver was estranged from the Church (1838–1848), he was true to his testimony of the Book of Mormon. In fact, as proof of his ongoing testimony, he admitted the error of his ways and eventually rejoined the Church. This raises a serious problem for the critics. They must now answer the difficult question, "If Oliver distanced himself from the Church and renounced his testimony of the Book of Mormon, as the critics claim, why in the world would he rejoin the Church and reaffirm his testimony? What would he gain from that? What would be the motive?" The motive is clear—he wanted to make amends with God and the Church he knew to be true. When Oliver asked for readmission to the Church, George A. Smith recorded, "He bore testimony, in the most positive terms, to the truth of the Book of Mormon, the restoration of the priesthood to the earth, and the mission of Joseph Smith as the prophet of the last days."[15]

David Whitmer was with Oliver Cowdery when he passed away. Of that experience, David wrote: "I was present at the deathbed of Oliver Cowdery, and his last words were, 'Brother David, be true to your testimony to the Book of Mormon.' . . . Many witnesses yet live in Richmond, who will testify to the truth of these facts, as well as to the good character of Oliver Cowdery."[16]

Do Oliver Cowdery's final words in life sound like those of a charlatan, a man desiring to foist a hoax on his fellow man, a man who had recanted his testimony? Or are they the words of a man who wanted to bear his final, truthful testimony to the world so he could stand before God at the judgment bar with a clear conscience and declare that he was faithful to his testimony to the very end?

## David Whitmer

David Whitmer gave scores of interviews and recollections of his interaction with the angel who showed him the golden plates. There are minor differences in some of these accounts—some no doubt because the interviewer intentionally or inadvertently misrecorded David's words, in other cases because David may have emphasized one point more than another or remembered a fact he had not disclosed in a prior interview.[17] That is human nature. To now suggest, as some critics do, that David's multiple accounts should be discredited because of minor inconsistencies over decades of time is simply to ignore human nature.[18] The critics have become so preoccupied with the sideshow that they have missed the main event—the constant recurring thread that runs through David's accounts: he saw the angel and the plates.

For fifty years following David's excommunication from the Church, he lived in the non-Mormon community of Richmond, Missouri, yet he always held fast to his testimony. His friends and associates, while not believers in the Book of Mormon, grew to love and respect him, even to elect him as their mayor and to defend him when necessary. On one occasion a vehement anti-Mormon labeled David as disreputable. The local newspaper editorial in Richmond, while not agreeing with David's theological views, defended his integrity in these words: "If a life of probity, of unobtrusive benevolence and well doing for well-nigh a half century, marks a man as a good citizen, then David Whitmer should enjoy the confidence and esteem of his fellowmen."[19]

In 1881, twenty-one of Richmond's leading citizens, none of whom publicly acknowledged the truth of the Book of Mormon, signed a statement declaring that they had known David for more than forty years as "a man of the highest integrity, and of undoubted truth and veracity."[20]

A reporter from the *St. Louis Republican* wrote in July 1884, "The honesty and excellent character of the Whitmer family are substantiated by the people of Richmond without exception."[21]

Thomas Marsh, at one time the senior member of the Quorum of the Twelve Apostles, who became disaffected with the Prophet Joseph, sought out Oliver Cowdery and David Whitmer, fellow dissenters from the Church, to seek the truth about the Book of Mormon. Thomas Marsh wrote of this experience: "I enquired seriously at David if it was true that he had seen the angel, according to his testimony as one of the witnesses of the Book of Mormon. *He replied, as sure as there is a God in heaven, he saw the angel, according to his testimony in that book.* I asked him, if so, how he did not stand by Joseph? He answered, in the days when Joseph received the Book of Mormon, and brought it forth, he was a good man filled with the Holy Ghost, but he considered he had now fallen. I interrogated Oliver Cowdery in the same manner, who answered me similarly."[22]

Since David Whitmer was the last surviving witness, he was interviewed extensively. Historian Richard Lloyd Anderson compiled some of David's responses to interviews during the last decade of David's life. He did so in a composite form, a portion of which is below:

"Q: Is your published testimony accurate?

"A: As you read my testimony given many years ago, so it stands as my own existence, the same as when I gave it, and so shall it stand throughout the cycles of eternity.

"Q: Did you handle the plates?

"A: I did not handle the plates—only saw them.

"Q: How clearly could you see the plates?

"A: [T]he angel stood before us, and he turned the leaves one by one. [H]e held the plates and turned them over with his hands, so that they could be plainly visible.

"Q: Did the angel turn all the leaves before you as you looked on it?

"A: No, not all, only that part of the book which was not sealed, and what there was sealed appeared as solid to my view as wood.

"Q: Can you describe the plates?

"A: They appeared to be of gold, about six by nine inches in size, about as thick as parchment, a great many in number and bound together like the leaves of a book by massive rings passing through the back edges. The engraving upon them was very plain and of very curious appearance.

"Q: Is it possible that you imagined this experience?

"A: [O]ur testimony is true. And if these things are not true, then there is no truth; and if there is no truth, there is no God; and if there is no God, there is no existence. But I know there is a God, for I have heard His voice and witnessed the manifestation of His power.

"Q: Do you remember the peculiar sensation experienced upon that occasion?

"A: Yes, I remember it very distinctly. And I never think of it, from that day to this, but what that spirit is present with me."[23]

In the summer of 1833, vigilantes in Independence, Missouri, forced many members of The Church of Jesus Christ of Latter-day Saints from their homes. John P. Greene, a former Methodist minister who had joined the Church, recalled that David Whitmer and others were threatened with death unless they denied the Book of Mormon:

"When the mob again assembled, they went to the houses of several of the leading Mormons; and taking Isaac Morley, David Whitmer, and others, they told them to bid their families farewell, for they would never see them again. Then driving them at the point of the bayonet to the public square, they stripped and tarred and feathered them, amidst menaces and insults. The commanding officer then called twelve of his men, and ordering them to cock their guns and present them at the prisoners' breasts, and to be ready to fire when he gave the word—he addressed the prisoners, threatening them with instant death unless they denied the book of Mormon and confessed it to be a fraud; at the same time adding that if they did so, they might enjoy the privileges of citizens. David Whitmer, hereupon, lifted up his hands and bore witness that the Book of Mormon was the Word of God. The mob then let them go."[24] Does that sound like a man with an ulterior motive, a man attempting to perpetrate a fraud on his fellow man?

Given the numerous witnesses of David's integrity, some critics came up with the theory that he, Oliver Cowdery, and Martin Harris were hypnotized or deluded in some fashion. Joseph Smith III, who was present when one man raised such a possibility, recorded the reaction of David Whitmer:

"How well and distinctly I remember the manner in which Elder Whitmer arose and drew himself up to his full height—a little over six feet—and said, in solemn and impressive tones:

"'No sir! I was not under any hallucination, nor was I deceived! I saw with these eyes, and I heard with these ears! *I know whereof I speak!*'"[25]

In an interview with Nathan Tanner Jr. on April 13, 1886, David said: "I have been asked if we saw those things with our natural eyes. Of course they were our natural eyes. *There is no doubt that our eyes were prepared for the sight, but they were our natural eyes nevertheless.*"[26]

In an extended interview with Orson Pratt and Joseph F. Smith on September 7–8, 1878, David said, "I saw them [the plates, the sword of Laban, the Liahona, and the Urim and Thummim] just as plain as I see this bed (striking his hand upon the bed beside him), and I heard the word of the Lord as distinctly as I ever heard anything in my life declaring that they (the plates) were translated by the gift and power of God."[27] Again and again David testified of the reality of this sacred experience.

David was frustrated by the many people who misquoted him. To one reporter of the *Kansas City Journal* (June 1, 1881) he said, "I have been imposed upon and misrepresented so many times by persons claiming to be honorable newspaper men that I feel a delicacy in allowing my name to come before the public in newspaper print again."[28]

Critics have quoted John Murphy,[29] who declared that in a conversation with David Whitmer, David denied his testimony. Here is David Whitmer's response, which critics seldom if ever quote:

"It having been represented by one John Murphy, of Polo, Caldwell County, Mo., that I, in a conversation with him last summer, denied my testimony as one of the three witnesses to the BOOK OF MORMON.

"To the end, therefore, that he may understand me now, if he did not then; and that the world may know the truth, I wish now, standing as it were, in the very sunset of life, and in the fear of God, once and for all to make this public statement:

"*That I have never at any time denied that testimony or any part thereof, which has so long since been published with that Book, as one of the three witnesses.* Those who know me best, well know that I have always adhered to that testimony. And that no man may be misled or doubt my present views in regard to the same, I do again affirm the truth of all of my statements, as then made and published.

"He that hath an ear to hear, let him hear; it was no delusion!"[30]

After David learned that it had been reported in two encyclopedias that he had denied his testimony of the Book of Mormon, he responded with this unequivocal statement:

"It is recorded in the American Cyclopaedia and the Encyclopaedia Britannica, that I, David Whitmer, have denied my testimony as one of the three witnesses to the divinity of the Book of Mormon: and that the two other witnesses, Oliver Cowdery and Martin Harris, denied their testimony to that Book. *I will say once more to all mankind, that I have never at any time denied that testimony or any part thereof. I also testify to the world, that neither Oliver Cowdery or Martin Harris ever at any time denied their testimony. They both died affirming the truth of the divine authenticity of the Book of Mormon.*"[31] One might ask, "Why is this personal and powerful testimony, which was given near the end of David's life, never cited by the critics?"

In October 1886, the *Omaha Herald* reported: "Newspaper reporters are not admitted to his [David's] presence, and it is no wonder when one recalls the shameful misrepresentations which have been sent out as interviews. The last of these was written by an unprincipled penny-a-liner who, when he was told emphatically that he could not see Mr. Whitmer, sent off to his paper the sensational announcement that the 'White-haired Hero of Hill Cumorah' had just been stilled in death, and that with his latest breath he gurgled: 'The Book of Mormon is a fraud.'"[32] Such is the extreme to which some critics have gone in an attempt to discredit the testimony of the witnesses to the Book of Mormon.

A correspondent for the *Chicago Times* interviewed David on October 14, 1881, when David was seventy-six years of age, and substantiated his consistent testimony: *"Mr. Whitmer's beliefs have undergone no change since his early manhood."*[33]

James H. Hart, a Missouri businessman, reported in 1883 that David said: "I have been visited by thousands of people, believers and unbelievers, men and ladies of all degrees, sometimes as many as 15 in one day, and have never failed in my testimony. And they will know someday that my testimony is true."[34]

Less than three years before David Whitmer died, a law student and member of The Church of Jesus Christ of Latter-day Saints named James H. Moyle, who had just graduated from the University of Michigan, interviewed David for two and a half hours in what he called a cross-examination. Critics have drawn from this interview a single isolated comment: "There was only one thing that did not fully satisfy me. . . . He was somewhat spiritual in his explanations and not as materialistic as I wished." Again, the critics only disclosed a small portion of the truth. What they failed to disclose was that Mr. Moyle further wrote, "He [David] declared to me that the testimony which he had published to the world was true and that he had not denied any part of it." And then Mr. Moyle gave his conclusion after more than two hours of intense interrogation: "I then concluded, as I now believe, that jealousy and disappointment had soured his soul [about Joseph Smith and other Church leaders], but nothing could obliterate his testimony of the divinity of the Book of Mormon."[35]

David Whitmer died in January 1888. The local paper, the *Richmond Conservator,* recounted his final testimony: "On Sunday evening before his death he called the family and his attending physician, Dr. George W. Buchanan, to his bedside, and said 'Doctor do you consider that I am in my right mind?' to which the Doctor replied, 'Yes, you are in your right mind, I have just had a conversation with you.' He then addressed himself to all present and said: 'I want to give my dying testimony. You must be faithful in Christ. I want to say to you all that the bible and the record of the Nephites, The Book of Mormon, are true so you can say that you have heard me bear my testimony on my death bed.'"[36]

With passion and consistency—never wavering—David Whitmer reaffirmed his testimony again and again and again. To suggest he denied his testimony is a 24-carat falsehood. It is a fabrication of the highest order. David had multiple opportunities to deny or dilute his testimony, but he never chose to do so.[37] Why? Because he saw what he saw, and he heard what he heard, just as he testified on numerous occasions during his life.

## Martin Harris

While many contemporaries of Martin Harris could not accept the Book of Mormon, they could not honestly discount his integrity. Some critics argue that he was superstitious and gullible,[38] but there is little room for debate about his honorable character. E. B. Grandin, the non-Mormon printer of the Book of Mormon, was well acquainted with Martin Harris. He wrote of him: "Mr. Harris was among the early settlers of this town [Palmyra] and has ever borne the character of an honorable and upright man, and an obliging and benevolent neighbor. He had secured to himself by honest industry a respectable fortune—and he has left a large circle of acquaintances and friends to pity his delusion."[39]

The question was occasionally asked if the plates were real or an intangible object comprising part of a "spiritual vision." Critics point to a statement by Martin Harris that he saw the plates with "the eyes of faith and not with the natural eyes"[40] and similar statements suggesting the plates were not a real and tangible object. That has never seemed like much of an argument to me. Of course Martin Harris needed faith to see the angel and the plates, and no doubt he was spiritually transfigured in some way to behold the divine messenger who showed him the plates (see Moses 1:14). Thus, he saw the angel and the plates, both as real as can be, with an eye of faith.

David Whitmer confirmed Martin Harris's observation and dismissed this argument of the critics as much ado about nothing. In a letter dated April 2, 1887, he wrote: "Of course we were in the spirit when we had the view, for no man can behold the face of an angel, except in a spiritual view, but we were in the body also, and everything was as natural to us, as it is at any time."[41]

Lest there be any question about the reality of the plates, Martin Harris addressed the issue on more than one occasion. When confronted by a group of teenagers, Martin Harris declared:

"Well, just as plain as you see that chopping block, I saw the plates; and sooner than I would deny it I would lay my head upon that chopping block and let you chop it off."[42]

Robert Aveson, a printer, had a long interview with Martin Harris, who was then ninety-one years of age, and asked him directly about seeing the plates. Martin responded: "It is not mere belief, but is a matter of knowledge. I saw the plates and the inscriptions thereon. I saw the angel, and he showed them unto me."[43]

Martin Harris responded to another question about whether or not he was sure he had seen the plates by gesturing to his hand and saying: "Gentlemen, do you see that hand? Are you sure you see it? Are your eyes playing you a trick or something? No. Well, as sure as you see my hand so sure did I see the angel and the plates."[44]

On repeated occasions, Martin Harris made it clear that he saw the plates and they were a tangible object. It seems so misleading that critics never quote any of these statements that give us an accurate picture of what Martin actually saw.

In a letter to Hanna B. Emerson dated January 1871, Martin summarized the testimony he had repeatedly and consistently given during his lifetime:

"No man ever heard me in any way deny the truth of the Book of Mormon, the administration of the angel that showed me the plates: nor the organization of the Church of Jesus Christ of Latter Day Saints under the administration of Joseph Smith, Jun., the prophet whom the Lord raised up for that purpose in these latter days, that he may show forth his power and glory."[45]

George Godfrey shared this encounter he had with Martin Harris shortly before Martin's death:

"A few hours before his death and when he was so weak and enfeebled that he was unable to recognize me or anyone, and knew not to whom he was speaking, I asked him if he did not feel that there was an element at least, of fraudulence and deception in the things that were written and told of the coming forth of the Book of Mormon, and he replied as he had always done so many, many times in my hearing and with the same spirit he always manifested when enjoying health and vigor and said: 'The Book of Mormon is no fake. I know what I know. I have seen what I have seen and I have heard what I have heard. I have seen the gold plates from which the Book of Mormon is written. An angel appeared to me and others and testified to the truthfulness of the record, and had I been willing to have perjured myself and sworn falsely to the testimony I now bear I could have been a rich man, but I could not have testified other than I have done and am now doing for these things are true.'"[46]

## Conclusion

While all of the Three Witnesses were excommunicated from the Church and had personal differences with the Prophet Joseph Smith, the overwhelming evidence confirms they never denied their testimonies, contrary to any secondhand or hearsay statements presented by critics. Faithful Latter-day Saints have used this fact as an argument to support the witnesses' testimonies: namely, that after the Three Witnesses were excommunicated, it would have been a perfect time to expose Joseph and his alleged fraud, to get even, to seek personal revenge for their excommunications, but they never chose to do so because they knew their testimonies were true.

Critics, however, refute this and say that the reason the Three Witnesses did not deny their testimonies was because they did not want to ruin their reputation and admit they had participated in a fraud. It is interesting to note that in this line of reasoning, critics acknowledge that the Three Witnesses never denied their testimonies, yet on other occasions critics claim they have evidence that they did deny their testimonies. It is one or the other, not both.

This argument of the critics further breaks down when one realizes that each of these witnesses reaffirmed his testimony of the Book of Mormon near or at the time of his death, when there was far less reason, if any, to protect his mortal reputation. If these witnesses had been deceiving the people, as the critics allege, then the logical thing would have been to keep quiet on their deathbeds or, alternatively, to confess their sin of deception so they could face God with a clear conscience. But instead all three chose to voluntarily reaffirm their testimonies. Why? Because they wanted to face God with their final witness on their lips that they had remained true to their testimonies to the very end.

In spite of the attempted character assassination of the Three Witnesses and the utterly false claims that some of them denied their testimonies, Harry Beardsley, a critic of Joseph Smith, made this candid confession about the Three Witnesses based on his information in the 1920s: "In this particular instance, they apparently spoke what they believed to be the truth, when they asserted that they had seen the plates. All three later apostatized . . . and during their periods of apostasy were approached by numerous foes of the Mormons and enterprising journalists who sought to obtain from them statements refuting their testimony. *All remained steadfast until death in their assertion that they had seen the plates and that they believed* The Book of Mormon *to be of divine origin.*"[47]

Any suggestion that the Three Witnesses denied their testimonies is pure fantasy in light of their repeated personal statements to the contrary. As powerful as the testimonies of Oliver, David, and Martin are, the Lord provided even more testimonies to silence the critic and to strengthen the believer. The next chapter discusses the testimonies of the Eight Witnesses and makes some concluding comments about the power and evidentiary weight of all eleven witnesses.

---

NOTES

1. In addition to these eleven witnesses, Mary Whitmer saw the plates; also, Emma Smith and William Smith lifted or touched them while the plates were covered in cloth (see Johnson and Reeder, *The Witness of Women,* 29–31).
2. "The Valueless Testimony of the Book of Mormon Witnesses."
3. Hinckley, "Be Not Deceived," 46.
4. See "The Valueless Testimony of the Book of Mormon Witnesses"; Runnells, "Letter to a CES Director."
5. Martin Harris made it clear from his own testimony, as cited in this chapter, that he saw the plates as shown to him by the angel, but he did not handle them.
6. Lucy Smith, *Biographical Sketches,* 139.
7. See Runnells, "Letter to a CES Director." Some modern intellectuals claim that only the gullible or the naïve would believe in angels, yet believing Christians know that the New Testament is replete with stories of angelic visitations, such as the angelic visits to the mother of Jesus; Zacharias; Peter, James, and John on the Mount of Transfiguration; the women at the tomb; Cornelius; Peter and John in prison; and John on the Isle of Patmos. If God is the same yesterday, today, and forever, then why would we not have angelic visitations today?
8. James Hart wrote a poem principally focused on the witnesses to the Book of Mormon (in Cook, *David Whitmer Interviews,* 104). In it he asks a lawyer who was acquainted with the witnesses about their character. One of the stanzas reads as follows:

   "And Mr. Cowdery, I have known him too;
   More truthful man than he I never knew.
   And as lawyer he was shrewd and bright,
   And always made an honorable fight."
9. See http://www.josephsmithpapers.org/paper-summary/letter-to-the-church-in-caldwell-county-missouri-16-december-1838/6. All three witnesses became estranged from the Prophet Joseph during the tumultuous crisis of 1837–38 in Kirtland and then the expulsion of the Saints from Missouri.
10. Other critics have argued that Oliver was a distant relative of Joseph and therefore had a built-in conflict of interest that adversely affected his integrity, yet I have seen no evidence whatsoever presented of this purported bias.

11. In Anderson, *Investigating the Book of Mormon Witnesses,* 44.
12. In *Seneca Advertiser,* May 5, 1848. This article was copied verbatim as an endorsement in the *Walworth County Democrat* and then republished (May 30, 1848) by Horace A. Tenney in the *Wisconsin Argus* at Madison several weeks after Cowdery's defeat for public office.
13. In Schaefer, "'The Testimony of Men,'" 109.
14. Letter from Elizabeth Cowdery to David Whitmer, Mar. 8, 1887, Southwest City, MO, in Anderson, *Investigating the Book of Mormon Witnesses,* 63; emphasis added. To refute Oliver's testimony of the Book of Mormon, the critics have cited a letter by Judge W. Lang, a law partner of Oliver Cowdery, which appeared in an anti-Mormon flyer in 1881, more than thirty years after Oliver's death. It is considered by some as a possible forgery (the letter is no longer extant). The letter claims to represent Oliver's discussions on the subject with Mr. Lang, who summarized these alleged conversations and his impressions as follows:

    "The plates were never translated and could not be, were never intended to be. What is claimed to be a translation is the 'Manuscript found' [referring to the Spaulding manuscript], worked over by Cowdery. He was the best scholar amongst them. Rigdon got the original at the job printing office in Pittsburg. As I have stated . . . I say to you that I do know, as well as can now be known that Oliver revised the 'manuscript,' and Smith and Rigdon approved of it before it became the 'Book of Mormon.'"

    I can imagine what an attorney might do with this witness and his letter on cross-examination; it would be nothing less than devastating. Semitrucks could drive through some of the gaping holes in his testimony. Following are some examples:

    *First:* Mr. Lang claimed that Oliver Cowdery "worked over" and "revised" the Solomon Spaulding manuscript into what is now the Book of Mormon. What Mr. Lang didn't know at the time was that three years later, in 1884, the Spaulding manuscript would be found by scholars who were not members of The Church of Jesus Christ of Latter-day Saints. As already discussed in chapter 2, these scholars said there was "*no* resemblance between these two books in general or in detail." If that is the case, how did Oliver merely rework and revise a manuscript that had no resemblance whatsoever to the Book of Mormon? And why would Oliver state that he was the principal scribe as Joseph translated to him the Book of Mormon, if in fact he was the one who wrote it?

    *Second:* Mr. Lang stated that Joseph Smith and Sidney Rigdon approved the "rewrite" before it became the Book of Mormon. This is pure fiction. Chapter 2 of this book provides compelling historical evidence from multiple reliable sources that Sidney never met Joseph until *after* the Book of Mormon was published.

    *Third:* Mr. Lang claims that Rigdon got the original manuscript at the job printing office in Pittsburgh, even though there is no hard evidence of this whatsoever.

    *Fourth:* Either Mr. Lang or the anti-Mormon flyer of 1881 conveniently forgot to mention that Oliver Cowdery, after his alleged conversations with Mr. Lang, rejoined The Church of Jesus Christ of Latter-day Saints from which he had been excommunicated and bore powerful witness of the truth of the Book of Mormon. Why rejoin if he knew and had disclosed to Mr. Lang that the Book of Mormon was a fraud?

15. As set forth in a letter written by George A. Smith on October 31, 1848, to Orson Pratt and published in the *Millennial Star,* Vol. 11, in 1849; reprinted in Wells, "Oliver Cowdery," 229.
16. David Whitmer, *An Address to All Believers in Christ,* 13. Shortly before his death, Oliver said to Jacob Gates: "Jacob, I want you to remember what I say to you, I am a dying man, and what would it profit one to tell you a lie? I know . . . that this Book of Mormon was translated by the gift and power of God. My eyes saw, my ears heard, and my understanding was touched, and I know that whereof I testified is true. It was no dream, no vain imagination of the mind—it was real" (in Faulring, "The Return of Oliver Cowdery," 153).
17. Lyndon W. Cook, who collected and commented on the interviews of David Whitmer, wrote, "Although he was misquoted on this point [that he handled the plates], Whitmer made it abundantly clear that the three witnesses did not handle the plates, the table on which they lay, nor any of the ancient artifacts" (*David Whitmer Interviews,* xiv, footnote 5).
18. See, for example, "The Valueless Testimony of the Book of Mormon Witnesses."
19. In *Richmond Conservator,* Jan. 9, 1885.
20. In Jenson, "The Three Witnesses," 211.
21. In Cook, *David Whitmer Interviews,* 151.
22. Marsh, "History of Thos. Baldwin Marsh," 2; emphasis added.
23. Anderson, *Investigating the Book of Mormon Witnesses,* 80–82.
24. Greene, *Facts Relative to the Expulsion of the Mormons,* 17.
25. In Joseph Smith III, *Joseph Smith III and the Restoration,* 312; emphasis added.
26. In Cook, *David Whitmer Interviews,* 192–193; emphasis added.
27. In Cook, *David Whitmer Interviews,* 26.
28. In Cook, *David Whitmer Interviews,* 59.
29. See Vogel, *Early Mormon Documents,* 5:63.
30. David Whitmer, *An Address to All Believers in Christ,* 8–9; emphasis added.
31. David Whitmer, *An Address to All Believers in Christ,* 13; emphasis added. Some critics believe that this quotation of David should be tempered by the following statement from the same publication: "If you believe my testimony to the Book of Mormon; if you believe that God spake to us three witnesses by his own voice, then I tell you that in June 1838, God spake to me again by his own voice from the heavens, and told me to 'separate myself from among the Latter Day Saints'" (27). One response to this is that David had the Spirit when he saw the angel and golden plates but lost the Spirit and his ability to recognize it when he claimed the Spirit told him to separate from the Latter-day Saints. Why? Because this claim came at a time when

he had been excommunicated from the Church and lost the gift of the Holy Ghost. For further corroboration of this, see the observations of James H. Moyle during his interviews with David Whitmer, as quoted in Cook, *David Whitmer Interviews,* 158–70.

32. In Cook, *David Whitmer Interviews,* 194.
33. In Cook, *David Whitmer Interviews,* 78.
34. In Cook, *David Whitmer Interviews,* 95–96.
35. In Cook, *David Whitmer Interviews,* 159–70.
36. In Cook, *David Whitmer Interviews,* 226.
37. After reviewing all the available interviews, letters, and other sources concerning the testimony of David Whitmer, Lyndon Cook concluded, "At the center of all the interviews was his undying faith in the authenticity of the Book of Mormon, his faith that Joseph Smith had been divinely called, and that by miraculous power God had again restored his truth to the earth" (*David Whitmer Interviews,* xxvi).
38. See Runnells, "Letter to a CES Director."
39. In *Wayne Sentinel,* Jan. 21, 1824.
40. See Kelley and Braden, *The Braden and Kelley Debate,* 173.
41. In Cook, *David Whitmer Interviews,* 247.
42. In Lundwall, *Assorted Gems of Priceless Value.*
43. Aveson, "Three Witnesses to the Book of Mormon."
44. Statement of William M. Glenn to O. E. Fischbacher, May 30, 1943, Cardston, Alberta, Canada, cited in *Deseret News,* Oct. 2, 1943.
45. In "Correspondence," *The True Latter Day Saints' Herald,* Oct. 15, 1875, 630.
46. Godfrey, "Testimony of Martin Harris," from an unpublished manuscript copy in the possession of his daughter, Florence (Godfrey) Munson of Field, Utah; quoted in Ricks, *The Case of the Book of Mormon Witnesses,* 117.
47. Beardsley, *Joseph Smith and His Mormon Empire,* 67; emphasis added.

# CHAPTER 8

# The Eight Witnesses

Similar to the Three Witnesses, the Eight Witnesses of the golden plates were true to their testimonies to the very end, even though some of them also left the Church. The conclusion of their testimonial statement, as published in the Book of Mormon, reads, "We lie not, God bearing witness of it." What God-fearing man would make such a statement to condemn himself, unless he knew with absolute assurance his testimony was true? Following are some evidences witnessing that these courageous men stayed true to their testimonies.[1]

## Hyrum Smith

After months of imprisonment in Liberty Jail, Hyrum Smith wrote:

"I felt a determination to die, rather than deny the things which my eyes had seen, which my hands had handled, and which I had borne testimony to wherever my lot had been cast."[2]

While Hyrum and Joseph were in Carthage Jail, about to meet the fate of martyrs, Hyrum read to Joseph words of comfort from the Book of Mormon. Before the final shots would take their lives, Joseph bore a fervent testimony of the divinity of the Book of Mormon to their prison guards. Elder Jeffrey R. Holland, in recounting these events, said:

"As one of a thousand elements of my own testimony of the divinity of the Book of Mormon, I submit this as yet one more evidence of its truthfulness. In this their greatest—and last—hour of need, I ask you: would these men [Joseph and Hyrum] blaspheme before God by continuing to fix their lives, their honor, and their own search for eternal salvation on a book (and by implication a church and a ministry) they had fictitiously created out of whole cloth?

"Never mind that their wives are about to be widows and their children fatherless. Never mind that their little band of followers will yet be 'houseless, friendless and homeless' and that their children will leave footprints of blood across frozen rivers and an untamed prairie floor. Never mind that legions will die and other legions live declaring in the four quarters of this earth that they know the Book of Mormon and the Church which espouses it to be true. Disregard all of that, and tell me whether in this hour of death these two men would enter the presence of their Eternal Judge quoting from and finding solace in a book which, if *not* the very word of God, would brand them as imposters and charlatans until the end of time? *They would not do that!* They were willing to die rather than deny the divine origin and the eternal truthfulness of the Book of Mormon."[3]

That is powerful logic. Why, in their moment of extremity, in the moment preceding their brutal and unwarranted deaths, would Joseph and Hyrum seek refuge and comfort and hope in a book they knew to be a total fraud? Such an act would be both senseless and futile.

## Jacob Whitmer

The son of Jacob Whitmer told Andrew Jenson, a Church historian in the late 1800s, "My father Jacob Whitmer was always faithful and true to his testimony to the Book of Mormon and confirmed it on his death bed."[4]

## Hiram Page

William McLellin told of a tragic experience involving Hiram Page in Missouri during the year 1833 when the mobs were rampaging against the Saints. Page was being beaten unmercifully in the woods. Even though he begged for mercy, there was none. Finally, one of the mob said, "If you will deny that damned book [referring to the Book of Mormon], we will let you go." Page replied, "How can I deny what I know to be true." In response, the mob continued to beat him until they thought he was about to die. Then, as recorded by McLellin, one of the mob said, "Now what do you think of your God, when he don't save you? Well said he [Page], I believe in God —Well, said one of the most intelligent among them, I believe the damned fool will stick to it though we kill him. Let us let him go. But his life was nearly run out. He was confined to his bed for a length of time. So much for a man who knows for himself."[5] One might appropriately ask, "What motivation is there to perpetuate a lie under these dire circumstances?"

On May 30, 1847, after he had disassociated from the Church, Hiram Page wrote a letter to an excommunicated member of the Church in which he declared, "As to the book of Mormon, it would be doing injustice to myself, and to the work of God of the last days, to say that I could know a thing to be true in 1830 [when he gave his testimony of the reality of the golden plates], and know the same thing to be false in 1847."[6]

Hiram Page's son reported: "I knew my father to be true and

faithful to his testimony of the divinity of the Book of Mormon until the very last. Whenever he had an opportunity to bear his testimony to this effect, he would always do so, and seemed to rejoice in having been privileged to see the plates."[7]

## John Whitmer

In 1836 John Whitmer gave this powerful testimony of the Book of Mormon:

"It may not be amiss in this place, to give a statement to the world concerning the work of the Lord, as I have been a member of this church of Latter Day Saints from its beginning; to say that the book of Mormon is a revelation from God, I have no hesitancy; but with all confidence have signed my name to it as such. Therefore I desire to testify to all that will come to the knowledge of this address; that I have most assuredly seen the plates from whence the book of Mormon is translated, and that I have handled these plates, and know of a surety that Joseph Smith, jr. has translated the book of Mormon by the gift and power of God, and in this thing the wisdom of the wise most assuredly has perished: therefore, know ye, O ye inhabitants of the earth, wherever this address may come, that I have in this thing freed my garments of your blood, whether you believe or disbelieve the statements of your unworthy friend and well-wisher."[8]

About two years after making this statement, John Whitmer was excommunicated from the Church. He was bitter and upset. When asked by Theodore Turley about the Book of Mormon, he responded, "I cannot read it, and I do not know whether it is true or not." Unfortunately, the critics often fail to put this quote in context. When put in context, one realizes that John Whitmer was not questioning the truth of the Book of Mormon, rather he was responding to a question about the engravings on the golden plates. He replied that he could not read the engravings and therefore could not verify if the translation was correct. So there would be no mistake, however, about the reality of his divine experience, he later commented in the same interview: "I handled those plates; there were fine engravings on both sides. I handled them."[9]

John Whitmer never rejoined the Church, but as the years passed and the bitterness subsided, he again reaffirmed the reality of the plates. In 1876, just two years before his death, John Whitmer wrote a letter to Mark Forscutt, a leader in what was then called the Reorganized Church of Jesus Christ of Latter Day Saints. The letter included this persuasive testimony:

"Oliver Cowdery lived in Richmond, Mo., some 40 miles from here, at the time of his death. I [John Whitmer] went to see him and was with him for some days previous to his demise. I have never heard him deny the truth of his testimony of the Book of Mormon under any circumstances whatever. Neither do I believe that he would have denied, at the peril of his life; so firm was he that he could not be made to deny what he has affirmed to be a divine revelation from God. . . .

" . . . *I have never heard that any one of the three or eight witnesses ever denied the testimony that they have borne to the Book as published in the first edition of the Book of Mormon.* There are only two of the witnesses to that book now living, to wit., David Whitmer, one of the three, and [I] John Wh[itmer], one of the eight. Our names have gone forth to all nations, tongues and people as a divine revelation from God. And it will bring to pass the designs of God according to the declaration therein contained."[10]

## Samuel Smith

When Phineas Young asked Samuel Smith if he was one of the witnesses to the Book of Mormon, Samuel replied, "Yes, I know the book to be a revelation from God, translated by the gift and power of the Holy Ghost, and that my brother Joseph Smith Jun., is a Prophet, Seer and Revelator."[11]

## Christian and Peter Whitmer

Christian and Peter Whitmer were brothers-in-law to Oliver Cowdery. Oliver wrote of their faithful adherence to their testimonies:

"Among those who have gone home to rest, we mention the names of our two brothers-in-law, Christian and Peter Whitmer, jr., the former died on the 27th of November 1835, and the other the 22nd of September last, in Clay County, Missouri. By many in this church, our brothers were personally known: they were the first to embrace the new covenant, on hearing it, and during a constant scene of persecution and perplexity, to their last moments, maintained its truth—they were both included in the list of the eight witnesses in the Book of Mormon, and though they have departed, it is with great satisfaction that we reflect, that they proclaimed to their last moments, the certainty of their former testimony: The testament is in force after the death of the testator. May all who read remember the fact, that the Lord has given men a witness of himself in the last days, and that they have faithfully declared it till called away."[12]

## Joseph Smith Sr.

While there is no known statement from Joseph Smith Sr. discussing his original testimony as one of the Eight Witnesses, his life of service and devotion to the very end, in spite of intense persecution, is perhaps his greatest and most enduring testimony of that truth to which he, like the other seven, bore solemn witness.

## The Bottom Line

Richard Anderson noted: "I've got about two hundred times [documented statements] when one of the witnesses said, 'I did sign the statement.' 'The statement means what it says.' 'I saw the angel.' 'I saw the plates.' Or in the case of the eight witnesses, 'I handled the plates.' So, two hundred very positive and specific statements in many cases and I'm dealing today with about eight or ten documents [with negative comments allegedly from or about the Book of Mormon witnesses], in other words, five percent. And the question is: 'Do you believe the 95 percent or do you believe the five?'"[13]

To put this in perspective, suppose you are the judge in an auto accident case, and there are twenty witnesses. Further, suppose that nineteen of the witnesses were consistent in their testimonies as to how the accident occurred. Now suppose one witness testified that what he saw was in opposition to the other nineteen. As judge, whom will you believe? Yes, there is a possibility—very remote—that the lone dissenter is right, but, absent other evidence, the rational, impartial mind is going to side with the nineteen witnesses. And so it is with the Book of Mormon. The impartial and unbiased judge must admit that the testimonies of the eleven witnesses, as supported by overwhelming historical evidence, are a very convincing evidence of the truth of the Book of Mormon.

The eleven witnesses had every possible opportunity to expose Joseph and the Book of Mormon as a fraud but never did so. Some were excommunicated, some had personal differences with the Prophet, some joined other churches, one was shot and killed, and at least two were told to deny their testimonies or be killed. Many, if not all, were interviewed multiple times—by apostates, by nonbelievers, by journalists seeking a sensational story, by the curious, and by the honest in heart—but no matter the circumstance, no matter the pressure put on them to recant, they would not. Through thick and thin, these men never yielded to that temptation, never succumbed to the pressure to deny their testimonies.

In summary, what factors must be present for witnesses to make a compelling argument in court?

*First:* Were there multiple witnesses, and were their testimonies consistent with each other? In this case, eleven men of integrity bore remarkably consistent testimonies of the Book of Mormon.

*Second:* Have these testimonies stood the test of time, or have there been material changes as the years have passed? History verifies that each of the eleven witnesses bore the same testimony throughout his entire life.

*Third:* Did the witnesses bear the same testimony even when it was contrary to their own best interests, or was there some diluting, hedging, or even retraction of the original testimony? Again, the historical evidence is clear—it reflects that the eleven witnesses continued to bear courageous and powerful testimony of the Book of Mormon even though some were excommunicated, ridiculed, pressured by peers, or threatened with death. There was no wavering even under the most adverse of circumstances.

*Fourth:* Did these eleven men bear testimony even though there was no ulterior motive for doing so, such as money, fame, or power? Yes.

*Fifth:* Did these men continue to bear testimony even on their deathbeds, when a man is most inclined to tell the truth before meeting his Maker? Yes.

As one considers this list of factors, one is inevitably led to the conclusion that the testimonies of the eleven witnesses are compelling, even irrefutable evidence of the divine origin of the Book of Mormon.

Every argument seems to have a "bottom line"—a point at which you cut through all the chaff, all the distractions, all the red tape, and you find the core or essence of the issue. Richard Anderson was asked at a religious conference, "So are we to understand that every claim or assertion that one of the witnesses denied their testimony comes from a secondary or hearsay source?" Mr. Anderson replied, "I think so. I don't know of an exception. *And you can't find anything where any of them wrote that they denied their testimony.*"[14]

It didn't matter—rain, sleet, snow, earthquake, hurricane, tornado, or whatever the minions of the evil one could figuratively throw at these witnesses—imperfect as these men may have been as mortals, they were true to the mark, true to their testimonies of the Book of Mormon to the very end. *And that is the bottom line.*

---

NOTES

1. I express appreciation to FairMormon for making these testimonies so readily accessible. See "The Eight Witnesses and Their Experience Viewing the 'Gold' Plates."
2. Hyrum Smith, "Communications: To the Saints Scattered Abroad," 23.
3. Holland, "Safety for the Soul," 89; emphasis in original.
4. In Jenson, Stevenson, and Black, "Historical Landmarks," 2.
5. "W.E. McLellin's Book," circa 1871, as published in Schaefer, "'The Testimony of Men,'" 109.
6. Hiram Page, letter to William E. McLellin, 63.
7. Philander Page, in Jenson, "The Eight Witnesses," 614.
8. John Whitmer, "Address," 286–87.
9. In Vogel, *Early Mormon Documents,* 5:241. This interview is also printed with minor editing in *History of the Church,* 3:307–8.
10. Peterson, "Not Joseph's, and Not Modern," 207–8; emphasis added.
11. In Young, "History of Brigham Young," 277; cited in Anderson, *Investigating the Book of Mormon Witnesses,* 139.
12. Cowdery, "The Closing Year," 426.
13. Anderson, "Explaining Away the Book of Mormon Witnesses."
14. Anderson, "Explaining Away the Book of Mormon Witnesses"; emphasis added.

CHAPTER 9

# Another Testament of Christ's Divinity

The Bible is certainly a magnificent witness of Jesus Christ and His divinity, but the crowning witness of the Savior and His Atonement is to be found in the Book of Mormon, particularly in its account of the visit of the resurrected Christ to the Nephites.

One of the prime purposes of the Book of Mormon, as announced on its title page, is "to the convincing of the Jew and Gentile that Jesus is the Christ, the Eternal God, manifesting himself unto all nations." Accordingly, the doctrine, ordinances, and stories as contained in the Book of Mormon have a common underlying goal—to point us to Jesus Christ as the Savior and Redeemer of the world.

No wonder, as Susan Easton Black observed, the Savior is referenced or mentioned in the Book of Mormon "on an average of every 1.7 verses."[1] In comparison, she further notes that a form of Christ's name is used an average of once every 2.1 verses in the New Testament. In other words, she observes, "the name of the Savior appears nearly 25 percent more frequently in the Book of Mormon than even in the New Testament."[2]

Stephen H. Webb, the late Catholic theologian and philosopher, added his observations of this Christ-centered book: "Mormonism is obsessed with Christ, and everything that it teaches is meant to awaken, encourage, and expand faith in him. I came to this conclusion when I read through the Book of Mormon for the first time."[3]

Suffice it to say, the Book of Mormon is inundated with references to the Savior and His godly attributes—His overarching love, His infinite power, His tender mercies, and His incomparable Atonement. This is a book with multiple witnesses and undeniable evidences of Jesus Christ and His divinity, thus honoring its subtitle as "Another Testament of Jesus Christ." President Gordon B. Hinckley gave this testimony: "Hand in hand with the Bible, whose companion volume it is, it stands as another witness to a doubting generation that Jesus is the Christ, the Son of the living God."[4]

President Ezra Taft Benson taught: "Much of the Christian world today rejects the divinity of the Savior. They question His miraculous birth, His perfect life, and the reality of His glorious resurrection. The Book of Mormon teaches in plain and unmistakable terms about the truth of all those. *It also provides the most complete explanation of the doctrine of the Atonement. Truly, this divinely inspired book is a keystone in bearing witness to the world that Jesus is the Christ.*"[5]

## The Atonement of Jesus Christ

The Atonement of Jesus Christ is the greatest evidence we have that Jesus is the divine Son of God—our Redeemer and our Savior. Nonetheless, many in the Christian world struggle to understand the depth and breadth of the Atonement of Jesus Christ, even though it is the central doctrine of all Christianity. The clarity and expansiveness of this doctrine as taught in the Book of Mormon, however, should be beyond honest dispute. The Old and New Testaments have some scattered doctrinal gems on the Atonement, which we greatly appreciate, but the Book of Mormon has numerous sermons, even entire masterpieces on the subject.[6] It is of interest to note that the word *atonement* appears only once in the King James Version of the New Testament (Romans 5:11), while it appears more than twenty-five times in the Book of Mormon.[7]

Book of Mormon prophets realized how important it was to possess a thorough understanding of Christ's Atonement. Lehi, while counseling his son Jacob, said, "How great the importance to make these things [the Atonement of Jesus Christ] known unto the inhabitants of the earth, that they may know that there is no flesh that can dwell in the presence of God, save it be through the merits, and mercy, and grace of the Holy Messiah" (2 Nephi 2:8). Jacob caught the significance of that counsel, for while preaching to his people, he asked, "Why not speak of the atonement of Christ, and attain to a perfect knowledge of him" (Jacob 4:12). And King Benjamin taught in his farewell sermon that our study of the Atonement is critical to our salvation: "I say unto you, if ye have come to a knowledge of the goodness of God, and his matchless power . . . and also, the atonement which has been prepared from the foundation of the world . . . and should be diligent in keeping his commandments . . . I say, that this is the man who receiveth salvation" (Mosiah 4:6–7).

Our understanding of Christ's Atonement is meant to be much more than an intellectual assent to this fundamental doctrine; it is also designed to be the cornerstone of our testimonies, the mainspring of our hope, and the prime source of our motivation. It is, in the ultimate sense, the key to our salvation.

What then is the Atonement of Jesus Christ, and how does the Book of Mormon expand our scope and depth of understanding on this most supernal of all religious events? The Atonement of Jesus Christ is the supreme manifestation of His infinite love and power, expressed through His infinite suffering in the Garden of Gethsemane and on the cross of Calvary. The culmination of His Atonement was achieved when Jesus Christ exercised His power to rise from the tomb as a resurrected, glorified being. Its purpose was to overcome the four key obstacles that prevent men and women from becoming like God and having a fulness of joy. These obstacles are:

- Physical death, caused by the Fall of Adam
- Spiritual death, caused by the Fall of Adam and by our personal sins
- Afflictions and infirmities "of every kind" (Alma 7:11), such as discouragement, illness, rejection, unfairness, loneliness, and abuse
- Human weaknesses and imperfections that prevent us from becoming more like God

That is why Jesus is called the Savior of the world: because He can literally save us from those conditions that otherwise prevent us from becoming like Him and having eternal joy.

For many years, I thought of Christ's Atonement as addressing only the first two obstacles mentioned above—physical and spiritual death. Not only did the Book of Mormon give me new insights as to how the Savior, through His Atonement, overcame these two obstacles, but, in addition, it enlightened my mind as to how the Atonement of Jesus Christ can help us combat our mortal afflictions and infirmities. It also enlightened my mind as to how the Atonement of Jesus Christ can help us overcome our weaknesses and imperfections so we can become more like the Savior. *It would be difficult, if not impossible, for us to gain this additional understanding without the doctrinal insights offered by the Book of Mormon.* Following are some of those insights found in the Book of Mormon that can help us gain a greater appreciation for and understanding of the Savior's Atonement and His infinite powers.

## Christ's Resurrection Overcomes Physical Death

The Bible has multiple accounts of witnesses to Christ's Resurrection: the women at the tomb (see Matthew 28:1–10; Luke 24:1–10), the Apostles (see Luke 24:36–43; John 20:19–20), the two disciples on the road to Emmaus (see Luke 24:13–32), and more than five hundred brethren at one time (see 1 Corinthians 15:6). There is no greater witness, however, in all recorded scripture of the Savior's Resurrection than His appearance to the Nephites when a multitude of about 2,500 went forth one by one "and thrust their hands into his side, and did feel the prints of the nails in his hands and in his feet . . . and did see with their eyes and did feel with their hands, and did know of a surety and did bear record" (3 Nephi 11:15) that He was the Son of God. Who can read that account and not feel the witness of the Spirit testifying of its truthfulness?

Both the Bible and the Book of Mormon confirm that all men, women, and children, whether righteous or wicked, will be raised from the grave as a consequence of Christ's Resurrection (see 1 Corinthians 15:20–22; Alma 12:8, 14–15). There are some in Christianity, however, who believe that we are "resurrected" as spirits, without the "limitations" of a physical body. The Book of Mormon dispels this untruth: "The soul shall be restored to the body, and the body to the soul; yea, and every limb and joint shall be restored to its body; yea, even a hair of the head shall not be lost" (Alma 40:23).

The Book of Mormon also helps us understand that as resurrected beings we will stand in the presence of God to be judged, with a perfect knowledge of all our guilt and righteousness (see 2 Nephi 9:14–16).

In these doctrinal explanations, the Bible and the Book of Mormon act as complementary and supplementary witnesses of Christ's Resurrection.

## Christ, through the Atonement, Can Overcome Spiritual Death by Cleansing Us of Our Sins and Removing Our Guilt

Repentance is possible only because of Christ's Atonement. Samuel the Lamanite confirmed this truth when he told the Nephites that the Savior, through His Atonement, made possible "the condition of repentance" (Helaman 14:18).

Once we have emerged from the waters of baptism and received the Holy Ghost, or thereafter repented, there is no black mark on our right ankle that reads "2010 sin," no stain behind our left ear that says "2015 transgression." There is no such thing as a spotted or cream-colored repenter in God's kingdom; rather it is as Moroni promised: "Ye become holy, without spot" (Moroni 10:33; see also Isaiah 1:18). What a beautiful, all-encompassing promise!

The Book of Mormon further helps us understand that this miraculous healing is not just reserved for those who lived after the time of Christ's suffering in the garden and on the cross, but that its effects are retroactive. King Benjamin declared that those who lived in his time, about 130 years before Christ, "might receive remission of their sins, and rejoice with exceedingly great joy, even as though he had already come among them" (Mosiah 3:13). Lest there be any misunderstanding on this point, the chapter heading to Alma 39 reads, "Christ's redemption is retroactive." In other words, the Book of Mormon clearly teaches that the atoning powers of Christ are infinite in time—not only prospectively but also retroactively.

In addition, the Book of Mormon helps us understand the expansiveness of Christ's cleansing powers by giving us specific examples of the depth to which one may sink and still be saved. It reveals to us that Christ's healing powers have extended and will extend to "the very vilest of sinners" (Mosiah 28:4), to one who was known as "a very wicked and an idolatrous man" (Mosiah 27:8), to those who had "gone astray" and "were full of all manner of wickedness" (Alma 13:17), to one who was called a "child of hell" (Alma 11:23), to those who were "in the darkest abyss" (Alma 26:3), and to those who acknowledged that they "were the most lost of all mankind" (Alma 24:11). In other words, the Book of Mormon makes it clear that the Savior, through His Atonement, has the power to cleanse all men and all women of all sins, except in the case of those who choose to reject the Atonement and who "would not be redeemed" (Mosiah 26:26; see also D&C 88:33). This knowledge should bring immeasurable comfort to all of us—to know that our sins, however egregious they may be, are not outside the reach of Christ's cleansing powers. Even if we are repeat offenders, the Book of Mormon gives us this hope: "But as oft as they repented and sought forgiveness, with real intent, they were forgiven" (Moroni 6:8; see also Mosiah 26:30). The Book of Mormon confirms and clarifies the unfathomable depths of Christ's cleansing and forgiving powers.

Even though we may believe in Christ and His cleansing powers, the question often arises: "How do I know if and when I have been forgiven of my sins?"[8] The Book of Mormon gives us some helpful insight in this regard. If we feel the Spirit in our lives when we pray or read the scriptures, teach or testify or render service, or at any other time, then that is our witness that we have been forgiven—or, alternatively, that the cleansing process is taking place, because the Lord "dwelleth not in unholy temples, but in the hearts of the righteous" (Alma 34:36; see also Mosiah 2:37; Alma 7:21; Helaman 4:24).

In most cases, the cleansing process takes time because the change in our nature takes time, but in the interim, we can proceed with confidence that God approves of our progress to a sufficient degree that we can enjoy some measure of His Spirit.[9] President Henry B. Eyring taught the same principle: "If you have felt the influence of the Holy Ghost, you may take it as evidence that the Atonement is working in your life."[10]

Some have asked, "But if I am forgiven, why do I still feel guilt?" Perhaps in God's mercy the memory of that guilt is a warning, a spiritual "stop sign" of sorts, at least for a time, that cries out when additional temptations confront us: "Don't go down that road. You know the pain and anguish it can bring." In this sense, it serves as a protection, not a punishment.

Will our guilt ever go away? The Book of Mormon gives us additional insights on this issue. To the repentant, the Lord promises that the time will come when "their joy shall be full forever" (2 Nephi 9:18; see also Revelation 21:4), meaning there will come a time when we will no longer be troubled by our past sins. Although Christ's Atonement does not alter the past, in some miraculous way Christ has the power to wipe away all the sorrow and pain associated with our former misdeeds. Because of His Atonement, Christ has that healing power.

I do not know if we will ever forget our sins, but the consequence will be the same as if we did, for the time will come (either in this life or the next) when the repentant will be at complete peace. Such was the case with the Book of Mormon prophet Enos, who sought for a remission of past sins. The scriptures record: "And there came a voice unto me, saying: Enos, thy sins are forgiven thee. . . . *Wherefore, my guilt was swept away.* And I said: Lord, how is it done? And he said unto me: Because of thy faith in Christ" (Enos 1:5–8; emphasis added). Enos had faith that Christ's Atonement could not only cleanse his sins but also remove his guilt. Such was also the case with the converted Lamanites. Their king, in the midst of confessing their "many murders," was nonetheless able to acknowledge that God "hath forgiven us of those our many sins and murders which we have committed, and *taken away the guilt from our hearts, through the merits of his Son*" (Alma 24:9–10; emphasis added).

Alma, while reflecting upon the Savior's Atonement and his sinful past, exclaimed: "While I was harrowed up by the memory of my many sins, . . . I cried within my heart: O Jesus, thou Son of God, have mercy on me. . . . And now, behold, *when I thought this, I could remember my pains no more; yea, I was harrowed up by the memory of my sins no more*" (Alma 36:17–19; emphasis added). So complete was this healing process that Alma then added, "There can be nothing so exquisite and sweet as was my joy" (Alma 36:21). Alma did not forget his sins. In fact, he was recalling them at that precise moment, but somehow the miracle of Christ's Atonement removed all, not just part, of his guilt associated with those wrongful deeds.

The people of King Benjamin listened to their king's glorious sermon on the Atonement of Jesus Christ and then declared that a mighty change had been wrought in their hearts. In response, King Benjamin declared: "Ye are born of him and have become his sons and his daughters. And under this head ye are made free" (Mosiah 5:7–8)—not only free from sin but also free from all its associated guilt.

But how is it that we can remember our sins and at the same time be free from guilt? Due to his mighty change of heart, Alma explained how this was possible. He declared unto the people that he, like the people of King Benjamin, "had been born of God" (Alma 36:23; see also verses 24, 26). In other words, as a repentant soul, his guilt was removed, because with perfect honesty he could now say, "I am not the man who committed those past sins, rather I am a new and different man, 'born of God'—a new creature in Christ [see Mosiah 27:26; 2 Corinthians 5:17]. I am no longer Alma the rebellious; I am now Alma the repentant."[11] The Book of Mormon enlightens our minds and comforts our hearts with this glorious truth that as we are born again, the Lord can remove not only our sins but also our guilt.

## The Power to Comfort Us in Our Afflictions

Some might wonder if the Savior's Atonement plays any part in our lives beyond raising us from the dead and cleansing us of our sins. The Book of Mormon makes clear that it does. Through His Atonement, the Savior acquired the powers to strengthen, support, and comfort us as we experience the afflictions and infirmities of life. The Bible gives us some beautiful insights into Christ's healing and comforting powers, particularly as recorded in Isaiah 53:3–5 and Isaiah 61:1–3. The Book of Mormon confirms these powers and gives us some additional insights into their breadth and origin.

Perhaps there are no more instructive verses in all of scripture that explain how and why the Savior suffered for us, and how that suffering enabled Him to be the ultimate Comforter, than these found in the book of Alma:

"And he shall go forth, suffering pains and afflictions and temptations of every kind; and this that the word might be fulfilled which saith he will take upon him the pains and the sicknesses of his people.

"And he will take upon him death, that he may loose the bands of death which bind his people; and he will take upon him their infirmities, that his bowels may be filled with mercy, according to the flesh, that he may know according to the flesh how to succor his people according to their infirmities" (Alma 7:11–12; see also Mosiah 3:7).

It is one thing to understand that the Savior has comforting and healing powers. It is another to know how these powers might be applied in our own lives. The Book of Mormon shares multiple ways in which this is accomplished. Sometimes the simple words from the Lord, "Be comforted," are sufficient. When the sons of Mosiah needed comfort as they began their mission to the Lamanites, "The Lord did visit them with his Spirit, and said unto them: Be comforted. And they were comforted" (Alma 17:10; see also Jacob 2:8).

Amulek counseled the persecuted poor among the Zoramites to "bear with all manner of afflictions," and then he gave them the eternal perspective that made this possible—"a firm hope that ye shall one day rest from all your afflictions" (Alma 34:40–41). The Atonement of Jesus Christ brings eternal perspective, eternal perspective brings hope, and hope brings comfort.

When Limhi and his people were in bondage to the Lamanites, they suffered great afflictions, "and there was no way that they could deliver themselves out of their hands" (Mosiah 21:5). Then the Lord stepped in with His comforting powers "and began to soften the hearts of the Lamanites that they began to ease their burdens" (Mosiah 21:15).

On a similar occasion, when Alma and his people were in bondage, the Lord chose yet another way to comfort His people:

"I will also ease the burdens which are put upon your shoulders, that even you cannot feel them upon your backs, even while you are in bondage; and this will I do that ye may stand as witnesses for me hereafter, and that ye may know of a surety that I, the Lord God, do visit my people in their afflictions.

"And . . . the Lord did strengthen them that they could bear up their burdens with ease" (Mosiah 24:14–15).

The Book of Mormon not only helps us understand that God can comfort us, but it also gives us specific examples as to how that might occur—by sharing the power of His words, by enhancing our eternal perspective, by softening the hearts of our enemies, and by strengthening us so we can more easily bear the burdens at hand. No doubt the Lord can comfort us in other ways, such as removing the affliction entirely, if He so desires.[12] Recognizing all this, it is no wonder that Alma should say: "For I do know that whosoever shall put their trust in God shall be supported in their trials, and their troubles, and their afflictions, and shall be lifted up at the last day" (Alma 36:3).

These insights from the Book of Mormon, along with specific examples of their application, can strengthen our faith in the Savior's healing powers and in His divine nature.

## The Power to Overcome Our Weaknesses and Perfect Us

One of the glorious insights into the Atonement of Jesus Christ, as taught in the Book of Mormon, is that the Savior can not only cleanse us but also perfect us. The doctrine that we can become Christlike because of Christ's Atonement is considered blasphemous by some Christians, even though it is clearly taught in the Bible.[13] Nonetheless, this is the crowning aim and achievement of Christ's Atonement: to take a mortal with all of his or her weaknesses and imperfections and convert those weaknesses not only to strengths but even more—to godlike attributes (see Moses 1:39). The Book of Mormon clarifies this doctrine that unfortunately is so confusing to those who rely upon the Bible alone.

King Benjamin addressed this topic in his final sermon. He spoke of the need to "[put] off the natural man and [become] a saint through the atonement of Christ the Lord" (Mosiah 3:19). In other words, the way to become saintly, meaning godly, is to avail oneself of Christ's grace (His enabling powers) made possible by the Atonement. Moroni was lamenting his weakness in his writing skills when the Savior said, "I give unto men weakness that they may be humble; and my grace is sufficient for all men that humble themselves before me; for if they humble themselves before me, and have faith in me, then will I make weak things become strong unto them" (Ether 12:27). If one weakness can become a strength through the Atonement of Jesus Christ, why cannot all weaknesses become strengths? And as each weakness becomes a strength, the road to perfection is traveled.

The prophet Mormon also testified that we can become godlike, inviting us to "pray unto the Father with all the energy of heart . . . that ye may become the sons of God; that when he [Christ] shall appear we shall be like him, . . . that we may be purified even as he is pure" (Moroni 7:48). Moroni also bore witness of this possibility to become pure and perfect like the Savior, but in addition revealed to us the means by which this might be accomplished:

"*Yea, come unto Christ, and be perfected in him,* and deny yourselves of all ungodliness; and if ye shall deny yourselves of all ungodliness, and love God with all your might, mind and strength, then is his grace sufficient for you, *that by his grace ye may be perfect in Christ;* and if by the grace of God ye are perfect in Christ, ye can in nowise deny the power of God.

" . . . *Then are ye sanctified in Christ by the grace of God, through the shedding of the blood of Christ, . . . that ye become holy, without spot*" (Moroni 10:32–33; emphasis added).

We recognize that becoming holy or godly through Christ's Atonement is a step-by-step process, a struggle that involves successes and failures along the way, but Christ has given us the comforting assurance that He will be with us each step of the path in that pursuit (see D&C 84:88; Abraham 1:18).

Because the Savior provided the way to become more like Him through His Atonement, He could command us to "be perfect even as I, or your Father who is in heaven is perfect" (3 Nephi 12:48), and He could further command, "What manner of men ought ye to be? Verily I say unto you, even as I am" (3 Nephi 27:27).

This doctrine of perfection as taught in the Book of Mormon is so consistent with the ultimate purpose of Christianity and biblical scripture that it is difficult to understand why other churches do not readily embrace it. For example, suppose you were to ask one of your Christian friends if all Christians should be striving to become more like Christ. No doubt your friend would respond "yes," since to say "no" would destroy the principal reason for the existence of Christianity, namely to become disciples of Christ and thus become more like Him and ultimately live with Him. But once he says "yes," he has crossed the line from which there is no return. Suppose you further asked, "Then to what extent can you become like Christ?" He might respond, "To a very small degree, since He is perfect and beyond our comprehension." You might then suggest, "Let's assume it's 1 percent. But if it's 1 percent, why not 5 percent? And if 5 percent, why not 10 percent? And if 10 percent, why not 50 percent? And so on. Once someone has acknowledged that it is possible to become like Christ to any degree, then what prevents such a person from becoming like Christ and our Father in Heaven to the degree commanded by Christ, namely: "Be ye therefore perfect, even as your Father which is in heaven is perfect" (Matthew 5:48).[14] In other words, if it is blasphemous to think we can become godlike, then at what point is it not blasphemous to become like God—90 percent, 50 percent, 1 percent? Is it more Christian to seek partial perfection than total perfection as the scriptures have commanded us to do?

Knowing that we are the spirit offspring of God (see Acts 17:26–29) and thus have His "spiritual DNA" embedded in our souls, and that we may live for eternity with God as our Father and guide, then what limits would we want to ascribe to man's spiritual progress?

This glorious truth and hope—that men and women, with all their weaknesses and imperfections, can eventually become godlike through the Atonement of Jesus Christ—is one of those pearls of great price, one of those plain and precious truths that was lost in the apostasy of Christ's original Church but restored through the Book of Mormon. How grateful we should be for this divine disclosure of infinite worth!

## Other Insights into Christ's Atonement

The Book of Mormon reveals not only the magnificent heights to which we can rise due to Christ's Atonement but also the tragic depths to which we must sink if there were no Atonement. Just as the crowning aim of the Savior's Atonement is to become at one with Christ, and at one like Him, Jacob discloses the tragic consequences that must exist without Christ's Atonement—we must become at one with the devil and at one like him, for as Jacob said, "our spirits must have become like unto him [the devil], and we become devils, . . . and to remain with the father of lies" (2 Nephi 9:9).

King Benjamin gave us other insights. He taught that the Atonement of Jesus Christ was planned in the premortal existence—"prepared from the foundation of the world" (Mosiah 4:6)—and that there was no plan B, no other way by which man can be saved, "neither are there any conditions [other than the Atonement of Jesus Christ] whereby man can be saved" (Mosiah 4:8; see also Mosiah 3:17).

As discussed in chapter 5 of this book, Mormon exposed the false doctrine of original sin and infant baptism. He declared: "He that saith that little children need baptism denieth the mercies of Christ, and setteth at naught the atonement of him and the power of his redemption" (Moroni 8:20; see also Moroni 8:22).

Some have expounded the theory that Christ's suffering was mitigated by the fact that He was half divine and therefore His divinity protected Him from hunger when He fasted, from exhaustion after a long day's work, and from suffering in Gethsemane and on the cross. Some have even speculated that Christ did not really bleed from every pore but merely sweat "as [though] it were great drops of blood" (Luke 22:44). King Benjamin refuted these misconceptions with this declaratory statement, "And lo, he shall suffer temptations, and pain of body, hunger, thirst, and fatigue, *even more than man can suffer, except it be unto death; for behold, blood cometh from every pore, so great shall be his anguish for the wickedness and the abominations of his people*" (Mosiah 3:7; emphasis added).

The Book of Mormon introduces a phrase not found in the Bible: "an infinite atonement" (2 Nephi 9:7; Alma 34:12), thus revealing the expansiveness, scope, and depth of Christ's saving powers.

In addition, the Book of Mormon teaches that if we embrace the Atonement of Jesus Christ, we can be of good cheer regardless of how dire our circumstances may be. Mormon wrote to his son Moroni of the Nephites' devastating losses in battle, of their depraved and degenerate condition, but then put it all in perspective: "My son, be faithful in Christ; and may not the things which I have written grieve thee, to weigh thee down unto death; but may Christ lift thee up, and may his sufferings and death, and the showing his body unto our fathers, and his mercy and long-suffering, and the hope of his glory and of eternal life, rest in your mind forever" (Moroni 9:25; see also John 16:33).

We learn a great lesson from this revealed truth. Because of the Atonement of Jesus Christ, we are in the driver's seat as to our eternal destiny. There is no external force or person or event—no disaster, financial loss, divorce, sickness, or abuse—that can rob us of our exaltation, provided we exercise faith in the Savior and follow Him. We can be optimistic about life because, as Nephi taught: "Cheer up your hearts, and remember that ye are free to act for yourselves—to choose the way of everlasting death or the way of eternal life" (2 Nephi 10:23; see also 2 Nephi 2:27).

Nowhere is the Savior's Atonement taught more powerfully, more concisely, and more expansively than in the Book of Mormon. It restores much that has been lost or mystified on this most sublime of all gospel truths. In this regard, Elder Jeffrey R. Holland has noted: "Much of this doctrine [of the Atonement of Jesus Christ] has been lost or expunged from the biblical records. It is therefore of great consequence that the Book of Mormon prophets taught that doctrine in detail and with clarity."[15]

## Roles and Titles for Christ

The Book of Mormon also bears witness of Jesus Christ through its references to His multiple titles. It contains at least 101 different names of Christ that refer to His divine roles—such as "Messiah" (1 Nephi 1:19), "Mighty God" (2 Nephi 6:17), "Savior" (1 Nephi 10:4), "Beloved Son" (2 Nephi 31:11), "Christ" (2 Nephi 10:3), "Counselor" (2 Nephi 19:6), "Eternal God" (1 Nephi 12:18), "God of Abraham" (1 Nephi 19:10), "Holy Child" (Moroni 8:3), "Immanuel" (2 Nephi 18:8), "Jehovah" (Moroni 10:34), "Lamb of God" (1 Nephi 10:10), "Lord of the vineyard" (Jacob 5:8), "Mediator" (2 Nephi 2:28), "Prince of Peace" (2 Nephi 19:6), "Redeemer" (1 Nephi 10:6), "Supreme Creator" (Alma 30:44), and a host of others.[16] Each of these titles helps us gain a greater insight into the roles of Jesus Christ. Each serves as a witness of His divine identity.

## Christ's Divine Attributes

Perhaps there is no greater demonstration of Christ's love and compassion in all scripture (excepting His Atonement) than that recorded in 3 Nephi 17. The Lord, obviously moved by the multitude's desire for Him to stay among them, said, "Behold, my bowels are filled with compassion towards you." He then invited them to bring forth their sick and afflicted, and "he did heal them every one as they were brought forth unto him." He then knelt with the multitude and "prayed unto the Father" things that were so great and marvelous that they "cannot be written." So moved were the people by His words and the feelings of the moment that they bore this record: "No one can conceive of the joy which filled our souls at the time we heard him pray for us unto the Father." The Savior wept and then "took their little children, one by one, and blessed them" (see 3 Nephi 17:6–21). The Savior's concern—His love and compassion for the one—were manifested again and again. His love seemed to flow from every pore, every breath.

Nephi noted, "He [Christ] doeth not anything save it be for the benefit of the world; for he loveth the world, *even that he layeth down his own life that he may draw all men unto him*" (2 Nephi 26:24; emphasis added). That was the foundation of His leadership and ministry: He did not compel or force people unto Him—rather He drew them unto Him. Inspired by His love, compassion, and sacrifice, people naturally heeded His call to come unto Him and be like Him.

Christ was and is the perfect God and exemplar. His divine attributes are spoken of again and again in the Book of Mormon. One cannot read this book without knowing that He is "the Lord

Omnipotent" (Mosiah 3:5), that He has "all wisdom, and all power, both in heaven and in earth" (Mosiah 4:9), that we are "encircled about eternally in the arms of his love" (2 Nephi 1:15), that He is "filled with mercy" (Alma 7:12), and that we are the frequent recipients of His "tender mercies" (1 Nephi 1:20; 1 Nephi 8:8). Knowing all this, how could we not love Him with all our heart, might, mind, and strength? How could Joseph Smith, if a fraud, plant these divine impressions in our minds and sacred feelings in our hearts?

## The Book of Mormon Brings Us to Christ

Not only does the Book of Mormon teach us about Christ, it brings us to Christ. A member of our congregation who had been less active in the Church for some time shared his testimony of how the Book of Mormon transformed his life. With his permission, I share some excerpts from an address he gave: "Just a year ago, I would not have been able to imagine being here and speaking in church. But last October something happened. I started to read the Book of Mormon. As I did so, it became delicious to me. . . . I would read for hours at a time. On an airplane, in a hotel room, at home, I didn't want to put it down. By January, I had finished the book. By April, I had read it again.

"During this time, I changed. My world changed. A heart that had become hardened was softened. Faith that had long been extinguished was found again and began to grow. I wanted to repent. I wanted to grow closer to the Savior. I wanted to become more like the Savior. . . .

"I stand before you today a new man because of this experience. A changed man. . . . Of course, it is the Savior that heals people and changes lives, but the Book of Mormon has the power to bring people to Christ." My friend is but one of many who have been brought to Christ through the Book of Mormon.

## Conclusion

I believe that individuals who honestly read the Book of Mormon can learn by the Spirit "that Jesus is the Christ, the Eternal God, manifesting himself unto all nations," exactly as declared on the book's title page. This book is indeed a witness, a divine witness, even the crowning witness of Jesus Christ, His Atonement, and His divinity.

---

NOTES

1. Black, *Finding Christ through the Book of Mormon,* 5.
2. Black, *Finding Christ through the Book of Mormon,* 15.
3. Stephen H. Webb, "Mormonism Obsessed with Christ."
4. Hinckley, "Four Cornerstones of Faith," 6.
5. Benson, *Witness and a Warning,* 18; emphasis added.
6. There are many magnificent chapters on the Atonement of Jesus Christ in the Book of Mormon, such as 2 Nephi 2; 2 Nephi 9; 2 Nephi 25; Jacob 4; Mosiah 3–5; Mosiah 15; Alma 34; Alma 40–42; Helaman 14; and 3 Nephi 11.
7. "Where Did Joseph Smith Get His Doctrinal Ideas About Christ?"
8. The Doctrine and Covenants gives this test: "By this ye may know if a man repenteth of his sins—behold, he will confess them and forsake them" (D&C 58: 43).
9. Lest there be any misunderstanding, this does not eliminate the need for confession, when required, because confession is often necessary to both hasten and complete the repentance process.
10. Eyring, "How to Receive the Holy Ghost," 48.
11. That was the realization of Scrooge in Dickens's *A Christmas Carol.* He had so transformed his life that he could rightfully declare, "I am not the man I was." Likewise, William Shakespeare, in his comedy *As You Like It,* wrote of the conversion of a man who at one time had attempted to have his younger brother killed. When asked about this misdeed, the man replied, "'Twas I; but 'tis not I: I do not shame to tell you what I was, since my conversion so sweetly tastes, being the thing I am" (act 4, scene 3, lines 134–37).
12. I am not sure if Jesus acquired all of these comforting powers as a result of His Atonement or if some are independent powers possessed by the Savior, but it seems plausible that Christ knows which comforting powers to use in each of our trials because, as a part of His Atonement, He suffered all our afflictions and thereby knows "according to the flesh *how to succor his people according to their infirmities*" (Alma 7:12; emphasis added).
13. See Genesis 3:22; Matthew 5:48; John 10:32–34; Acts 17:28; Romans

8:16–17; Ephesians 4:12–13; Philippians 2:5–6; Philippians 3:14; 2 Peter 1:4; Revelation 3:21; Revelation 21:7.

14. The word *perfect* as used in this scripture comes from the Greek word *telios.* Some have suggested this might be translated as "finished" or "completed," resulting in a connotation other than godly perfection—perhaps meaning a complete or mature Saint. When read in context, however, this scripture seems to require a conclusion of godly perfection, since the type of completeness or perfection to which it is referring is "*even* as your Father which is in heaven is perfect." In other words, God is not perfect like a mature Saint or in any other relative sense.
15. Holland, *Christ and the New Covenant,* 199.
16. For additional names and explanations of them, see Black, *Finding Christ through the Book of Mormon.*

## CHAPTER 10

# Does the Bible Prophesy of the Book of Mormon?

### Prophecies about the Book of Mormon

A number of years ago, someone asked me, "If the Book of Mormon is such a critical witness of the Savior, why isn't the Book of Mormon prophesied of by name in the Bible?"

I replied by asking, "Do you believe that Jesus Christ is the Son of God, the Savior of us all?"

"Of course," he replied.

I added further, "If Jesus Christ is our Savior—the very foundation of Christianity, I assume He would be prophesied of in the Old Testament."

"He is," the man replied.

I then asked, "Can you find the name of Jesus Christ specifically mentioned anywhere in the Old Testament?"

He replied, in essence, "Well, the Old Testament does not mention the name of Jesus Christ—I admit that—but it does prophesy of Him in such a way that any reasonable person should know that it's referring to Jesus Christ."

He was right—the Old Testament does not mention Jesus Christ by name, but it does prophesy of Him with such specificity that we ought to recognize those prophecies as speaking of Him. For example, it prophesies that He would be born in Bethlehem (see Micah 5:2) of a virgin (see Isaiah 7:14), that He would suffer the sins of the world (see Isaiah 53:3–5), that He would ride a donkey into Jerusalem (see Zechariah 9:9), that He would be betrayed for thirty pieces of silver (see Zechariah 11:12–13), that He would be crucified (see Psalm 22:15–18), and that He would cry out, "My God, my God, why hast thou forsaken me?" (Psalm 22:1). But even with all these specific references, many, if not most, of the people in the meridian of time could not accept that Jesus Christ was the literal fulfillment of those prophecies. Nonetheless, the prophecies were there to be discerned by the spiritually enlightened.

And so it is with the Book of Mormon. The Bible prophesies of its coming forth and its purpose, not by name, but by events and descriptions that are sufficiently clear and precise that honest seekers of the truth who are familiar with the Book of Mormon can discern their fulfillment. What, then, are some of these prophecies?

## Prophesied Blessings for Joseph and His Descendants

Jacob, also known as Israel, had twelve sons, whose descendants are collectively known as the house of Israel. One of those sons, Joseph, who inherited the birthright (see 1 Chronicles 5:1–2), had two sons, Ephraim and Manasseh. Lehi was a descendant of Manasseh (see Alma 10:3), and Ishmael (who accompanied Lehi to the Americas) was a descendent of Ephraim.[1] Thus, these two families that composed the first generation of the Nephite-Lamanite civilization were direct descendants of Joseph (see 1 Nephi 6:2; 3 Nephi 10:17). Why is this important? Because the Bible prophesies that descendants of Joseph—referring to Lehi, Ishmael, and perhaps others (see 3 Nephi 10:17)—would leave their homeland of Jerusalem, cross the ocean, come to a blessed land, have a great posterity, and record their history into a book that would be given to one who is unlearned. This book would come forth in our day and be another witness (in addition to the Bible) of Jesus Christ. The following is evidence of such:

## A Blessed Land

Genesis 49:22–26 speaks of Joseph as a "fruitful bough" and states that certain "branches" or descendants of Joseph, referring at least to Lehi and Ishmael (see 1 Nephi 15:12; 2 Nephi 10:22), would cross the "wall"—likely meaning the ocean (which was a wall to the people), and that they would find their way to a blessed land (see Deuteronomy 33:13), which would be the land of their inheritance (see 3 Nephi 15:12–13; 3 Nephi 16:16). These descendants of Joseph were further promised "blessings of the breasts, and of the womb" (Genesis 49:25), meaning they would have a great posterity, as evidenced by the populous Nephite and Lamanite civilizations.

The book of Deuteronomy further describes this blessed land, which Joseph's descendants would inherit, as "precious" on five different occasions (see Deuteronomy 33:13–16). What was this land of their inheritance but the precious land of the Americas, which Lehi also referred to as "this *precious* land of promise" (2 Nephi 1:10; emphasis added; see also Ether 2:7–12). If the Nephites and Lamanites are not the descendants of Joseph as prophesied, and their precious land is not the Americas, then where are Joseph's descendants who crossed the ocean, their great posterity, and their precious land, all as prophesied in Genesis 49:22–26 and Deuteronomy 33:13–16?

## "Speak Out of the Ground"

But there is more. Isaiah spoke of a people who, *like* the people of Jerusalem ("it shall be unto me *as* Ariel [Jerusalem]" (Isaiah 29:2; emphasis added), would have an enemy "camp against" them, "lay siege against [them] with a mount" and "raise forts against [them]" (Isaiah 29:3). Who are those other people that are likened to those destroyed in Jerusalem?[2]

Nephi gave the answer. He used phrases similar to Isaiah's to describe the destruction of his own people: "The Lord God shall have camped against them . . . and shall have laid siege against them with a mount, and raised forts against them; and after they shall have been brought down low in the dust, . . . the words of the righteous shall be written" (2 Nephi 26:15). In addition, Isaiah told us that these people would "speak out of the ground," meaning their records would be brought forth out of the earth. Isaiah then referred to these records as a "book," which is delivered to someone who is unlearned (see Isaiah 29:1–12). What an appropriate description of the Book of Mormon.[3] The Nephites were destroyed, as prophesied, and their people did speak out of the ground through the golden plates that had been buried in the earth (see 2 Nephi 26:16; Mormon 8:26). And these plates were delivered to someone who was unlearned: namely, Joseph Smith.

## "A Fruitful Field"

Isaiah also prophesied of a book that would come forth when "Lebanon shall be turned into a fruitful field, and the fruitful field shall be esteemed as a forest" (Isaiah 29:17). What is Lebanon, and has it yet become a fruitful field and esteemed as a forest? And what is the book that is to come forth in that time period? Lebanon is a mountain range; as explained by one Bible scholar, it is "mentioned nine times in the Bible as either part of the Promised Land [Israel] or the northern boundary of the Promised Land."[4]

Some years ago, I traveled to the Holy Land. Knowing of the devastation that had taken place during the Ottoman rule, I was surprised to see the number of trees that forested the mountainsides. I asked our guide how this could possibly be. He said that commencing about 1900, the Israelis had planted more than 100 million trees in Israel. For years I thought that might be an overestimation, so I researched it, and to my further surprise I learned that more than 250 million trees have been planted since 1901.[5] In this way, Israel (Lebanon) has become, and is currently becoming, a forest, as prophesied by Isaiah, and it is in this day when the Book of Mormon has come forth.

As Isaiah said, "in that day [when Lebanon is esteemed as a forest] shall the deaf hear the words of the book, and the eyes of the blind shall see out of obscurity, and out of darkness" (Isaiah 29:18). If any book meets the requirements of that prophecy, it is the Book of Mormon. It has restored many of the plain and precious truths lost from the Bible and thus helped the spiritually deaf and blind to hear and see once again.

## "The Stick of Judah and the Stick of Joseph"

No wonder Ezekiel prophesied that the stick of Judah (meaning the record of the Jews, known as the Bible) and the stick of Joseph (meaning the record of Joseph's descendants, known as the Book of Mormon) shall be joined into one stick or book, "and they shall become one in thine hand" (see Ezekiel 37:17)—in essence, complementary witnesses of Jesus Christ. The Lord further tells us that these two books "shall grow together, unto the confounding of false doctrines . . . and also to the knowledge of my covenants" (2 Nephi 3:12).

The Book of Mormon is also consistent with the law of

witnesses, as taught by Paul: "In the mouth of two or three witnesses shall every word be established" (2 Corinthians 13:1). The Bible is one witness of Jesus Christ, the Book of Mormon is a second witness, and the records of the lost ten tribes, yet to be revealed, will be at least one more witness (see 2 Nephi 29:13).

## "Other Sheep"

In the New Testament, Christ referred to the Book of Mormon people when He spoke to His disciples in Jerusalem: "And other sheep I have, which are not of this fold: them also I must bring, and they shall hear my voice; and there shall be one fold, and one shepherd" (John 10:16). Who were these other sheep that Christ would visit? In at least partial fulfillment of that prophecy, the resurrected Savior appeared to the Nephites, who heard the voice and became a part of His fold, exactly as prophesied (see 3 Nephi 15:21–24).

## "The Birthright Was Joseph's"

The foregoing prophecies of the Book of Mormon are further confirmed by the fact that Judah, a son of Jacob, received great blessings, "but the birthright was Joseph's" (1 Chronicles 5:2). This becomes significant when one realizes that Judah received the following blessings:

- A great posterity—the Jewish race
- A promised land—the country of Israel
- The Savior—born through Judah's lineage
- A book—the Bible, which is the record of God's dealings with the house of Israel, particularly the Jews, and Christ's ministry among them

Did Joseph, who received the birthright, receive blessings equal to or greater than Judah's? He did. He received the following:

- A great posterity—including the Nephite and Lamanite civilizations
- A promised land—the Americas
- The Savior—who personally visited Joseph's descendants and guided their chosen prophets
- A book—the Book of Mormon, which is the record of God's dealings with Joseph's descendants in the Americas and the resurrected Christ's personal ministry among them

And so, just as the Savior was prophesied of in the Bible—not by name, but by events and descriptions—so too the Book of Mormon was prophesied of in the Bible, not by name, but by events and descriptions. To those who are familiar with the Book of Mormon, these prophecies are clear and revealing and convincing.[6]

Some might claim that Joseph Smith wrote the Book of Mormon in such a way to make it look like it was a fulfillment of the foregoing scriptures. If that is the case, this "unlearned" boy seems to have become more savvy and brilliant all the time—not only having read the numerous books referred to in previous chapters, but now also becoming a master scriptorian, all by the age of twenty-three—in spite of the fact that he was married and trying to eke out a living on the frontier to support his wife. But of greater consequence, if these biblical scriptures do not apply to the Book of Mormon, then to what people and what book are they referring?

---

NOTES

1. See Ludlow, *Companion to Your Study of the Book of Mormon,* 199.
2. Some believe that Isaiah 29:1–8 applies only to Jerusalem and not to the people of the Book of Mormon. However, the chapter heading to the Latter-day Saint edition of the scriptures, in referring to these same verses, reads, "Nephites shall speak as a voice from the dust."
3. The *Faithlife Study Bible,* sponsored by Evangelical Christians, commented on Isaiah 29:11 as follows: "The prophet's message is like a document sealed

up for a future audience that will be able to understand it. A seal could only be broken by one with proper authority." This is consistent with the fact that the words of the Book of Mormon were sealed for a future audience in our dispensation who would be able to understand them, and that the one with the proper authority who could break the seal, or translate it by the power of God, was Joseph Smith.

4. Horn, "Lebanon in the Holy Scriptures."
5. See Jewish National Fund, "We Are JNF."
6. Other scriptures that refer to the Book of Mormon and its people include Genesis 11:8; Psalm 85:11; and Revelation 14:6–7.

PART IV

# Gaining a Personal Testimony of the Book of Mormon

# CHAPTER 11

# How Can I Know if the Book of Mormon Is True?

## The Role of Science and Academia in Gaining a Testimony

Throughout this book I have referred to cultural, linguistic, archaeological, and other scientific evidences that support claims made in the Book of Mormon. Lest there be any question, my intent has not been to prove the truthfulness of the Book of Mormon by these or any other scientific or academic means, although I do believe that in the future many more such evidences will surface and thus become additional witnesses of the book's divine authenticity. For the time being, it seems that God has given us sufficient evidences not to replace our faith but to support our faith.

The nature of science and academia suggests to me that there will be a growing reservoir of external and internal evidences to support the Book of Mormon, yet there will always be some question or obstacle that will cause concern for those who are trying to prove spiritual truths with intellectual evidence alone. As knowledge evolves, what may be a seeming contradiction will one day become another confirmation. Yet, in the interim, how many people will become spiritual casualties along the way? How many were deterred from discovering the truth of the Book of Mormon because cement or metal plates or barley had not yet been discovered? How many lost their testimonies or criticized the Book of Mormon because they thought Alma was only a woman's name or were persuaded that Joseph Smith had the creative and theological genius to write such a book without divine assistance?

Fortunately, we do not have to be in a state of spiritual quandary. President Russell M. Nelson gave these assuring words: "You don't have to wonder about what is true. You do not have to wonder whom you can safely trust. Through personal revelation you can receive your own witness that the Book of Mormon is the word of God."[1]

Suffice it to say, it is good when scientific, historical, and cultural evidence can inspire someone to investigate the Book of Mormon, provided such investigation is motivated by a desire to seek a spiritual confirmation, or when such evidence acts in a supporting, not primary role. Reliance on the Spirit will produce a testimony built on rock. But if the scientific, historical, and cultural evidence becomes the foundation of one's testimony because one has not yet paid the price to receive a spiritual witness, then that testimony will be prone to crack or collapse with every tremor of intellectual concern. It will be a testimony built on sand (see Matthew 7:24–27).

One cannot discover a spiritual truth by intellectual means alone. Paul taught, "No man can *say* that Jesus is the Lord, but by the Holy Ghost" (1 Corinthians 12:3; emphasis added). Joseph Smith taught that this passage should read, "No man can *know* that Jesus is the Lord but by the Holy Ghost."[2] The Lord further taught that we cannot come to know Him "with the carnal neither natural mind, but with the spiritual" (D&C 67:10). And Nephi warned that in our day that false teachers would "teach with their learning, and deny the Holy Ghost, which giveth utterance" (2 Nephi 28:4; see also 2 Nephi 9:28–29).

Archaeology and other scientific or academic evidences are not the conclusive test for a testimony, but neither should they be discounted as a means that can strengthen our testimonies. At some point, science, academia, and the Spirit will converge, and eventually science and academic research will be one more confirming witness of what we hopefully have already learned spiritually—that the Book of Mormon is the word of God.

Elder Matthew Cowley, an Apostle, shared this valuable insight: "I know very little about the outside evidences of the Book of Mormon, but I have a testimony of the divinity of this book, and that testimony has come to me from within the two covers of the book itself. To me, archaeology, and all that archaeologists discover, which may in a way prove the genuineness of the book—these discoveries are lost in the spirit of the book itself, and if you can't find a testimony within the covers of this book, there is no need to look elsewhere."[3]

In truth, the Book of Mormon does not need to be defended by outside sources; it is its own best witness. Its genius lies in the inherent converting power found within the text itself.

## Voluntary versus Compulsory Faith

Some skeptics have said: "Unless I can see and touch the golden plates, I will not believe." (Yet I imagine that many of those same people believe in the Ten Commandments even though they have not seen and handled the original stone tablets.)[4] A similar circumstance occurred when the Apostle Thomas said of the resurrected Lord, "Except I shall see in his hands the print of the nails, and put my finger into the print of the nails, and thrust my hand into his side, *I will not believe.*" Thereafter Thomas saw the resurrected Lord and beheld the print of the nails in His hands and thrust his own hand into the Savior's side. After he had done so, the Savior said to Him: "Be not faithless, but believing. . . . Thomas, because thou hast seen me, thou hast believed: blessed are they that have not seen, and yet have believed" (John 20:25, 27, 29). This experience should be a poignant lesson to those who will not believe without physical proof of the Book of Mormon.

The Zoramites were another case in point. Those who were cast out of their city because of their exceeding poverty became humble. Alma then observed, "And now, because ye are compelled to be humble blessed are ye." Then he made this profound observation: "Yea, he that truly humbleth himself, . . . the same shall be blessed—yea, much more blessed than they who are compelled to be humble" (Alma 32:13, 15). Alma further noted, "Therefore, blessed are they who humble themselves without being compelled to be humble . . . , without being brought to know the word, or even compelled to know, before they will believe" (Alma 32:16).

Nephi knew that the day would come when the truth of the Book of Mormon could not be denied: "Christ will show unto you, with power and great glory, that they are his words, at the last day" (2 Nephi 33:11).

However, those who gain a spiritual testimony of the Book of Mormon through their faith and diligence, without relying principally on scientific proofs, are no doubt much more blessed than those who become believers because they are intellectually driven or "compelled" to accept the Book of Mormon due to the scientific, historical, and cultural evidence that has been discovered and will yet be emerging.[5]

But one might ask, "If the end result is the same—Thomas, after seeing, believed, and the Zoramites, after being compelled to do so, became humble—why are those who believed without seeing, and those who were humble without being compelled, more blessed? Why the difference in the Lord's pronounced blessings?"

I do not profess to have the full answer, but perhaps the following thoughts provide some insights. First, knowledge in and of itself does not necessarily lead to action, particularly in spiritual matters—only faith does that. The devils know and believe that Jesus is the Christ, but because they have no faith, they are not motivated to worship and serve Him (see Acts 19:13–16; James 2:19–20).

In essence, knowledge is an intellectual understanding of truth, while faith is a principle of action—it motivates us to live what we believe (see Hebrews 11:17–40). Thus, those who have faith in Jesus Christ and in the Book of Mormon will have greater motivation to live the teachings of the Savior than those who have been compelled to believe and thus attained intellectual assent alone. Because of this, faith results in greater spiritual growth than the acquisition of knowledge alone.

Second, faith is not only a means but an end. It not only motivates us but, as we perfect our faith, it also becomes a godly attribute and thus a source of godly power.[6] Accordingly, if we discover truth only through knowledge and not through faith, we forfeit the opportunity to develop this godly attribute that both motivates us to action and becomes a source of divine power.

## The Spirit Is the Ultimate Witness of Truth

The story is told of a church that evidently lost some of its parishioners to The Church of Jesus Christ of Latter-day Saints. In an effort to counterattack, the church put on its marquee the following message: "Don't read the Book of Mormon—that is how they get you." And in fact, that *is* how the Spirit does "get you": by bearing witness of the truth of that sacred book.

I have no doubt that many critics of the Church and of the Book of Mormon are intelligent people, but recognizing and receiving spiritual truth is not a function of one's IQ; rather it is a function of one's faith and humility and willingness to live God's commandments. Then and only then can spiritual truth come.

Of all the witnesses to the Book of Mormon, there is none more certain or sure than that of the Spirit. It is the witness of all witnesses—the evidence of all evidences. Moroni confirmed this truth. He made it clear that the way to know for sure if the Book of Mormon is the word of God is to apply the spiritual test God has decreed for this spiritual book, as set forth in Moroni 10:4: "And when ye shall receive these things, I would exhort you that ye would ask God, the Eternal Father, in the name of Christ, if these things are not true; *and if ye shall ask with a sincere heart, with real intent, having faith in Christ, he will manifest the truth of it unto you, by the power of the Holy Ghost*" (emphasis added). Hopefully, we will never underestimate the power of this promise.

This spiritual test, however, is not for the faint of heart; it is not a casual prayer or an occasional reading of the scriptures; it is not designed for those who desire only to satisfy their curiosity. It is much more than a turning of pages. It requires diligent study, sincere pondering, intense petitions to God, a never-give-in attitude, and, in many cases, fasting. It requires a humility and spiritual integrity that once the answer comes we will follow the directed course to the end, whatever it may be. It requires a willingness to endure rebuffing and rejection from friends and loved ones, to give up wealth or fame or power for the kingdom, to give away all our sins to know the truth (see Alma 22:18). In essence, it requires a willingness to submit our will to God's will, no matter how inconvenient or difficult the task may be. This is asking "with a sincere heart, with real intent." Then our hearts and minds will be receptive to the whisperings of the Spirit, as Moroni promised.

Amulek paid such a price for his conversion. The scriptures tell us he gave up "all his gold, and silver, and his precious things . . . for the word of God, he being rejected by those who were once his friends and also by his father and his kindred" (Alma 15:16).

I have a friend who joined the Church while I was in Canada serving a mission. He is extremely bright. Recently I received a letter from him. After his baptism, he said: "I descended into a dark, skeptical period where I began to question everything about Church history and certain doctrines, and eventually rejected the truthfulness of the restored gospel, and had my name withdrawn from the Church records. My addiction to websites that were severely critical of Mormonism had persuaded me to abandon the Church altogether and I began to attend other Christian denominations in the hope of finding God's true church on earth."

In spite of this, he married a Latter-day Saint woman who was faithful and patient, and who prayed constantly that the eyes of his spiritual understanding would be opened. Eventually he felt prompted to return to the Church and to study its teachings. He resolved to view only faith-promoting websites. He read and studied the scriptures diligently with an open heart and mind. "One day," he said, "while reading the Book of Mormon in my room, I paused and knelt down and gave a heartfelt prayer and felt resoundingly that Heavenly Father whispered to my spirit that the Church and the Book of Mormon were definitely true. My 3.5-year period of reinvestigating the Church led me back wholeheartedly and convincingly to its truthfulness." He said that his happiest moments were being reconverted and rebaptized into the Church and being sealed to his wife and family in the temple for time and eternity. At the time of his letter, he was serving as elders quorum president in his ward.[7]

In a subsequent letter to me, this friend wrote: "I would also like to point out that the *primary factor in helping me gain a spiritual testimony of the Book of Mormon was that I changed my focus or criterion on what would make it true for me. Initially, I wanted the Book of Mormon to be proven to me historically, geographically, linguistically, and culturally. But when I changed my focus to what it teaches about the gospel of Jesus Christ and His saving mission, I began to gain a testimony of its truthfulness.* I felt in my heart and mind that what the Book of Mormon teaches about Jesus Christ and gospel principles are true, and therefore it must be an inspired Word of God. *Seeking after scientific proof for the Book of Mormon had shackled, bound, and blinded me, but seeking after spiritual enlightenment empowered me to be set free to receive the light and testimony of its beauty and truthfulness.*"[8]

What a thoughtful and uplifting observation! If we will focus our study of the Book of Mormon on Jesus Christ—His mission and His message—then our testimonies will blossom and we will eventually find that certain witness for which we seek.

In the course of my friend's transformation, he replaced an intellectual testimony built on sand with a spiritual testimony built on rock. After all his intellectual studies, he discovered there was only one sure way to know the truth about the Book of Mormon, and that happened when he was upon his knees.

The Lord has declared that He will reveal truth to us by way of our minds and our hearts: "Yea, behold, I will tell you in your mind and in your heart, by the Holy Ghost. . . . Now, behold, this is the spirit of revelation" (D&C 8:2–3). What happens when someone rejects either the mind or heart as a means for learning and detecting truth? Paul gave the answer. He observed that individuals who are proud and vain in their supposed intellectual supremacy and dismiss the feelings of their hearts will, as a consequence, also have their minds darkened as a source of truth. In other words, one cannot pick and choose one source of truth (such as the mind) and reject the other source (the heart) without peril of losing both. Paul spoke of the Gentiles who "walk . . . in the vanity of their mind." And then he tells us the consequence: "Having the understanding [mind] darkened . . . because of the blindness of their heart" (Ephesians 4:17–18). The prophet Abinadi taught a similar principle when speaking to King Noah and his wicked priests: "Ye have not applied your hearts to understanding; therefore, ye have not been wise" (Mosiah 12:27).

## Why Is It Important for Me to Know the Book of Mormon Is True?

President Boyd K. Packer shared the following experience: "The story is told of two frivolous girls clattering through a great museum and then flippantly remarking as they left the building that it hadn't impressed them much. One of the doorkeepers standing by commented to them, 'Young ladies, this museum is not on trial here today. Its quality cannot be contested. You are the ones who are on trial.'"[9]

And so it is with the Book of Mormon—it is not on trial. It is we who are on trial to see if we will read it with a sincere heart and real intent to discover and live its truths. President Ezra Taft Benson spoke to this point: "The Book of Mormon is not on trial—the people of the world, including the members of the Church, are on trial as to what they will do with this second witness for Christ."[10] Moroni testified of this truth: "Ye shall see me at the bar of God; and the Lord God will say unto you: Did I not declare my words unto you, which were written by this man[?] . . . And God shall show unto you, that that which I have written is true" (Moroni 10:27, 29). Then we will be on trial before God as to whether we accepted or rejected His words as found in the Book of Mormon.

Why is it critical for each of us to gain a testimony of the Book of Mormon? Because as we do so, it will become our personal iron rod. Mists of darkness may come, ridicule may confront us, unanswered questions may arise, but through it all we will have our iron rod to cling to—to keep us on the straight and narrow path that leads to eternal life (see 1 Nephi 15:24). The questions may continue, but they will be just that—questions, not doubts.

As certain as can be, the time will come when each of us will be faced with an intellectual question we cannot answer or a crisis that tries our faith to the very core. At that moment, we cannot draw from the oil of another's lamp—we cannot rely on another's testimony—we must stand independent and firm in our own testimony to weather the storm. Otherwise, we will fall.

If we want the truth badly enough, if we are willing to pay the requisite price and be unrelenting in that quest, the answer will eventually come. There is a touching scene in a movie on the life of Martin Luther, entitled *Luther.* He is about to be tried for heresy. Just before the trial begins, his friend and longtime spiritual mentor—a priest—rebukes Luther for turning the world upside down with his teachings, spurring the world on in a revolt of Protestants against Catholics. Then, in a stirring moment, Luther grabs his friend's arm and says, "You wanted me to change the world; did you think there would be no cost?"[11]

Likewise, there is a cost for gaining a testimony of the Book of Mormon. Alma, who had seen an angel from heaven, nonetheless had to pay a price for his testimony. He said, "*Behold, I have fasted and prayed many days that I might know these things of myself. And now I do know of myself that they are true;* for the Lord God hath made them manifest unto me by his Holy Spirit; and this is the spirit of revelation which is in me" (Alma 5:46; emphasis added).

Are we willing to pay a similar price for a testimony of Jesus Christ and the Book of Mormon? If so, the answer will come, as promised by Moroni.

## Testimony of Edna Bush

In the 1960s, I served a mission for the Church in the Washington, DC, area. There I met an extremely intelligent convert to the Church by the name of Edna Bush. Many years earlier she had traveled to Salt Lake City, where she toured Temple Square and left with the impression that members of The Church of Jesus Christ of Latter-day Saints were good people but mighty gullible to believe in golden plates and an angel Moroni.

Later, two sister missionaries from the Church knocked on her door and presented her with a copy of the Book of Mormon. She said, "I decided I would read it and prove it false once and for all." But as she read it, the ammunition she expected to find did not materialize. Instead, she became a recipient of the promise of Moroni: "God . . . will manifest the truth of it unto you, by the power of the Holy Ghost" (Moroni 10:4). As a consequence, she was baptized a member of the Church. She became a dedicated student of the Book of Mormon and contributed articles on that subject to Church magazines.[12]

On one occasion, this good woman took my missionary companion and me down into her basement. On the shelf, I believe there were more than a hundred paperback copies of the Book of Mormon. Each one had a title on the spine, such as "repentance," "resurrection," or "faith." She explained that she had read each one of the books from cover to cover, focusing on the topic listed on the spine. She then took out a scroll and unrolled it across the floor. I do not recall its exact length—probably eight to twelve feet. On it were various timelines tracking all the major travels and events of the Book of Mormon people. It was detailed and most impressive. She then turned to me and said, "Elder Callister, if there were major errors in this book, I would have found them long ago." Her intellectual analysis was most impressive, but it was not the foundation of her testimony. Of course, it may have been a stepping-stone, and rightfully so, but the testimony that is rock solid, that does not waver with each transient scientific discovery, is hewn from a humble and prayerful heart.

## Young People Can Gain Testimonies

The Spirit can come to young people as well as adults. President Boyd K. Packer shared the following account:

"A 15-year-old son of a mission president attended high school with very few members of the Church.

"One day the class was given a true-or-false test. Matthew was confident that he knew the answers to all except for question 15. It read, 'Joseph Smith, the alleged Mormon prophet, wrote the Book of Mormon. True or false?'

"He could not answer it either way, so being a clever teenager, he rewrote the question. He crossed out the word *alleged* and replaced the word *wrote* with *translated.* It then read, 'Joseph Smith, the Mormon prophet, translated the Book of Mormon.' He marked it true and handed it in.

"The next day the teacher sternly asked why he had changed the question. He smiled and said, 'Because Joseph Smith did not *write* the Book of Mormon, he *translated it,* and he was not an *alleged* prophet, he was a prophet.'

"He was then invited to tell the class how he knew that."[13]

That young boy later became the chief justice of the Utah Supreme Court.

As a boy of about fifteen or sixteen I read the account of the 2,000 sons of Helaman. This story had a particular appeal to me as a young man. I marveled at their bravery and the Lord's protecting hand. Then a voice came to my mind—not an audible voice, but a discernible one: "That story is true."

Some years ago, I was attending one of our worship services in Toronto, Canada. A fourteen-year-old girl was the speaker. She said that she had been discussing religion with one of her friends at school. Her friend said to her, "What religion do you belong to?"

She replied, "The Church of Jesus Christ of Latter-day Saints." Her friend looked puzzled. Sensing her unfamiliarity with the Church's correct name, she explained, "We are sometimes called Mormons."

Her friend responded: "I know that church, and I know it is not true."

"How do you know?" came the reply.

"Because," said her friend, "I have researched it."

"Have you read the Book of Mormon?"

"No," came the answer, "I haven't."

Then this sweet young girl responded, "Then you haven't researched my Church because I have read every page of the Book of Mormon and I know it is true."

## Personal Testimony

I am continually asking questions about the history and doctrine of the Church, including the Book of Mormon. For most of these questions I find answers that are intellectually and spiritually satisfying to me. For some questions, I feel I have some helpful insights but not yet the complete picture, and for the balance I am still searching for further enlightenment. For example, for every 100 questions I have, perhaps there are 70 or so for which I feel I have good answers, 20 or so for which I have partial insights,[14] and the balance of which I simply say, "I do not know the answer at the current time."[15]

Unfortunately, some people want perfection in every prophet and an immediate answer to every doctrinal question. In other words, they want prophets without imperfections and a religion without faith, and they can't have it. Why? Because no such thing exists.

I have a testimony of this miraculous book, the Book of Mormon, that it will bring us closer to God than any other book. Combined with the Spirit, it is the most powerful, convincing witness we have of the divinity of the Savior, the prophetic mission of Joseph Smith, and the truth of this Church. The Lord has provided us with an abundance of prophecies, scientific discoveries, and rational evidence to highlight the truthfulness of this book, and thus the honest searcher of truth should say: "This book merits further investigation; this book has the hallmarks of a divine work. I will put it to the test as Moroni has invited me to do." And for those who do so, the Lord has promised that He "will manifest the truth of it unto you, by the power of the Holy Ghost" (Moroni 10:4).

I am not an archaeologist or scientist, but I have felt the impressions of the Spirit of which Moroni testified, and when I read the Book of Mormon, I am so moved. Such has been my personal experience, and such is my testimony that this book is God-given, that it is of divine origin, that it is the word of God.

---

NOTES

1. Russell M. Nelson, "Revelation for the Church, Revelation for Our Lives," 95.
2. *Joseph Smith Papers,* "History, 1838–1856, volume C-1 Addenda," 26.
3. Cowley, "Testimony through Reading the Book of Mormon," 7–8.

4. The Lord made it clear in Doctrine and Covenants 5:7 that if people will not believe the words of the Book of Mormon, they will not believe in Joseph Smith and the Book of Mormon, even if they saw the plates from which it was translated.
5. This same principle is taught in Ether 12:6 and Doctrine and Covenants 76:74–79.
6. *Lectures on Faith* teaches: "Faith is not only the principle of action, but of power also, in all intelligent beings, whether in heaven or on earth. [It is] the principle of power which existed in the bosom of God. Take this principle or attribute—from the Deity, and he would cease to exist" (3).
7. Letter to author dated February 18, 2017.
8. Letter to author dated May 1, 2017; emphasis added.
9. Packer, *Teach Ye Diligently,* 177.
10. Benson, "A New Witness for Christ," 8.
11. Thomasson and Gavigan, *Luther.*
12. For more information on the life of Edna K. Bush and her passion for the Book of Mormon, see Bush, "The Book of Mormon and My Conversion"; *Dissecting the Book of Mormon;* and "Magnificent Messages."
13. Packer, "The Book of Mormon: Another Testament of Jesus Christ," 63–64.
14. See 1 Nephi 11:17; Words of Mormon 1:7.
15. Chad Webb, administrator of the Church's seminaries and institutes of religion, gave the following inspired counsel concerning the difference between doubting and intelligent inquiry: "There is an interesting example in the history of the Church that illustrates the difference between doubting—which often leads to darkness and uncertainty—and patient and intelligent inquiry—which leads to understanding and spiritual confirmation. When Joseph Smith received the vision concerning the three degrees of glory, which is in section 76 of the Doctrine and Covenants, many members of the Church, including Brigham Young, initially had a difficult time accepting it as a revelation from the Lord because it departed significantly from the mainstream Christian view of one heaven and one hell. However, listen to how Brigham chose to respond: 'My traditions were such, that when the Vision came first to me, it was so directly contrary and opposite to my former education, I said, wait a little; I did not reject it, but I could not understand it' [in *Deseret News—Extra,* Sept. 14, 1852, 24]. Brigham decided to exercise patience, to pray, to ponder and to seek clarification from the prophet. But while he sought further understanding, he did not let go of what he had come to love in the restored gospel. And soon, he obtained his own witness from the Holy Ghost" (Chad H. Webb, "That They May Know").

CHAPTER 12

# How Can I Recognize the Promptings of the Holy Ghost?

Moroni testified that we can know of the truth of the Book of Mormon "by the power of the Holy Ghost" (Moroni 10:4). But what does that mean? How can we know when we have been a recipient of that power and that promise? Hopefully, the following will be helpful in answering those soul-searching questions.

## Why Is It Important to Recognize the Promptings of the Holy Ghost?

Addressing missionaries, *Preach My Gospel* reads: "The Spirit speaks quietly, through your feelings as well as your mind. One great challenge for you and those you work with is to recognize the quiet, subtle promptings of the Holy Ghost."[1] This is a challenge for every current and future member of Christ's Church.

Accordingly, we might all ask, "How can I learn to recognize the promptings of the Spirit?" Sometimes these promptings may come from the Light of Christ, which is given to all men and women (see Moroni 7:13–16; D&C 84:44–47); other times they may come from the Holy Ghost. If we can recognize these divine promptings, then they can be a frequent, reinforcing witness to us of the reality and divinity of God the Father, His Son Jesus Christ, the Book of Mormon, and the Restoration of Christ's Church. Then we will know for ourselves, in spite of any secular or theological arguments to the contrary, that the Book of Mormon is true. Then our testimonies will be founded on the personal light of divine revelation, not the borrowed light of another.[2] Then we will have the witness of the Spirit, which is the only sure and certain witness of spiritual truth (see 1 Corinthians 12:3).

## The Promptings of the Spirit Are Real

President Boyd K. Packer shared an experience of John Burroughs, a naturalist:

"One summer evening [he] was walking through a crowded park. Above the sounds of city life, he heard the song of a bird.

"He stopped and listened! Those with him had not heard it. He looked around. No one else had noticed it.

"It bothered him that everyone should miss something so beautiful.

"He took a coin from his pocket and flipped it into the air. It struck the pavement with a ring, no louder than the sound of a bird. Everyone turned; they could hear that!

"It is difficult to separate from all the sounds of city traffic the song of a bird. But you can hear it. You can hear it plainly if you train yourself to listen for it."[3]

In a similar manner, the whisperings and impressions of the Spirit are all around us, but they will be drowned out and smothered by the noise of the secular world if we do not train our spiritual ears to hear them and our hearts to feel them. Part of our spiritual education is to learn how to recognize those promptings and then act on them.

I have a high school friend who became one of the premier radiologists in Hawaii. Other radiologists would send him their X-rays when they had difficulty interpreting them. Through his experience and schooling, he had acquired expertise and skill that eluded many others. In each case, he saw the same film as his colleagues, but the difference was in his ability to recognize and read what was indiscernible to them. So it is with the Spirit. No doubt the Spirit sends many messages, but they are discernible only to those whose spiritual education, experience, and worthiness have trained and prepared them to receive and recognize them.

On one occasion, I visited a teachers quorum meeting with four or five young men present. The teacher invited each to share an experience when he had felt the Spirit. No one responded. I do not doubt that each had had one or more such experiences in his life, but perhaps some were too shy to share their feelings, or perhaps some had simply failed to recognize the Spirit when the moment came.

A similar problem can exist in the mission field. Missionaries teach the truths of the gospel, often with great power and authority. Investigators may feel good when they initially hear these truths, but if they are unable to recognize the accompanying impressions as promptings of the Spirit, they may ultimately dismiss them as mere emotional or psychological feelings. That is why it is so important for missionaries to not only teach the doctrine by the Spirit but also teach their investigators how to recognize the Spirit when He comes. For similar reasons it is important for all of us to recognize the promptings of the Spirit.

## The Voice of God versus the Voices of the World

The voice of God is vastly different from the voices of the world. We live in a world of high drama and action thrillers, fast-paced entertainment and loud music. As a result, many people expect spiritual impressions to come in a dramatic way—an audible voice or a vision or some thunderous witness from the heavens. But the Lord usually works in much more subtle and serene ways. The newly born Savior was laid in a manger; His Atonement commenced in a quiet garden; the Restoration of Christ's Church began in a secluded grove; and His truths are often revealed in the intimacy of a searching heart or the solitude of a reflective mind (see D&C 8:2–3). There is something sacred and divine in the quiet and seemingly anonymous works of God. The Lord taught this lesson to Elijah:

"And he said, Go forth, and stand upon the mount before the Lord. And, behold, the Lord passed by, and a great and strong wind rent the mountains, and brake in pieces the rocks before the Lord; but the Lord was not in the wind: and after the wind an earthquake; but the Lord was not in the earthquake:

"And after the earthquake a fire; but the Lord was not in the fire: and *after the fire a still small voice*" (1 Kings 19:11–12; emphasis added).

The Savior's appearance in ancient America is another case in point. The Father's voice, which introduced His Beloved Son, was described as follows: "It was not a harsh voice, neither was it a loud voice; nevertheless, and notwithstanding it being a small voice it did pierce them that did hear to the center" (3 Nephi 11:3).

Suffice it to say, the voice of God thrives in a quiet, reverent setting.

## How Can I Recognize the Promptings of the Spirit?

The question is often asked, "How can I distinguish between my own psychological or emotional feelings and the still small voice of the Spirit?" Recognizing spiritual promptings requires pondering, studying the scriptures, exercising spiritual integrity, manifesting humility, and testing the promptings that come against the promises of the Lord. Fortunately, there are certain feelings of the heart and impressions to the mind that come only from heaven. Those feelings and impressions are divinely directed.

In the world of science, results are measured in liters, volts, light years, and the like. In the spiritual world, results are measured in what are known as the fruits of the Spirit, such as love, peace, goodness, and joy (see Galatians 5:22–23). Fortunately, even Satan, the great counterfeiter, cannot duplicate these fruits. The Lord confirmed this truth when He taught:

"Every good tree bringeth forth good fruit [such as love, peace, and joy]; but a corrupt tree bringeth forth evil fruit [such as contention, turmoil, and unhappiness].

"A good tree cannot bring forth evil fruit, *neither can a corrupt tree [Satan] bring forth good fruit. . . .*

*"Wherefore by their fruits ye shall know them"* (Matthew 7:17–18, 20; emphasis added; see also Moroni 7:11).

A few of the fruits of the Spirit are discussed below. As you read them, see if you can identify with some of those fruits as you have read the Book of Mormon, learned about the gospel of Jesus Christ, and done your best to live righteously.

### *Peace*

The Savior said, "My peace I give unto you: not as the world giveth, give I unto you" (John 14:27). Peace is one fruit of the Spirit. The Lord made it clear that peace cannot be duplicated by the evil one: "There is no peace, saith the Lord, unto the wicked" (Isaiah 48:22).

Oliver Cowdery, an early leader in the Church, had been in the home of Joseph Smith's father and prayed to know whether the Book of Mormon was true. While there, he received a convincing witness of this sacred book, which came in the form of an undeniable peace.

Time passed, and human nature evidently took its toll. Perhaps Oliver began to wonder if the feelings on that occasion had really been an impression from heaven or just some psychological feeling or passing moment of self-delusion. Whatever the reason, Oliver went to Joseph and asked him to request a revelation from God that would be a witness to him of the truthfulness of the Book of Mormon. Joseph sought such a revelation. It came as follows:

"Verily, verily, I say unto you [Oliver], if you desire a further witness, cast your mind upon the night that you cried unto me in your heart, that you might know concerning the truth of these things.

*"Did I not speak peace to your mind concerning the matter? What greater witness can you have than from God?"* (D&C 6:22–23; emphasis added).

In this revelation the Lord confirmed that Oliver had previously received peace from Him about the Book of Mormon. Joseph had no knowledge of Oliver's prior experience; in fact, he only learned of it through this revelation. Oliver now knew with certainty that the peace he had received was a divine witness of the truth of the Book of Mormon. The Lord connected the dots for Oliver: the cause with the effect, the prompting of the Spirit with peace.

If you feel peace as you read the Book of Mormon, that is a witness from God to you, by the Spirit, that it is true. That peace may come as you read of the reality of the Resurrection, the goodness of God and His tender mercies, the certainty of complete forgiveness for those who repent, the power of the Savior to comfort, or our glorious divine destiny, but peace will come to the humble seeker of truth. It is a witness of the presence of the Spirit.

### *An Intent to Do Good*

If while reading the Book of Mormon you have a desire to be a better person, then that is your personal witness from the Spirit that what you are reading is from God. The prophet Mormon taught: *"Every thing which inviteth and enticeth to do good, and to love God, and to serve him, is inspired of God"* (Moroni 7:13; emphasis added; see also Moroni 7:16–17; Ether 4:11–12). After quoting this scripture, President Gordon B. Hinckley said: "That's the test, when all is said and done. Does it [the prompting] persuade one to do good, to rise, to stand tall, to do the right thing, to be kind, to be generous? Then it is of the Spirit of God."[4]

President Henry B. Eyring added this further insight: "It is not surprising that when we feel the influence of the Holy Ghost, we also can feel that our natures are being changed because of the Atonement of Jesus Christ. We feel an increased desire to keep His commandments, to do good, and to deal justly."[5]

Alma taught that we can recognize the Spirit when the word of God "beginneth to enlarge [our] soul" (Alma 32:28)—in other words, we feel more loving and kind and thoughtful. The Lord described the Spirit as "that Spirit *which leadeth to do good*—yea, to do justly, to walk humbly, to judge righteously" (D&C 11:12; emphasis added). If you feel an impression to be more Christlike—to be a better spouse or child or neighbor or friend or servant of the Lord—then that is the Spirit working upon you. On the other hand, Satan cannot and will not inspire you to be a better person. It is antithetical to his very nature and purpose.

The prompting to do good, to be better, is one of the fruits of reading the Book of Mormon, for Joseph Smith said that "a man would get nearer to God by abiding by its precepts, than by any other book."[6] Invitations to do good and be good are repeated themes in the Book of Mormon. Perhaps the most awe-inspiring and challenging invitation was given by the Lord Himself: "What manner of men ought ye to be? Verily I say unto you, even as I am" (3 Nephi 27:27).

The Lord gave His personal endorsement of this fruit of the Spirit: "For because of my Spirit he [the reader of the Book of Mormon] shall know that these things are true; *for it persuadeth men to do good. And whatsoever thing persuadeth men to do good is of me*" (Ether 4:11–12; emphasis added). I would be hard-pressed to think of a time when I read the Book of Mormon and did not want to be a better person. It is as though every page infuses that desire into the heart and soul of the reader.

After King Benjamin delivered his majestic sermon on the Atonement of Jesus Christ, his people declared that they knew his words were true "because of the Spirit of the Lord Omnipotent, which has wrought a mighty change in us, or in our hearts, that we have no more disposition to do evil, but to do good continually" (Mosiah 5:2). That impression "to do good continually" is a fruit of the Spirit.

### *Enlightened Understanding*

Another divine witness comes in the form of increased enlightenment and understanding. The Lord reminded Oliver Cowdery and Joseph Smith, "As often as thou hast inquired thou hast received instruction of my Spirit" (D&C 6:14). Lest there be any misunderstanding as to the source of this instruction and knowledge, the Lord showed the connection between the effect (increased knowledge) and the cause (the Spirit) as follows: "Thou knowest that thou hast inquired of me and I did enlighten thy mind; *and now I tell thee these things that thou mayest know that thou hast been enlightened by the Spirit of truth*" (D&C 6:15; emphasis added).

The Lord further confirmed this cause-and-effect relationship between the Spirit and enlightenment in these words: "I will impart unto you of my Spirit, which shall enlighten your mind" (D&C 11:13). Alma described the workings of the Spirit in similar terms: "It beginneth to enlighten my understanding" (Alma 32:28), and "Your mind doth begin to expand" (Alma 32:34). President Henry B. Eyring expressed his personal feelings on this subject: "The Holy Ghost is the Spirit of Truth. Almost always I have felt a sensation of light. Any feeling I may have had of darkness is dispelled."[7] Similar feelings came to King Lamoni, of whom it was recorded: "the dark veil of unbelief was being cast away from his mind" and it was replaced by "the light of everlasting life [which] was lit up in his soul" (Alma 19:6).

This enlightenment literally causes a transformation of our minds. It elevates us to a loftier plane so we have a higher intellectual and spiritual IQ, so to speak—a more refined capacity to think and reason as God does. Paul invited us to "be ye transformed by the renewing [or enlightening] of your mind" (Romans 12:2). Joseph Smith added, "A person may profit by noticing the first intimation of the spirit of revelation; for instance, when you feel pure intelligence flowing into you, it may give you sudden strokes of ideas."[8] I think we have all felt such enlightenment when we have diligently sought God's help in solving a problem or facing a trial, or when we have received ideas for a talk or lesson or a personal answer to a difficult challenge.[9]

President Russell M. Nelson shared an experience he had as a practicing heart surgeon: "I remember in an operating room, I have stood over a patient—unsure how to perform an unprecedented procedure—and experienced the Holy Ghost diagramming the technique in my mind."[10]

This enlightenment from the Spirit can enhance our eternal perspective (see Mosiah 5:3) and give us needed direction in life. It can help us better understand the doctrine we might be pondering. It can instill within us an understanding that we are the literal spirit children of God and that our divine destiny is nothing less than godhood. It can confirm to us the truths that are central to the gospel—the premortal existence, the nature of God, the gospel being preached to the dead, the need for continuing revelation, and the eternal nature of the family. If given the opportunity, the Spirit will flood the doctrinal blind spots in our minds with heavenly light. Joseph Smith and Sidney Rigdon were witnesses of this marvelous truth as they received a glorious vision of the heavenly kingdoms. They wrote, "By the power of the Spirit our eyes were opened and our understandings were enlightened, so as to see and understand the things of God" (D&C 76:12).

I grew up understanding that Jesus Christ, through the Atonement, could redeem me from physical and spiritual death, but when I learned from the Book of Mormon that the Savior, by virtue of His Atonement, could also perfect me, this thought was nothing short of a transcendent moment of heavenly enlightenment. These words of Moroni filled a blind spot in my gospel understanding: "Yea, come unto Christ, and be perfected in him, and deny yourselves of all ungodliness. . . . Then are ye sanctified in Christ by the grace of God, through the shedding of the blood of Christ" (Moroni 10:32–33).

These truths and insights that quicken our minds, deepen our doctrinal understanding, and give us newfound reservoirs of direction and hope are witnesses of the Spirit operating in our lives. An outpouring of the Spirit will cause the scriptures to take on a new vibrancy—they will be more readable and desirable and understandable than ever before. This enlightenment is a form of mental expansion and divine confirmation.

As we read and reread the Book of Mormon, we will be enlightened again and again with new insights into the Fall of Adam and the Atonement of Jesus Christ. In addition, we will receive clarifications and expansion of many other doctrinal principles, such as baptism, the gift of the Holy Ghost, the Light of Christ, the Resurrection, and the nature of ongoing revelation. The Book of Mormon is a treasure trove of doctrinal gems, waiting to enlighten the receptive mind by the power of the Spirit.

### *The Voice of the Lord in Our Mind*

When Enos prayed mightily for the welfare of his brethren, he recorded that "the voice of the Lord came into my mind again, saying: I will visit thy brethren according to their diligence in keeping my commandments" (Enos 1:10). Evidently, this was not an audible voice that came into his ears, rather a silent but discernible voice that came into his mind.

One time I was assigned with another leader of the Church to reorganize a stake. Our main responsibility was to interview members of the stake and call one of them to be the new stake president. I knew none of the twenty-five or so people we were interviewing. At one point, an interviewee walked into the room where the two of us sat. I was somewhat surprised when a voice came to my mind: "That is the stake president." I had previously participated in a number of stake reorganizations, and eventually the Spirit always revealed to us whom the stake president should be, but usually some struggle was required to receive that revelation. Never had I received such an immediate and powerful witness as this.

The interview then commenced. One of the interviewee's responses caused me to seriously doubt whether he should be the stake president. I was torn in my feelings. Logically, I could not recommend him, but spiritually a confirmation had come.

When all the interviews were completed, the other Church leader turned to me and said, "Who do you think the stake president should be?" I responded that if I were relying on the interview alone, I would not recommend the brother for whom I had concerns, but when he walked into the room, I received the distinct impression that this man was the Lord's chosen servant.

The other leader responded, "I had the same impression." The man was called.

Perhaps in this case the Lord gave me such a clear and powerful impression because He knew that otherwise I might be tempted to follow the logic of my mind rather than the impression of the Spirit—that I might be influenced more by my impressions of the outer man than the inner man.

That inaudible but discernible voice to our mind is another witness of the Spirit, another confirmation that may come to us of the truth of the Book of Mormon.

### *Delicious to the Taste*

On some occasions, the doctrine we hear or the impressions we receive are "delicious" to us, meaning they taste good spiritually (see Alma 32:28). When this happens, we need no external evidence to verify them; we have tasted of their goodness, and that is sufficient. As the Lord said, "You shall feel that it is right" (D&C 9:8), or, as Paul explained, "[You] have tasted the good word of God" (Hebrews 6:5).

When I read some of the Book of Mormon's expressions of divine eloquence, such as "Wickedness never was happiness" (Alma 41:10) or "If you believe all these things see that ye do them" (Mosiah 4:10), I feel of their innate goodness and truth. They taste delicious to me.[11]

One way to know the Book of Mormon is true is to realize that time and time again it teaches divine doctrine that is delicious to the spiritual taste.

### *Other Divine Witnesses*

Sometimes the divine witness comes in the burning of the bosom. The two disciples who walked with the Savior on the road to Emmaus acknowledged, "Did not our heart burn within us, while he talked with us by the way" (Luke 24:32; see also D&C 9:7–9). Other times it may cause a softening of our hearts (see Alma 24:8), bring us joy (see 1 Nephi 8:12; D&C 11:12–13), or cause our bones to quake within us (see D&C 85:6; 3 Nephi 11:3).

Paul tells us that some of the fruits of the Spirit are "love, joy, peace, longsuffering, gentleness, goodness, faith" (Galatians 5:22; see also verse 23). When any of these attributes or impressions envelop our hearts or penetrate our minds, it is a witness from God that what we are reading or listening to, what we are feeling, is from Him. As one might expect, these impressions are given for a reason, and that reason is to help us become more committed disciples of Jesus Christ. Accordingly, God holds us accountable for these divine witnesses and our subsequent conduct.

## Summary: Recognizing the Fruits of the Spirit

If we have not experienced the fruits of the Spirit, particularly in recent times, then we can benefit from this wise counsel of President Henry B. Eyring: "If you have difficulty in feeling the Holy Ghost, you might wisely ponder whether there is anything for which you need to repent and receive forgiveness."[12] As we put our lives in order, we are in essence fine-tuning the spiritual receiver that allows us to better recognize the divine promptings and feelings being transmitted by the Holy Ghost.[13]

Elder Richard G. Scott shared a similar sentiment: "The inspiring influence of the Holy Spirit can be overcome or masked by strong emotions such as anger, hate, passion, fear, or pride. When such influences are present, it is like trying to savor the delicate flavor of a grape while eating a jalapeno pepper. Both flavors are present, but one completely overpowers the other."[14]

We might all ask, "How can I know when the Holy Ghost is bearing witness to me of the truth of the Book of Mormon?" The Holy Ghost may do this in different and unique ways for every honest searcher after truth. For some it may be peace or warmth, for others a burning in the bosom, a greater love for the Savior, an increased desire to be more Christlike, enlightenment of the mind, or an impression to the heart that the doctrine being taught makes sense and tastes good. Or the impression may come as a combination of the foregoing. These and similar signs are the fruits of the Spirit that Paul described. As we experience any of these fruits, we are experiencing the witness of the Spirit. It is God's quiet but certain testimony to us that what we are hearing or reading or doing is true and good, that we are on the right course—that heavenly truths are being disclosed and confirmed.

Many of these fruits have been divine witnesses to me that the Book of Mormon is indeed the word of God. Likewise, they can be divine witnesses to everyone who reads this sacred book with pure intent, without prejudice or malice, but with an honest desire to know and live the truth.

---

NOTES

1. *Preach My Gospel,* 96.
2. In this regard, Elder Heber C. Kimball taught: "The time will come when no man nor woman will be able to endure on borrowed light. Each will have to be guided by the light within himself. If you do not have it, how can you stand?" (in Whitney, *Life of Heber C. Kimball,* 450).
3. Packer, "Prayers and Answers," 19.
4. *Teachings of Gordon B. Hinckley,* 261.
5. Eyring, "Gifts of the Spirit for Hard Times."
6. *Teachings of Presidents of the Church: Joseph Smith,* 64.

7. Eyring, "Gifts of the Spirit for Hard Times."
8. *Teachings: Joseph Smith,* 132.
9. Sometimes this enlightenment will continue to linger, as it did with Joseph Smith when he said, "I now resume the subject of the baptism for the dead, as that subject seems to occupy my mind, and press itself upon my feelings the strongest" (D&C 128:1).
10. Russell M. Nelson, "Revelation for the Church, Revelation for Our Lives," 94.
11. Several of these sublime statements are listed in chapter 6 of this book.
12. Eyring, "Gifts of the Spirit for Hard Times."
13. I also recognize that on some occasions good individuals might be wrestling with depression or other emotional issues, and thus for a time it might be more difficult for them to feel and enjoy the full fruits of the Spirit in their lives.
14. Scott, "To Acquire Spiritual Guidance," 8.

PART V

# SUMMARY

CHAPTER 13

# God's Crowning Witness

The following is intended to highlight and summarize some of the key points discussed previously in this book—in essence, a closing argument. Hopefully, it will lay out in a concise way a compelling case for the Book of Mormon as a work of God, and thus inspire one to read it, embrace its doctrine, and become a witness of its divine authenticity.

## The Keystone to Our Testimony

The Book of Mormon is not only the keystone of The Church of Jesus Christ of Latter-day Saints, but it can also become the keystone of our testimonies,[1] so that when trials or unanswered questions confront us, it can hold our testimonies securely in place. This book is the one weight on the scales of truth that exceeds the combined weight of all the critics' arguments against the Church. Why? Because if it is true, then Joseph Smith was a prophet, and if he was a prophet, then it gives credence to the fact that this is the restored Church of Jesus Christ, regardless of any historical or other arguments to the contrary. For this reason, the critics are intent on disproving the Book of Mormon, but the obstacles they face are insurmountable.[2] Why? Because this book is of divine origin.

## The Critics' Arguments Regarding the Origin of the Book of Mormon

### *Joseph Was a Creative Genius*

What must the critics do to prove that the Book of Mormon is man-made? First, the critics must explain how Joseph Smith, a twenty-three-year-old farm boy with limited education, created a book with hundreds of unique names and places as well as detailed stories and events. To do this, many critics propose that he was a creative genius who relied upon numerous books and other local resources to create the historical content of the Book of Mormon. But contrary to their assertion, there is not a solitary witness who claims to have seen Joseph with any of these resources that Joseph is supposed to have read or who can confirm a single conversation with him about these resources before the translation began.

### *Joseph Had a Prodigious Memory*

Even if this argument were true, it is woefully insufficient to explain the Book of Mormon's existence. One must also answer the question, "How did Joseph read all these resources, winnow out the irrelevant and erroneous, keep the intricate facts straight as to who was in what place and when, and then dictate it by perfect memory?" For when Joseph translated, he had no outline, no notes whatsoever. In fact, his wife, Emma, recalled: "He had neither manuscript nor book to read from. If he had had anything of the kind, he could not have concealed it from me."[3]

So how did Joseph perform this remarkable feat of dictating a book more than 500 pages in length without any notes? To do so, he not only must have been a creative genius, but he also must have had a photographic memory of prodigious proportions. But if this is true, why did his critics not call attention to this remarkable talent? In fact, to the contrary, Joseph's critics argued that he did not replace the 116 lost pages of the Book of Mormon because he could not remember what was in them.[4]

### *Joseph Was a Theological Genius*

But there is more. These arguments account only for the book's historical content. The real issues still remain—how did Joseph produce a book that radiates with the Spirit, and where did he get such profound doctrine, much of which clarifies or contradicts the Christian beliefs of his time (see chapter 5)?

For example, the Book of Mormon teaches, contrary to most Christian beliefs, that revelation continues today through living prophets of God (see Mormon 9:7–9), and that after death we go to a spirit world before going to heaven or hell (see Alma 40:11–15). It reveals the covenants made at baptism (see Mosiah 18:8–9) and the sacramental prayers (see Moroni 4; 5), neither of which are addressed in the Bible.

In addition, one might ask, "Where did Joseph get the powerful insight that because of Christ's Atonement, He can not only cleanse us but also perfect us?" (see Moroni 10:32–33). Where did he get the stunning sermons on faith in Alma 32 and Ether 12, or the remarkable sermons on mercy and justice as delivered by Amulek and Alma (see Alma 34; 42), or Nephi's masterful explanation of the doctrine of Christ (see 2 Nephi 31; 32), or the tender account of the Savior's ministry to the Nephites (see 3 Nephi 11–27)? Are we now to believe that Joseph Smith just dictated these sermons and accounts off the top of his head with no notes whatsoever?

Contrary to such a conclusion, God's fingerprints are all over the Book of Mormon, as evidenced by its majestic doctrinal truths, particularly its masterful sermons on the Atonement of Jesus Christ—all of which are compelling evidence of its divine authenticity.

If Joseph were not a prophet, then in order to account for these and many other remarkable doctrinal insights, the critics must also make the argument that he was a theological genius. But if that were the case, one might ask, "Why was Joseph the only 'genius' in the 1,800 years following Christ's ministry to produce such a wide array of unique and clarifying doctrines?"[5] Because it was revelation, not brilliance that was the source of these doctrinal insights.

### *Joseph Was a Naturally Gifted Writer*

Even if we suppose Joseph were a creative and theological genius, with a photographic memory, these talents alone do not make him a skilled writer. To explain the Book of Mormon's existence, critics must also make the claim that Joseph was a naturally gifted writer. Otherwise, how did he interweave scores of names, places, and events into a harmonious whole? How did he pen detailed war strategies, compose eloquent sermons, and coin phrases that are highlighted, memorized, and quoted, such as "To be learned is good if they hearken unto the counsels of God" (2 Nephi 9:29) or "Charity is the pure love of Christ" (Moroni 7:47)? These are messages that resonate with the heart, appeal to the mind, and stir men and women to action. To suggest that Joseph Smith possessed the skills necessary to write this monumental work in a single draft in approximately sixty-five working days is simply counter to the realities of life. It is one thing to have creative ideas; it is quite another to put them into a complex but coherent and harmonious whole, inundated with majestic doctrinal truths.

President Russell M. Nelson, an experienced and skilled writer, shared that he had more than forty rewrites of one general conference talk.[6] I have discovered that when I write on any doctrinal topic, I must make numerous rewrites, deletions, additions, and continuous refinements. Are we now to believe that Joseph Smith, on his own, dictated the entire Book of Mormon, which includes dozens of doctrinal sermons, in a single draft with mainly minor grammatical changes made thereafter?[7]

Joseph's wife, Emma, who knew him better than any other person, confirmed the impossibility of such an undertaking: "Joseph Smith [as a young man] could neither write nor dictate a coherent and well worded letter; let alone dictate a book like the Book of Mormon."[8]

### *Joseph Was a Very Lucky Guesser*

And finally, even if one accepts all of the foregoing arguments, dubious as they may be, the critics still face another looming obstacle. Joseph claimed that the Book of Mormon was written on golden plates. This claim received unrelenting criticism in his day, for "everyone" knew that ancient histories were written on papyrus or parchment—that is, until years later, when metal plates with ancient writings were widely discovered and made known to the world.[9] In addition, critics claimed that the use of cement, as described in the Book of Mormon, was beyond the technical expertise of early Americans—that is, until cement structures were found to exist in ancient America.[10] How do the critics now account for these and similar unlikely discoveries? Joseph, you see, must have been a very, very lucky guesser. Somehow, in spite of all the odds against him, against all existing scientific and academic knowledge, he guessed right when all the others were wrong.

## There Are Only Two Reasonable Options

When all is said and done, one might wonder how someone could believe that all these alleged factors and forces, as proposed by the critics, fortuitously combined in a way that enabled Joseph to write the Book of Mormon and thus foster a satanic fraud. But how would this make sense? In direct opposition to such an assertion, this book has inspired millions to reject Satan and to live more Christlike lives.

While someone might choose to believe the critics' line of reasoning, it is, for me, an intellectual and spiritual dead end. To believe such, I would have to accept one unproven assumption after another. In addition, I would have to disregard the testimony of every one of the eleven witnesses, each of whom was true to his testimony to the very end; I would have to reject the divine doctrine that fills page after page of this sacred book with its supernal truths; I would have to pretend there are no Bible prophecies about the Book of Mormon; I would have to dismiss the divine eloquence of the language and the multiplicity of inspired phrases that ring with heavenly sanction; I would have to ignore the fact that multitudes, including myself, have come closer to God by reading this book than any other; and, above all, I would have to deny the confirming whisperings of the Holy Spirit. This would be contrary to everything I know to be true.

With regard to the Book of Mormon, each of us stands at a crossroads. One road leads to the conclusion that the Book of Mormon is man-made and thus a fraud. The other leads to the conclusion that the Book of Mormon is of divine origin and thus the word of God. In other words, there are only two realistic options on the table—either Joseph Smith wrote the Book of Mormon with the intent to deceive or he translated it by the gift and power of God with the intent to bless and inspire his fellow man.

These two options are set forth below in diagram form:

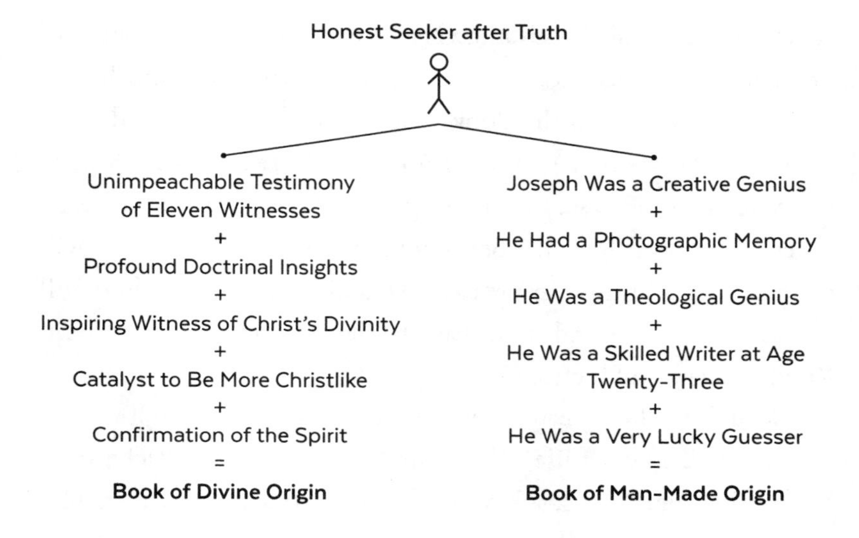


For the Book of Mormon to be man-made, as the critics claim, *each* of the steps leading to that conclusion must be in play at the same time. For the Book of Mormon to be of divine origin, *any one* of the steps leading to this conclusion is a convincing witness, but of course the sure and certain witness is the confirmation of the Spirit. For those who travel the road that leads them to the divine origin of the Book of Mormon, it will open the door to a multitude of promised blessings.

## Promised Blessings

Would you like greater power in your life to resist temptation? Then consider this promise of President Ezra Taft Benson: "There is a power in the book [the Book of Mormon] which will begin to flow into your lives the moment you begin a serious study of the book. You will find greater power to resist temptation. You will find the power to avoid deception. You will find the power to stay on the strait and narrow path."[11]

Would you like your home to be more heavenly—less

contentious and filled with more love? Then listen to the promise of President Marion G. Romney: "I feel certain that if, in our homes parents will read from the Book of Mormon prayerfully and regularly, both by themselves and with their children . . . the spirit of reverence will increase, mutual respect and consideration for each other will grow. The spirit of contention will depart. Parents will counsel their children in greater love and wisdom. Children will be more responsive and submissive to the counsel of their parents. Righteousness will increase."[12]

Would you like greater revelation to guide you through the trials and challenges of life? Then this promise of Elder Richard G. Scott is for you: "The Book of Mormon . . . teaches how to resolve the problems and challenges that we face today that were foreseen by the Lord. In that book he has provided the way to correct the serious errors of life, but this guidance is of no value if it remains locked in a closed book."[13]

Would you like to overcome pornography or any other addiction that plagues you? Then read and reread this promise of President Russell M. Nelson: "I promise that as you daily immerse yourself in the Book of Mormon, you can be immunized against the evils of the day, even the gripping plague of pornography and other mind-numbing addictions."[14]

Would you like an increased measure of the Spirit and a strengthening of your testimony? Then President Gordon B. Hinckley has a promise you will want to read and ponder: "Brothers and sisters, without reservation I promise you that if you will prayerfully read the Book of Mormon, regardless of how many times you previously have read it, there will come into your hearts an added measure of the Spirit of the Lord. There will come a strengthened resolution to walk in obedience to his commandments, and there will come a stronger testimony of the living reality of the Son of God."[15]

Who would not want each of these blessings promised by prophets of God? If the honest seeker after truth will take the time to humbly read the Book of Mormon with intensity, ponder its truths, and give ear to the sweet fruits of the Spirit, then he or she will eventually receive the fulfillment of these promises made by prophets of God.

The Book of Mormon is one of God's most priceless gifts to us. It is both sword and shield—it sends the word of God into battle to fight for the hearts of the just, and it serves as an arch defender of the truth. As Saints, we have not only the privilege to defend the Book of Mormon but the opportunity to take the offense—to preach with power its divine doctrine and to bear testimony of its crowning witness of Jesus Christ.

As I bring this book to a close, I feel I have only scratched the surface in highlighting the temporal, intellectual, and spiritual evidences of the Book of Mormon. The deeper one dives, the more one realizes there is no bottom to its divine insights and disclosures. Every vantage point rings with truth—whether it be linguistics, archaeology, authorship, doctrine, or the Spirit. Every page bears witness of its divine authenticity. The Lord Himself bore witness of its veracity: "As your Lord and your God liveth it [the Book of Mormon] is true" (D&C 17:6).

This book focuses on a case for the Book of Mormon, but in one sense the Book of Mormon does not need a case presented on its behalf. It is its own best witness—its own best evidence. It is the unmitigated word of God from beginning to end; it teaches the doctrine of Christ in purity; it bears witness of the Savior with precision and power; and it invites the Spirit in unrestrained proportions. Every aspect of the Book of Mormon bears witness of its divine origin because, in fact, it is divinely inspired.

I bear my solemn witness that the Book of Mormon was

translated by the gift and power of God. It is God's crowning witness of the divinity of Jesus Christ, the prophetic calling of Joseph Smith, and the absolute truth of The Church of Jesus Christ of Latter-day Saints. It is all it claims to be. It is the word of God. May it become the keystone of our testimonies, so it may be said of us, as it was of the converted Lamanites: "[They] never did fall away" (Alma 23:6).

---

NOTES

1. In this regard, President Ezra Taft Benson wrote: "There are three ways in which the Book of Mormon is the keystone of our religion. It is the keystone in our witness of Christ. It is the keystone of our doctrine. It is the keystone of testimony" ("The Book of Mormon—Keystone of Our Religion," 5).
2. Attempts to discredit the Book of Mormon have been discussed in earlier chapters.
3. In Joseph Smith III, "Last Testimony of Sister Emma," 289–90.
4. Michael R. Ash observed: "As far as I can tell, there is no evidence to support the belief that Joseph Smith had an uncanny or photographic memory. From a critic's perspective, such a proposition runs counter to other anti-Mormon claims. For example, the critics have also claimed that when Joseph Smith lost the first 116 pages of the Book of Mormon translation . . . he had forgotten what he had written, so he started anew" ("The King James Bible and the Book of Mormon").
5. Certainly, others such as Luther expounded doctrine, but Luther's doctrinal insights were largely in reaction to the Catholic dogma of the day and fall far short of the depth and breadth of correct doctrine revealed by Joseph Smith as set forth in chapter 5 of this book.
6. President Nelson confirmed this fact to the author, via an email from his secretary, dated August 18, 2017, and gave permission to include it in the author's general conference message of October 2017 (see Callister, "God's Compelling Witness: The Book of Mormon," 108).
7. Antonin Scalia, a former justice of the U.S. Supreme Court, was one of the keenest minds of our generation. He stated that while serving as a law professor he tried to teach his students two truths about improving their writing skills: "(1) the realization . . . that there is an immense difference between writing and good writing; and (2) the recognition that it takes time and sweat to convert the former into the latter" (*Scalia Speaks,* 58–59). This second truth would hardly be consistent with the assertion that Joseph Smith wrote the Book of Mormon from a single draft in approximately sixty-five working days.
8. In Joseph Smith III, "Last Testimony of Sister Emma," 290.

9. See chapter 3 of this book.
10. See Grant, in Conference Report, April 1929, 129; Sorenson, "Digging into the Book of Mormon, Part 2," 19.
11. Benson, "The Book of Mormon—Keystone of Our Religion," 7.
12. Romney, "The Book of Mormon," 67.
13. Scott, "True Friends That Lift," 76.
14. Russell M. Nelson, "The Book of Mormon: What Would Your Life Be Like without It?," 63.
15. Hinckley, "The Power of the Book of Mormon," 6.

# Works Cited

Anderson, Richard Lloyd. "Explaining Away the Book of Mormon Witnesses." Address at the Aug. 2004 FairMormon conference. fairmormon.org/conference/august-2004/explaining-away-the-book-of-mormon-witnesses.

———. *Investigating the Book of Mormon Witnesses.* Salt Lake City, UT: Deseret Book, 1981.

Anderson, Robert D. *Inside the Mind of Joseph Smith: Psychobiography and the Book of Mormon.* Salt Lake City, UT: Signature Books, 1999.

*The Ante-Nicene Fathers: The Writings of the Fathers down to A.D. 325.* Ed. Alexander Roberts and James Donaldson. New York: Scribner's Sons, 1903.

*The Apostolic Fathers.* Trans. J. B. Lightfoot. New York: The Macmillan Company, 1898.

Ash, Michael R. "Archaeological Evidence and the Book of Mormon." FairMormon. fairmormon.org/archive/publications/archaeological-evidence-and-the-book-of-mormon.

———. "The King James Bible and the Book of Mormon." FairMormon. fairmormon.org/wp-content/uploads/2012/02/King_James_Bible_and_the_Book_of_Mormon.pdf.

Aveson, Robert. "Three Witnesses to the Book of Mormon." *Deseret News,* Apr. 2, 1927.

Bancroft, George. *History of the United States,* vol. 1. New York: D. Appleton and Co., 1888.

Barnhart, Edwin, and Vejas G. Liulevicius. *Maya to Aztec: Ancient Mesoamerica Revealed.* Chantilly, VA: The Teaching Company, 2015.

Beardsley, Harry M. *Joseph Smith and His Mormon Empire.* Boston: Houghton Mifflin, 1931.

Benson, Ezra Taft. "The Book of Mormon and the Doctrine and Covenants." *Ensign,* May 1987, 83–85.

———. "The Book of Mormon—Keystone of Our Religion." *Ensign,* Nov. 1986, 4–7.

———. "A New Witness for Christ." *Ensign,* Nov. 1984, 6–8.

———. *A Witness and a Warning: A Modern-Day Prophet Testifies of the Book of Mormon.* Salt Lake City, UT: Deseret Book, 1988.

Bercot, David W. *What the Early Christians Believed about Baptism.* Audio recording. Scroll Publishing. youtube.com/watch?v=K9RGxS4wkMI.

Black, Susan Easton. *Finding Christ through the Book of Mormon.* Salt Lake City, UT: Deseret Book, 1987.

"Book of Mormon and DNA Studies." Gospel Topics, topics.lds.org.

Boylan, Robert. "Responding to a Critique of Tad Callister's October 2017 General Conference Talk on the Book of Mormon." Scriptural Mormonism, Oct. 5, 2017. scripturalmormonism.blogspot.com.

Brodie, Fawn. *No Man Knows My History: The Life of Joseph Smith, the Mormon Prophet.* New York: Knopf, 1945.

Bush, Edna K. "The Book of Mormon and My Conversion." *Ensign,* June 1972, 28–31.

———. *Dissecting the Book of Mormon: A Fresh Approach to the Book of Mormon.* St. Petersburg, FL: Edna K. Bush, 1968.

———. "Magnificent Messages." *Instructor,* Nov. 1967, 460.

Callister, Tad R. "God's Compelling Witness: The Book of Mormon." *Ensign,* Nov. 2017, 107–9.

Campbell, Alexander. *Delusions: An Analysis of the Book of Mormon.* Boston: Benjamin H. Greene, 1832.

Campbell, Gordon. *Bible: The Story of the King James Version, 1611–2011.* Oxford: University Press, 2010.

Chase, Lance D. "Spaulding Manuscript." In *Encyclopedia of Mormonism.* Ed. Daniel H. Ludlow. New York: Macmillan, 1992.

Cheesman, Paul R. *Ancient Writing on Metal Plates: Archaeological Finds Support Mormon Claims.* Bountiful, UT: Horizon, 1985.

Clark, John E. "Archaeological Trends and Book of Mormon Origins." *BYU Studies Quarterly* 44, no. 4 (Dec. 1, 2005):83–104.

Clynes, Tom. "Laser Scans Reveal Maya 'Megalopolis' Below Guatemalan Jungle." *National Geographic,* Feb. 1, 2018. news.nationalgeographic .com/2018/02/maya-laser-lidar-guatemala-pacunam.

Columbus, Christopher. *The Book of Prophecies.* Trans. Blair Sullivan. Eugene, OR: Wipf and Stock, 1997.

Cook, Lyndon W., ed. *David Whitmer Interviews: A Restoration Witness.* Orem, UT: Grandin Book Company, 1991.

"Correspondence." *The True Latter Day Saints' Herald* 22 (Oct. 15, 1875):628–32.

Cowdery, Oliver. "The Closing Year." *Latter Day Saints' Messenger and Advocate* 3, no. 3 (Dec. 1836):425–29.

Cowley, Matthew. "Testimony through Reading the Book of Mormon." *Relief Society Magazine* 53 (Jan. 1953):6–12.

Davis, Nicola. "Laser scanning reveals 'lost' ancient Mexican city had as many buildings as Manhattan." *Guardian*, Feb. 15, 2018.

"Did Joseph Smith obtain the names Cumorah and Moroni from a map of the Comoros Islands?" FairMormon. fairmormon.org/answers /Book_of_Mormon/Plagiarism_accusations/Comoros_Islands_and _Moroni.

Durant, Will. *The Story of Civilization, Volume 3—Caesar and Christ: A History of Roman Civilization and of Christianity from Their Beginnings to AD 325.* New York: Simon and Schuster, 1935.

"Early Christian Belief in a Pre-Mortal Existence." FairMormon. https:// www.fairmormon.org/evidences/Premortal_Life.

Ehrman, Bart D. *Misquoting Jesus: The Story behind Who Changed the Bible and Why.* New York: Harper Collins, 2005.

"The Eight Witnesses and Their Experience Viewing the 'Gold' Plates." Fair Mormon. fairmormon.org/answers/Book_of_Mormon/Witnesses /Eight_witnesses.

Ellis, Nancy Rigdon. "Correspondence." *Saints' Herald* 31 (May 31, 1884):1.

*Encyclopedia of Early Christianity.* Ed. Everett Fergusson. New York and London: Garland Publishing, 1990.

Etzenhouser, Rudolph. *From Palmyra, New York, 1830, to Independence, Missouri, 1894.* Independence, MO: Ensign Publishing House, 1894.

Eyring, Henry B. "Gifts of the Spirit for Hard Times." Brigham Young University devotional address, Sept. 10, 2006. speeches.byu.edu/talks/henry-b-eyring_gifts-spirit-hard-times.

———. "How to Receive the Holy Ghost." *New Era,* June 2014, 48.

Fairchild, James H. "Solomon Spaulding and the Book of Mormon." *Bibliotheca Sacra* 42, no. 165 (January 1885):173–74.

*Faithlife Study Bible.* Ed. John D. Barry, Douglas Mangum, Derek R. Brown, and Michael S. Heiser. Grand Rapids, MI: Zondervan, 2017.

Farrer, Austin. "Grete Clerk." In Jocelyn Gibb, comp. *Light on C. S. Lewis.* New York: Harcourt and Brace, 1965.

Faulring, Scott H. "The Return of Oliver Cowdery." In *The Disciple as Witness: Essays on Latter-day Saint History and Doctrine in Honor of Richard Lloyd Anderson.* Ed. Stephen D. Ricks, Donald W. Parry, and Andrew H. Hodges. Provo, UT: Foundation for Ancient Research and Mormon Studies, 2000, 117–73.

Fields, Paul J., G. Bruce Schaalje, and Matthew Roper. "Examining a Misapplication of Nearest Shrunken Centroid Classification to Investigate Book of Mormon Authorship." *Mormon Studies Review* 23, no. 1 (2011):87–111.

Finkelstein, Israel, and Neil Asher Silberman. *The Bible Unearthed: Archaeology's New Vision of Ancient Israel and the Origin of Its Sacred Texts.* New York: Touchstone, 2001.

Fiske, John. *Studies in Religion.* Cambridge, MA: Riverside Press, 1903.

*Gold Plates Used Anciently.* Salt Lake City, UT: The Church of Jesus Christ of Latter-day Saints, 1963.

Grant, Heber J. In Conference Report, Apr. 1929, 128–31.

Greene, John P. *Facts Relative to the Expulsion of the Mormons from the State of Missouri under the "Extermination Order."* Cincinnati, OH: R. P. Brooks, 1839.

Hamblin, William J. "An Apologist for the Critics: Brent Lee Metcalfe's

Assumptions and Methodologies." *Review of Books on the Book of Mormon* 6, no. 1 (1994):434–523.

———. "Sacred Writing on Metal Plates in the Ancient Mediterranean." *FARMS Review* 19, no. 1 (2007):37–54.

Hart, James H. *Mormon in Motion: The Life and Journals of James H. Hart.* New York: Windsor Books, 1978.

Hinckley, Gordon B. "Be Not Deceived." *Ensign,* Nov. 1983, 44–46.

———. "Four Cornerstones of Faith." *Ensign,* Feb. 2004, 3–7.

———. "The Power of the Book of Mormon." *Ensign,* June 1988, 2–6.

———. *Teachings of Gordon B. Hinckley.* Salt Lake City, UT: Deseret Book, 1997.

Holland, Jeffrey R. *Christ and the New Covenant: The Messianic Message of the Book of Mormon.* Salt Lake City, UT: Deseret Book, 1997.

———. "Safety for the Soul." *Ensign,* Nov. 2009, 88–90.

Horn, Cornelia B. "Lebanon in the Holy Scriptures." *Journal of Maronite Studies* 4, no. 1 (Jan.–June 2000). maronite-institute.org/MARI/JMS/january00/Lebanon_In_The_Holy_Scriptures.htm.

Howells, Rulon S. *His Many Mansions: A Compilation of Christian Beliefs.* New York: Greystone Press, 1940.

Hunt, Gilbert J. *The Late War between the United States and Great Britain,* 3rd ed. New York: Daniel D. Smith, 1819.

Hyman, David S. *Precolumbian Cements: A Study of the Calcareous Cements in Prehispanic Meso-American Building Construction.* Baltimore, MD: Johns Hopkins University, 1970.

Ivins, Anthony W. In Conference Report, Apr. 1929, 8–17.

Jenson, Andrew. "The Eight Witnesses." *Historical Record* 7 (Oct. 1888):609–22.

———. "The Three Witnesses." *Historical Record* 5 (May 1887):195–219.

Jenson, Andrew, Edward Stevenson, and Joseph S. Black. "Historical Landmarks." *Deseret Evening News,* Sept. 17, 1888, 2.

Jewish National Fund. "We Are JNF." jnf.org/menu-3/about-jnf.

Johnson, Chris, and Duane Johnson. "A Comparison of the Book of Mormon and The Late War Between the United States and Great Britain." wordtreefoundation.github.io/thelatewar.

Johnson, Janiece, and Jennifer Reeder. *The Witness of Women: Firsthand*

*Experiences and Testimonies from the Restoration.* Salt Lake City, UT: Deseret Book, 2016.

Johnson, Paul. *A History of Christianity.* New York: Atheneum, 1976.

Kelley, E. L., and Clark Braden. *The Braden and Kelley Debate: Public Discussion of the Issues between the Reorganized Church of Jesus Christ of Latter Day Saints and the Church of Christ (Disciples).* N.p.: The Old Paths Book Club, 1955.

King, David. *Baptism: Sprinkling and Pouring versus Immersion.* Birmingham, England: J. Fauloonbridge, 1865.

Lamb, Martin Thomas. *The Golden Bible, or the Book of Mormon: Is It from God*? New York: Wang and Drummond, 1887.

"Last Days of Oliver Cowdery." *Deseret News,* Apr. 13, 1859, 48.

*Latter-day Saints' Messenger and Advocate,* Oct. 1834, 14.

*Lectures on Faith.* Salt Lake City, UT: Deseret Book, 1985.

Lewis, C. S. *Mere Christianity.* New York: Harper Collins, 2001.

———. *Miracles: A Preliminary Study.* New York: Harper Collins, 2000.

Livingston, Tyler. "Another Look at Barley in the Book of Mormon." FairMormon, Apr. 17, 2010. fairmormon.org/blog/2010/04/17/another-look-at-barley-in-the-book-of-mormon.

"Lost Books." In LDS Bible Dictionary. Salt Lake City, UT: The Church of Jesus Christ of Latter-day Saints, 2013.

Ludlow, Daniel H. *A Companion to Your Study of the Book of Mormon.* Salt Lake City, UT: 1976.

Lund, John L. *MesoAmerica and the Book of Mormon: Is This the Place?* Salt Lake City, UT: The Communications Company, 2007.

Lundberg, Marilyn J. "The Copper Scroll." West Semitic Research Project. wsrp.usc.edu/educational_site/dead_sea_scrolls/copperscroll.shtml.

Lundwall, N. B., comp. *Assorted Gems of Priceless Value.* Salt Lake City, UT: Zion's Press, 1944.

Madsen, Truman G. "B. H. Roberts after Fifty Years: Still Witnessing for the Book of Mormon." *Ensign,* Dec. 1983, 10–19.

———. *Defender of the Faith: The B. H. Roberts Story.* Salt Lake City, UT: Bookcraft, 1980.

Manchester, William. *A World Lit Only by Fire: The Medieval Mind and the Renaissance—Portrait of an Age.* New York: Little, Brown, 1993.

Mann, Charles C. *1491: New Revelations of the Americas Before Columbus,* 2nd ed. New York: Random House, 2011.

Marsh, Thomas. "History of Thos. Baldwin Marsh." *Deseret News,* Mar. 24, 1858, 2.

Martin, Walter. *The Maze of Mormonism.* Santa Ana, CA: Vision House, 1978.

McConkie, Bruce R. *Doctrines of the Restoration: Sermons and Writings of Bruce R. McConkie.* Ed. Mark McConkie. Salt Lake City, UT: Bookcraft, 1989.

McLerran, Dan. "Lost Civilizations of North America." *Popular Archaeology,* Jan. 2011. popular-archaeology.com/issue/january-2011/article/lost-civilizations-of-north-america.

Midgley, Louis C. "Who Really Wrote the Book of Mormon? The Critics and Their Theories." In Noel B. Reynolds, ed. *Book of Mormon Authorship Revisited: The Evidence for Ancient Origins,* 101–39. Provo, UT: Foundation for Ancient Research and Mormon Studies, 1997.

Morain, William D. *The Sword of Laban: Joseph Smith Jr. and the Dissociated Mind.* Washington, DC: American Psychiatric Press, 1998.

"Moses." In *Harper's Bible Dictionary.* Ed. Paul J. Achtemeier et al. San Francisco, CA: Harper and Row, 1985.

Moyle, James H. "A Visit to David Whitmer." *The Instructor* 80 (Sept. 1945):400–404.

Nelson, N. L. "The Dictionary of Slander." *The Mormon Point of View* 1, no. 2 (Apr. 1, 1904): 155–96.

Nelson, Russell M. "The Book of Mormon: What Would Your Life Be Like without It?" *Ensign,* Nov. 2017, 60–63.

———. "Revelation for the Church, Revelation for Our Lives." *Ensign,* May 2018, 93–96.

———. "Truth—*and More.*" *Ensign,* Jan. 1986, 69–73.

"New Evidence for Horses in America." Book of Mormon Central, Jan. 29, 2018. bookofmormoncentral.org/blog/new-evidence-for-horses-in-america.

Nibley, Hugh W. "Checking on Long-Forgotten Lore." In *The Collected Works of Hugh Nibley,* 5:105–23. Ed. John W. Welch, Darrell L. Matthews, and Stephen R. Callister. Salt Lake City, UT: Deseret Book, 1988.

———. "The Dead Sea Scrolls: Some Questions and Answers." In *The Collected Works of Hugh Nibley,* 1:245–51. Ed. John W. Welch, Gary P. Gillum, and Don E. Norton. Salt Lake City, UT: Deseret Book, 1986.

———. "Lehi the Winner." In *The Collected Works of Hugh Nibley,* 5:105–23. Ed. John W. Welch, Darrell L. Matthews, and Stephen R. Callister. Salt Lake City, UT: Deseret Book, 1988.

———. "New Approaches to Book of Mormon Study." In *The Collected Works of Hugh Nibley,* 8:54–126. Ed. John W. Welch. Salt Lake City, UT: Deseret Book, 1989.

———. "A Permanent Heritage." In *The Collected Works of Hugh Nibley,* 5:242–63. Ed. John W. Welch, Darrell L. Matthews, and Stephen R. Callister. Salt Lake City, UT: Deseret Book, 1988.

———. "Preface." In *The Collected Works of Hugh Nibley,* 7:xi–xv. Ed. John W. Welch. Salt Lake City, UT: Deseret Book, 1988.

———. "Prophets in the Wilderness." In *The Collected Works of Hugh Nibley,* 7:264–90. Ed. John W. Welch. Salt Lake City, UT: Deseret Book, 1988.

———. *Since Cumorah.* Salt Lake City, UT: Deseret Book, 1967.

———. "A Twilight World." In *The Collected Works of Hugh Nibley,* 5:153–71. Ed. John W. Welch, Darrell L. Matthews, and Stephen R. Callister. Salt Lake City, UT: Deseret Book, 1988.

Ogden, D. Kelly. "Why Does the Book of Mormon Say That Jesus Would Be Born in Jerusalem?" *Ensign,* Aug. 1984, 51–52.

Packer, Boyd K. "The Book of Mormon: Another Testament of Jesus Christ." *Ensign,* Nov. 2001, 63–64.

———. "I Say unto You, Be One." Brigham Young University devotional address, Feb. 12, 1991. speeches.byu.edu.

———. "Prayers and Answers." *Ensign,* Nov. 1979, 19–21.

———. *Teach Ye Diligently.* Salt Lake City, UT: Deseret Book, 1975.

Page, Hiram. Letter to William E. McLellin. *Ensign of Liberty* 1 (Jan. 1848):63.

Parry, Donald W. "Why Is the Phrase 'and It Came to Pass' So Prevalent in the Book of Mormon?" *Ensign,* Dec. 1992, 29.

Peterson, Daniel C. "Chattanooga Cheapshot, or the Gall of Bitterness" (Review of *Everything You Ever Wanted to Know About Mormonism* by John Ankerberg and John Weldor). *Review of Books on the Book of Mormon 1989–2011,* 5, no. 1 (1993).

———. "Not Joseph's, and Not Modern." In *Echoes and Evidences of the Book of Mormon.* Ed. Donald W. Parry, Daniel C. Peterson, and John W. Welch. Provo, UT: Foundation for Ancient Research and Mormon Studies, 2002, 191–229.

Pratt, Parley P. *Mormonism Unveiled: Zion's Watchman Unmasked.* Painesville, OH: n.p., 1838.

———. *Plain Facts, Showing the Falsehood and Folly of the Rev. C. S. Bush, Being a Reply to His Tract Against the Latter-day Saints.* Manchester, England: W. R. Thomas, n.d.

*Preach My Gospel: A Guide to Missionary Service.* Salt Lake City, UT: The Church of Jesus Christ of Latter-day Saints, 2004.

*Proceedings of the International Churchill Societies, 1992–93.* Ed. Edmund Murray, Winston Churchill, and Martin Gilbert. London: Churchill Center, 1995.

Rappleye, Neal. "Why Did Alma Say Christ Would Be Born in Jerusalem? Surprising Evidence of the Book of Mormon." *LDS Living,* Dec. 21, 2017. ldsliving.com/why-did-alma-say-christ-would-be-born-in-jerusalem-surprising-evidence-of-the-book-of-mormon/s/87333.

*A Reformation Reader: Primary Texts with Introductions,* 2nd ed. Ed. Denis R. Janz. Minneapolis, MN: Fortress Press, 2008.

Reynolds, George. "The Originator of the 'Spaulding Story.'" *Juvenile Instructor* 17, no. 17 (Sept. 1, 1882):262–63.

Reynolds, Noel B. "Shedding New Light on Ancient Origins." *Brigham Young Magazine* 52, no. 1 (Spring 1998):36–45.

Richards, LeGrand. *A Marvelous Work and a Wonder,* rev. ed. Salt Lake City, UT: Deseret Book, 1972.

———. In Conference Report, Apr. 1955, 119–24.

Ricks, Eldin. *The Case of the Book of Mormon Witnesses.* Salt Lake City, UT: Olympus Publishing Company, 1961.

Riley, I. Woodbridge. *The Founder of Mormonism: A Psychological Study of Joseph Smith Jr.* New York: Dodd, Mead, and Company, 1902.

Roberts, B. H. In Conference Report, Apr. 1933, 117.

———. "Joseph Smith: An Appreciation." *Improvement Era* 36 (Dec. 1932):81.

———. *New Witnesses for God,* vol. 2. Salt Lake City, UT: Deseret News, 1909.

———. *Studies of the Book of Mormon.* Ed. Brigham D. Madsen. Urbana, IL: University of Illinois Press, 1985.

Romney, Marion G. "The Book of Mormon." *Ensign,* May 1980, 65–67.

Roper, Matthew P. "Joseph Smith, Central American Ruins, and the Book of Mormon." In *Approaching Antiquity: Joseph Smith and the Ancient World.* Ed. Lincoln H. Blumell, Matthew J. Grey, and Andrew H. Hedges. Provo, UT: Religious Studies Center, 2015, 141–62. rsc.byu.edu/es/archived/approaching-antiquity-joseph-smith-and-ancient-world/joseph-smith-central-american-ruins.

———. "Right on Target: Boomerang Hits and the Book of Mormon." Address at FairMormon Conference, Aug. 2001. fairmormon.org/conference/august-2001/right-on-target-boomerang-hits-and-the-book-of-mormon.

Roper, Matthew, Paul J. Fields, and G. Bruce Schaalje. "Stylometric Analyses of the Book of Mormon: A Short History." *Journal of the Book of Mormon and Other Restoration Scripture* 21, no. 1 (2012):28–45.

Runnells, Jeremy. "Letter to a CES Director." cesletter.org.

Santayana, George. *Life of Reason: Reason in Common Sense.* New York: C. Scribner's Sons, 1905.

Saturano, William. "The Thrill of the Find: Murals and Mysteries of the Maya." Presentation given at the Boston Museum of Science. youtube.com/watch?v=M0vZAVCOAaI.

Scalia, Antonin. *Scalia Speaks: Reflections on Law, Faith and Life Well Lived.* Ed. Christopher J. Scalia and Edward Whelan. New York: Crown Forum, 2017.

Schaefer, Mitchell K. "'The Testimony of Men': William E. McLellin and the Book of Mormon Witnesses." *BYU Studies,* 50 (2011), no. 1.

Scott, Richard G. *21 Principles: Divine Truths to Help You Live by the Spirit.* Salt Lake City, UT: Deseret Book, 2013.

———. "Realize Your Full Potential." *Ensign,* Nov. 2003, 41–43.

———. "To Acquire Spiritual Guidance." *Ensign,* Nov. 2009, 6–9.

———. "True Friends That Lift." *Ensign,* Nov. 1988, 76–77.

Seiglie, Mario. "The Exodus Controversy." *Virtual Christian Magazine* 4, no. 3 (Mar.–Apr. 2002):10–17.

Simons, Menno. *Menno Simons: His Life, Labors, and Teachings.* Comp. John Horsch. Scottdale, PA: Mennonite Publishing House, 1916.

Smith, Hyrum. "Communications: To the Saints Scattered Abroad." *Times and Seasons* 1, no. 1 (Dec. 1839): 20–24.

Smith, John L. "What about Those Gold Plates?" *Utah Evangel,* Sept. 1986, 8.

Smith, Joseph. "From Priest's American Antiquities." *Times and Seasons* 3, no. 15 (June 1, 1842):813–14.

———. *Teachings of Presidents of the Church: Joseph Smith.* Salt Lake City, UT: The Church of Jesus Christ of Latter-day Saints, 2007.

Smith, Joseph III. *Joseph Smith III and the Restoration.* Ed. Mary Audentia Smith Anderson. Independence, MO: Herald House, 1952.

———. "Last Testimony of Sister Emma." *Saints' Herald,* 26 (Oct. 1, 1879):289–90.

———. "The Spaulding Story Reexamined." *Saints' Herald* (Mar. 11, 1883).

Smith, Lucy. *Biographical Sketches of Joseph Smith, the Prophet, and His Progenitors for Many Generations.* Liverpool, England: S. W. Richards, 1853.

Smith, Lucy Mack. *History of Joseph Smith by His Mother.* Salt Lake City, UT: Bookcraft, 1958.

Sorenson, John L. *An Ancient American Setting for the Book of Mormon.* Provo, UT: Foundation for Ancient Research and Mormon Studies, 1996.

———. "Digging into the Book of Mormon: Our Changing Understanding of Ancient America and Its Scripture, Part 2." *Ensign,* Oct. 1984, 12–23.

Stuart, George. "Interview: George and David Stuart." *National Geographic Live* (Aug. 22, 2011). youtube.com/watch?V=JNP224ZUJWA.

Tertullian. *The Writings of Tertullian,* vol. 3. Ed. Anthony Uyl. Woodstock, Canada: Devoted Publishing, 2017.

Thomasson, Camille, and Bart Gavigan. *Luther.* Directed by Eric Till. Berlin, Germany: Eikon Film, 2003.

Tolworthy, Chris. "Cement in the Book of Mormon." exmormon.org.uk /tol_arch/atozelph/cement.htm.

Twain, Mark. *Roughing It.* Hartford, CT: American Publishing Company, 1899.

"The Valueless Testimony of the Book of Mormon Witnesses." The Interactive Bible. bible.ca/mor-witness-book.htm.

Vogel, Dan, comp. *Early Mormon Documents,* vol. 1. Salt Lake City, UT: Signature Books, 1996.

———, comp. *Early Mormon Documents,* vol. 5. Salt Lake City, UT: Signature Books, 2003.

———. *Indian Origins and the Book of Mormon: Religious Solutions from Columbus to Joseph Smith.* Salt Lake City, UT: Signature Books, 1986.

———. *Joseph Smith: The Making of a Prophet.* Salt Lake City, UT: Signature Books, 2004.

Walch, Tad. "President Monson, Others: President Packer a 'Diligent, Devoted Disciple of Christ.'" *Deseret News,* July 20, 2015. deseretnews.com/article/865632313/president-monson-to-speak-this-morning-at-president-packer's-funeral.html.

Webb, Chad H. "That They May Know How to Come unto Him and Be Saved." Brigham Young University–Hawaii devotional address, Mar. 22, 2016. devotional.byuh.edu/media160322.

Webb, Stephen H. "Mormonism Obsessed with Christ." *First Things,* Feb. 2012. firstthings.com/article/2012/02/mormonism-obsessed-with-christ.

Welch, John W. "B. H. Roberts: Seeker after Truth." *Ensign,* Mar. 1986, 56–62.

———. "The Discovery of Chiasmus in the Book of Mormon 40 Years Later." *Journal of Book of Mormon Studies* 16, no. 2 (2007):74–87, 99.

———. "How Much Was Known about Chiasmus in 1829 When the Book of Mormon Was Translated?" *FARMS Review* 15, no. 2 (2003):47–80.

———."The Laws of Eshnunna and Nephite Economics." *Pressing Forward with the Book of Mormon: The FARMS Updates of the 1990s.* Ed. John W. Welch and Melvin J. Thorne. Provo, Utah: Foundation for Ancient Research and Mormon Studies, 1999, 147–49.

———. "View of the Hebrews: 'An Unparallel.'" In *Reexploring the Book of Mormon.* Ed. John W. Welch. Salt Lake City, UT: Deseret Book, 1992, 83–87.

Wells, Junius F. "Oliver Cowdery." *Millennial Star* 83 (Apr. 13, 1911):225–29.

"What Can Stylometry Tell Us about Book of Mormon Authorship?" Book of Mormon Central, Dec. 12, 2017. knowhy.bookofmormoncentral.org/content/what-can-stylometry-tell-us-about-book-of-mormon-authorship.

"When Did Cement Become Common in Ancient America?" Book of Mormon Central. https://knowhy.bookofmormoncentral.org/content/when-did-cement-become-common-in-ancient-america.

"Where Did Joseph Smith Get His Doctrinal Ideas About Christ?" Book of Mormon Central. https://knowhy.bookofmormoncentral.org/content/where-did-Joseph-Smith-get-his-doctrinal-ideas-about-Christ.

Whitmer, David. *An Address to All Believers in Christ by a Witness to the Divine Authenticity of the Book of Mormon*. Richmond, MO: David Whitmer, 1887.

Whitmer, John. "Address." *Latter Day Saints Messenger and Advocate* 2 (Mar. 1836):285–88.

Whitney, Orson F. *Life of Heber C. Kimball,* 3rd ed. Salt Lake City, UT: Bookcraft, 1945.

"Why Hasn't Lehi's DNA Been Found?" Book of Mormon Central, Feb. 27, 2017. knowhy.bookofmormoncentral.org/content/why-hasn't-lehi's-dna-been-found.

Winchester, Benjamin. *Plain Facts, Shewing the Origin of the Spaulding Story*. Bedford, England: C. B. Merry, 1841.

Winebrenner, John. *The Ordinances: Baptism, Feet Washing, and the Lord's Supper*. Lebanon, PA: General Eldership of the Church of God, 1868.

Yamauchi, Edwin. "The Current State of Old Testament Historiography." In A. R. Millard, J. K. Hoffmeier, and D. W. Baker, eds., *Faith Tradition and History: Old Testament Historiography in Its Near Eastern Context.* Winona Lake, IN: Eisenbrauns, 1994, 1–36.

———. *The Stones and the Scriptures.* Westmont, IL: InterVarsity Press, 1973.

Young, Brigham. "History of Brigham Young," *Deseret News,* Feb. 3, 1858.

# INDEX